# THE WELLNESS UNIVERSE GUIDE TO

*Complete*

*Self-Care*

---

# 25 TOOLS
## FOR GODDESSES

---

# ANNA PEREIRA
### FOREWORD BY
# KARINA LEBLANC
OLYMPIC MEDALIST, UNICEF AMBASSADOR,
HONORARY CAPTAIN OF THE ROYAL CANADIAN NAVY

--------- Featuring: ---------

Del Adey-Jones, Ingrid Auer, Pat Bell, Stephanie Bailey,
Nicole Batiste, Carrie Hopkins-Doubts,
Lolita Guarin, Lidia Kuleshnyk, Donna Laitinen,
Rochel Marie Lawson, Birgit Lueders,
Rosemary Levesque, Carolyn McGee, David D McLeod,
Angela Medway-Smith, Rev. Jennifer Moore,
Tina Plantillas, Dr. Pamela Poston, Debbie Prediger,
Leah Skurdal, Victoria Soto, Nancy Stevens,
Dr. Patricia Talbot, Stacey Wharton

The Wellness Universe Guide to Complete Self-Care
25 Tools for Goddesses
Anna Pereira
ISBN Paperback: 978-1-954047-40-2
ISBN eBook: 978-1-954047-41-9

Visit www.TheWellnessUniverse.com and connect directly
to experts, attend classes, and read articles
that support your best life, mind, body, spirit.

Get your FREE JOURNAL to accompany your Goddess Journey.
Sign up for our newsletter. Visit:

www.TheWellnessUniverse.com

# DEDICATION

This world has been telling us who we are supposed to be for so long, many of us have disconnected from our unique Goddess energy. Within these unusual times, we may have found ourselves searching for who we are and why our life lacks the fire, resilience, joy, hope, positivity, and energy others speak of. Our Goddess energy volume has been turned down.

For every Goddess who seeks to bloom, open to the sun, and unfurl your petals, this book is for you.

Within you is a sacred Goddess. You seek something greater for yourself and to experience life unapologetically, with grace, compassion, fun, expression, inspiration, and confidence.

You have dreams and goals! You treasure the day and seek to exist in a wonderland of joy, balance, peace, and ease.

For those who are blessed and grateful to *know* you are a Goddess and inspired by your own ownership and expression to inspire your sister Goddesses to be where you are by sharing the tools in this book, this book is for you. Thank you for owning your Goddess energy and sharing this book.

To all of the brave souls who step up every day and serve the world with their wellness practice. To those who help the world transcend and transform to their highest and greatest good. To those who hold space to help just one person to make it through their day. To those whose legacy will be spoken of as "they made this a better world" by easing suffering, encouraging strength, teaching us to cope, and guiding us to healing, empowerment, love and peace; This book is dedicated to the servants of wellness, our Wellness Universe World-Changers. You heed the calling. You choose to serve. Thank you.

To those seeking wellness, inspiration, a better life. To those who have said, "I am a Goddess, and I am worthy of all of life's blessed experiences!" To those who are vulnerable and ready to heal the pain. To those who know there is a better life on the other side of wherever you are. To those who step up for themselves, families, loved ones, and community to show up as your best self. To the seekers of a better life experience. To those who know that love and peace start with you, this book is dedicated to you.

# TABLE OF CONTENTS

# INTRODUCTION

*"Every woman is a Goddess.*
*Each being a unique expression of the Divine."*

- Anna Pereira

Goddess energy comes from within. It's in your kindness, compassion, confidence, vulnerability, showing up, and knowing your boundaries. It's in being a great friend and a loving human. It includes having courage, an open heart, being adventurous, defining your values, being connected to your imagination and creativity, being free and open to your self-expression, being confident in your actions, and inspiring others. Whether a team player or a stand-alone victor, and always loving yourself through every challenge, falter, struggle, and success, *you* are a Goddess.

You are a force.

Your heart guides you.

Positive self-talk is the program that runs in your mind.

It's about progress, not perfection.

It's about telling yourself, "I love you," and, "You are doing great," and believing it.

It's showing up for those you love; this includes *you* at the top of the list.

It's empowering, encouraging, and embracing your sister Goddesses.

Treasuring the moment.

Being fearless when you need to be.

Staying grounded when under pressure.

Being vulnerable, asking for help, and sharing your load.

Seeing situations for what they truly are and being discerning from an empowered core.

Moving through pain and rising from the ashes ablaze.

Knowing you can do anything you put your heart, mind, and soul to.

And even if you don't achieve your vision, you find success in the journey.

Being kind, compassionate, and forgiving of yourself and others.

Knowing your boundaries and staying true to your beliefs.

Healing the wounds from your past and moving forward with grace.

Forging, forgiving, and feeling your way through it all.

Nourishing your mind, body, and spirit.

Respecting nature, the earth, and the heavens for all the glorious and bountiful blessings you are gifted daily.

Freedom. Total freedom.

It's not a superpower you achieve or a role you play; it's the essence you already are and always have been and that part of you that goes back to the stars once you journey back to source.

You are a firework.

You are a soft breeze.

You are creation.

You are unique Goddess energy.

Let us blissfully travel into this wonderland together. Let's live in it, in the here and now.

Tap into your Goddess energy with me through self-care and guidance. Through storytelling and tools from my dear friends and wellness experts within these pages from The Wellness Universe, allow this to be a joyous exploration into parts of you you're ready to ignite.

## FEAR NOT BEING THE GODDESS YOU ARE

Life is constantly changing and creates new circumstances and challenges. When we recognize and have an awareness around self-care, we can better and more quickly serve ourselves.

Do not fear your greatness, Goddess! Your Goddess energy will guide you to joy and wonderful experiences beyond imagination, of which you are so worthy of and all that you came to this Earth for.

I believe in you.

Are you ready to own your Goddess energy? Enjoy the journey of exploration, excavation, and implementation of wonderful tools, strategies, and resources that will empower you, sweet Goddess.

Let the stories you read and the tools shared within this guide help you to make changes for yourself that allow you to experience your wholeness in your power.

The world needs your greatness, inspiration, kindness, compassion, and courage, Dear Goddess. The Universe wants you to be all you intended to be and experience life fully expressing *your* unique Goddess energy.

Thank you for picking this book up. Your best version of you is essential for peace and love to flourish and helps make the world a better place.

Love,

Anna

# WHAT DOES LIVING IN YOUR UNIQUE GODDESS ENERGY MEAN TO YOU?

Goddesses around the globe shared their words with me to inspire your journey.

I asked this question to women whom I admire and inspire me. They shared their thoughts, personal stories, and inspiring quotes.

Before we get into the stories and self-care teachings from our world-renowned Goddess expert authors, healers, and teachers, be inspired by these Goddesses! Many share their journey on social media and have powerful messages that will inspire you.

Every woman is a Goddess. Let your wings unfurl and get connected to your divine power, essence, and inspire those around you to live in their Goddess energy too.


With Love,

Anna

# GODDESS LEPA

Being an empowered woman is living authentically. Don't be afraid to shake up the status quo and own it. Be your perfectly imperfect self and love it. March to your own tune and don't be bothered by what others think.

As women we need to own our power and put effort where we can make a difference. We must stand for what we believe in. A Goddess knows her power and lives with positive intentions and kindness.

**Lepa Galeb-Roskopp**, Found/Designer Misahara Jewelry

IG @lepagaleb @misaharajewelry

# GODDESS KATHELLEN

We are all unique and have our own paths to live. I learned so much in this world both high and low. Everything happens for a reason, to make you stronger for your next stop, or to teach you something. Being a Goddess means to try to be your best version of you every day and to not give up on your dreams, because anything is possible! I love this quote: "Feed your faith and your fears will starve." I take this to mean believe in what you are doing, whatever you are dreaming about, whatever you are working on, and nothing will stop you.

**Kathellen Sousa Feitoza**, Professional Athlete

IG @kathellensousa

# GODDESS JULIA

Good actions attract great people which brings good vibes and blessings. This, to me, is living in my Goddess energy.

Migrating to a new country can bring loneliness and a sense of being lost. Leaving behind the life I knew, my comforts, dear friends, beloved family, career, and so many other things—that was my life as I knew it. Brazil, in my case, was the country I left to start a new one in America.

But I didn't let any of that stop me. Arriving in the USA and not knowing a soul made life a little bit difficult. In my mother country I was surrounded by friends and family with a very active social way of life with purpose. With that in mind, I intentionally sought out friends that shared the same values of kindness and integrity and shared their goodness through being involved with social projects and charities.

Once I connected with some amazing women, I started thinking of how I could help more people, bring people together, and connect them. It came together naturally! A group of friends and I decided to raise money to donate to social projects in Brazil. We were delighted by the overwhelming support we received from our communities. Our project was lovingly embraced, and I was humbled.

The emotional support, connection, impact, and lives touched through good-hearted women coming together for a great cause was out of this world. And that's how Confraria do Bem—Goodwill Sisterhood—was born.

From a small idea, great women, and good intentions, we now have a powerful world-changing project connecting people that live in the USA and help make their lives better.

After all, we get out of life what we put into it.

One thing I'm always asked is, "Julia, how do you keep up with everything?" I reply, "Whenever you do something with your heart, selflessly, life becomes easy." And one last thing I live by: Don't do to others what you don't want others do to you.

**Julia Queiroz Primo**, Insurance Broker, business owner

IG @Julia_queiroz_primo

Facebook - Julinha Queiroz

Linkedin - Julia Queiroz Primo

# GODDESS VANESSA

Being a professional athlete, student, woman, sister, daughter, and most of all, a human being has taught me so many things along the way, the ups and the downs. Our self-dialogue is too often "I don't deserve this, that person is better than me anyway" or "They're older, they must know better than me, I should just listen to them and do as they say." That was my dialogue for so many years until one day I looked at myself in the mirror and kind of had a light switch realization. I changed from the "I'm not good enough to play on this team", "Coach is right, I'm too slow and untechnical", "Everyone else is prettier and skinner than me," to the "I'm a dang good soccer player, I know I can compete with the best, I'm a heck of an athlete and I don't care what people think of me." What my journey has taught me most of all is the power of belief. Believe in yourself, believe in your work, believe in your value and believe in your worth. You are your greatest advocate and your greatest supporter; you have to put yourself first because no one else will do it for you.

**Vanessa Gilles**, Professional Soccer Player, Olympic Gold Medalist

IG @Vanessagilles4

Twitter @VanessaGilles

# GODDESS BISILA

Goddess is a state of mind, it's an attitude that comes from within. It's the feeling and belief that everything you need is in you; it's an act of self-love. Every woman is a goddess, it's our responsibility to see how we can put our Goddess to service to humanity. This is the Goddess time and with all Goddesses coming together we can make a better world full of beauty and love! Enjoy the reading!

**Bisila Bokoko**

CEO BBES & BISILA BOKOKO Group

IG @bisilabokoko

# GODDESS MIKAELA

I work with women who are mentally and physically drained, yet they carry the guilt that they are not doing enough. They carry it in their workplace, for their children, partners, friends, parents, and for themselves. They have yet to realize that their life is about them. They are often lost, looking for the woman they once were or the woman they would like to be, seeking to leave behind the woman they think society and people around them want them to be.

They dive into the world of self-help and self-care. They go to yoga, find the time to go to the salon, join a 5am club, and every now and then there's a girl's night out, a massage, or some meditation. They become the victim of self-care and wellness. Instead of feeling empowered they transform self-help and wellness into another goal to achieve on an already infinite list of to-dos.

Again and again, they fail.

The search for wellness oftentimes contributes to stress, anxiety, judgment, shame, and guilt which turns into burnout. I've been there. I constantly used the argument "care for yourself so that you can care for your loved ones" until I finally got it! The why of why I should care for myself is ME. If I do it in the name of my loved ones, I am not fulfilling my own needs.

Thus, my wish for you, for us, every mother and woman, is that we stop caring for ourselves as an excuse for getting energy to care for others. Please, care for yourself because you deserve caring for yourself, as self-love. Because you are you, and because you are worth it all, and you deserve feeling good, for you.

This is living in your Goddess flow. In your Goddess energy!

**Mikaela Övén**, Mindfulness, Heartfulness & Parentalidade Consciente

Facebook: miafulness

IG @miafulness

# GODDESS TIPHANY

You DESERVE a love that makes your heart feel full not depleted. Remember to give attention where you feel joyfully energized and focus on intentions to transform chaos into peace.

Live in your Goddess energy daily.

**Tiphany Adams**

IG @Tiphanyadams

Facebook @officialtiphanyadams

YouTube @tiphanyadamswheelyfamous

# GODDESS ALAINA MICHELLE

When we move with love we will always win. To move with love means to always take action based on feeling good. When we feel good, we are truly aligned with self. When we are aligned with self, we always win. Even a loss is a win because it is when we lose that the light becomes even brighter. That's when we start again. The cycle is never ending, as we are infinite beings.

We think our love grows and expands. But it doesn't; its eternal.

It has always been there. It's everything. When we go through heartbreak, we think the love breaks between two people, or we fall out of love. We don't. Because love is infinite. It's the expectations we have that break our heart.

Love does not expand nor break us. Love has no price tag or time stamp. For us to give love to others we must fully understand that love is not an object. For us to receive love we must first learn how to love self. Love is infinite energy. I am Love.

Live Love. Give Love.

**Alaina Michelle**

IG @raemoonrose

Tiktok @raemoonrose

Facebook @raemoonrose

Twitter @raemoonrose

# GODDESS MARIE

What a perfect question to ponder, one that hits me more so this year than any other.

For me, its living in the confidence that I'm worthy of all that is good, beautiful, & amazing! I haven't felt that in a REALLY long time. It's about moving out of the darkness and into the LIGHT, even when I don't think I can. That energy made me take a leap of faith, moved me to change the things about my life that needed to be overhauled, unlocked my heart and I took control. I manifested what I had been seeking for by putting it out into the universe, praying on it and discovering what true self-care and self-love is…by opening myself up to endless possibilities of a life I'm happy to be living. That energy will continue to guide me all my days. I'm in tune with it, trust it and rely upon it. We all have that unique energy within us. For some, it just takes a little longer to have it revealed. So, when you hear it calling out to you, embrace it and revel in the fact that you are indeed a most spectacular Goddess!

**Marie Malzberg**, Producer, CNN

IG @tvreeny

# GODDESS ANDE

Goddess-tae! The Divine Goddess in me honors the Divine Goddess in you!

When you step fully into your Goddess energy, you are honoring your female divinity. Your oneness with the Universe, embracing all your feminine qualities -- inner beauty, wisdom, sexuality, and divine knowing, while spreading love everywhere you glow.

**Ande Lyons**, Host of the Startup Life LIVE Show

Twitter: @AndeLyons

Ins: @ande_lyons

YouTube: AndeLyons

# FOREWORD

Karina LeBlanc, Olympic Medalist, UNICEF Ambassador,
Honorary Captain of the Royal Canadian Navy

Have you ever met someone for the first time and immediately felt you were exactly where you were meant to be and the person in front of you was exactly who you needed to meet at that point in your life?

That's exactly how I felt the first time I met Anna. It was easy talking to her. For a very short while, we conversed as strangers. After all, we had just met. But it didn't take long before our conversation shifted to a deeper level as we shared with each other our vulnerabilities.

I've often thought of that very first conversation. How were we able to move the conversation so quickly from the kind of frivolous conversation you have with a stranger, to one where I felt comfortable to share so much so soon? I believe it's because on that day I met a truly authentic woman who has a deep understanding of herself and her own power within. A woman who values the potential of not only herself but also others. And a woman who knows how to inspire. My first conversation with Anna allowed me to see, with greater clarity, my own value and uniqueness in this world.

I know *25 Tools for Goddesses* is personal to Anna. After all, her life's purpose is to bring peace and true joy to everyone reading it and to inspire and empower all so that they see the greatness that they have within and start living the version of themselves they were put on this earth to be. 25 Tools for Goddesses, the fourth book in her self-care series, is like a toolkit for self-care and empowerment. The self-care practices and tools shared throughout the book are user-friendly. The true stories offer inspiration and cultivate confidence and that will encourage readers to be their best selves.

In life, when we step into understanding our own greatness and when we stop being afraid of the potential that lies within and bravely walk into the path that was meant for us, we begin to understand who we are and a new joy of what life is meant to be. You get to start over again living a life with purpose for a purpose. *25 Tools for Goddesses* is a must to take on your own journey of self-discovery.

Karina LeBlanc

www.KarinaLeBlanc.com

General Manager - Portland Thorns

Olympic Medalist, UNICEF Ambassador

Honorary Captain of Royal Canadian Navy

## CHAPTER 1

# HEART RECLAMATION

## USING VISUALIZATION
## TO TACK BACK YOUR LIFE

Anna Pereira

## MY STORY

"If you let this one get away, you will be alone forever."

The scene was just like watching a movie and hearing the echo, "FOREVER…
FOREVER…forever…" as the camera zooms in frame by frame, the look
of horror on my face, *is he right? Will I really be alone forever? Is J the best
thing that has ever entered my life? Am I such a terrible person? Not compatible?
Hard to get along with? Standards too high? Undeserving of love? Worthless?
Get away? Must I imprison someone to be loved?*

Why would my dad say this to me?

Oh, the thoughts that went through my head! I felt dizzy and nauseous
as if I were going to pass out. To consider being alone the rest of my life was
terrifying. To have these thoughts running through my mind brought back
all of the unworthy feelings, and more than feelings, at this point, they were
beliefs—deep, rooted, defining beliefs of not being worthy of love.

Then I shrugged it off. My dad has his own issues, and he was projecting
them again.

We were so much in love. He was a great guy. Funny, charming, a great circle of friends, social, stable career in IT for a global company, and easy on the eyes. A great love of my life. And the chemistry; Ai! Chihuahua! I gave J my entire heart, body, and soul.

## GROWING UP UNWORTHY

Riding bikes, playing with Barbies, kickball in the street, going to the park, exploring nature, digging in the dirt, salamander hunting, coloring contests, going to the beach, swimming in the pool, cartwheels in the front yard, a special trip to DQ for my favorite hot fudge brownie sundae; this was childhood.

Also, bullying, blame, shame, teasing, belittling, and ostracizing.

"Anna's corroded. Anna's corroded." The neighborhood bullies taunted me. I was picked last for teams. I was blamed for literally anything that went wrong, anytime, anywhere. I'm tearing up as I write this, revisiting these painful childhood memories and the heartless cruelties of children and the way they mock. And adults who had no compassion.

As I sit here now, I'm thinking, *corroded? Who the hell even uses that word? Let alone a child. What a strange word, 'corroded.'*

It indeed is a terrible word to be called. The definition from Merriam-Webster: *cor·rode | \ kə- ˈrōd \corroded; corroding*

*Definition of corrode*

*transitive verb*

*1: to eat away by degrees as if by gnawing*

*especially: to wear away gradually usually by chemical action*

*the metal was corroded beyond repair*

*2: to weaken or destroy gradually: UNDERMINE*

*manners and miserliness that corrode the human spirit*

*— Bernard De Voto*

And of course, something that is corroded is crusty, rusted, calcified, or has some sort of hideous layer that typically makes something appear to be useless or trash-worthy.

I still get emotional and can remember how hard it was growing up being me. My unruly, curly hair didn't help me either. Nappy. Frizzy head. Afro. I heard them all. The only solution was to cut it short.

Then I was called a boy.

There was no winning at the game of confidence, self-love, and self-worth. I had no coach. No team. No fans.

Getting back to the moment my dad shared his 'advice' with me. I was so in love with J. But he was not for me. He was medically diagnosed with a mental disorder that had him on medication. He was previously married to a woman for less than a year after dating her for ten. This was a clue that he had commitment issues.

We lived together. It was a short relationship, but I was head over heels and gave him all of my heart.

"I can't do this anymore." As I opened my eyes and rolled over that morning, those were his words.

"What?"

"I can't do this anymore."

"Do what?"

"I don't want to be here. I'm leaving."

At first, I thought he was just having an episode, like when he complained about his credit card bills, then went to the mall and returned with three new pairs of shoes and every pair was brown, just because.

"Okay."

Then reality set in. *He really is leaving.*

As he gathered his things, I was in complete crazy girlfriend mode. "Don't leave! I love you! You can't leave! Why are you leaving?" There were tears and screaming and falling to the floor in a heap.

Then the anger.

"Go take all of the lights down! There is no Christmas this year. You destroyed my Christmas! I can't believe you! Are you sure you want this?"

There was the desperation of a situation out of control and the ripping to shreds of my heart. I stood still in the middle of the room, feeling like I was falling into an abyss of surrealism.

I darted through the house chasing him, hysterical, begging, pleading, negotiating.

Later his friend showed up. In the dark, making no haste, they cut the thousands of white blinking lights off the bushes and hauled his stuff away. V (J's friend) removed his life, items, and every trace of J from our home.

*Oh my God. He can't wait to get out of here and my life*, I thought. I watched as if they executed a plan that had been in the works for some time now.

They went with arms full in and out like they were loading as many items into the escape vehicle as possible before the volcano erupted, and lava engulfed the house. V shot me a compassionate glance of pity as if to say, "I'm so sorry, Anna, this is just how it is."

He was gone.

My life was in pieces.

I was a pile on the floor.

The lava arrived, and I was left to burn.

I spent days and days in tears, torture, and pain, cursing him, God, and everything. And the words of my dad echoed in my head: "You will be alone forever."

I spun deeper and deeper into depression. Night after night, I felt like my heart was being ripped out and shredded. Emotional and physical pain twisted my insides and made me feel like I was bleeding out.

I howled in grief.

I had feelings of not wanting to live, asking God just to let me die.

It went on until I thought I had no more tears, pleading, negotiating, or begging inside of me, until I had no more anything left.

Then I found more tears, screaming, cursing, howling, begging, bargaining (with God) to make the pain go away. I was all alone through it all.

My best friend in the world, Jeanne, was my rock. She listened and supported and did all a best friend could do.

I talked, screamed, cried, and tried to hold it together, but kept falling apart for months.

I was desperate. I remained friends with his mom and dad. They loved me. I did all I could to grasp any thread that would give me hope of his return. But he never did.

J was gone forever.

Thank you, God, for knowing best!

Dear Reader, If you read the introduction to *The Wellness Universe Guide to Complete Self-Care, 25 Tools for Happiness*, my second book, I shared how I manifested my beloved husband of now 11 years.

Before I could manifest anything, there was something I needed to do: Take back my heart.

This awareness came after a conversation with a good friend of mine, Josh. He gave me some great rituals for cleansing and bathing with intention-infused sea salt and baking soda to cleanse my energy and bring positive things into my life.

"You have given your heart away. That's what we do when we love someone. You must take it back." And with that, he gave me a ritual that changed my life. I will share that tool with you later.

The gravity of this awareness hit me like a spear to my chest.

*Maybe I had been walking around all of this time without owning my heart?*

*When do I last remember loving myself with total ownership of me?*

Clearly, the fear of being alone, unloved, and unattached was the window to that epiphany.

*Single forever? I'd rather be dead, I thought.*

It's all clear now, of course. The lack of nurturing in my home, the neighborhood bullying, the growing up awkward were all the perfect ingredients to create a shit storm of a life for myself.

We were all in the ladies' room, lip-glossing it up and pumping Rave hairspray to get our 'guidette' styles as high as possible. I remember being so uncomfortable with who I was that I couldn't even look at myself in the mirror to fix my hair when hanging out with my girlfriends. I felt so ugly, embarrassed, and ashamed of my appearance.

Thinking about this makes me sad. What a poor, broken girl I was.

*How can someone so ugly be loved?* This is what went through my mind constantly.

This is the foundation for wrapping myself up in the validation of someone else. This is the foundation for seeking approval. This is the foundation for bad decisions, being manipulated, and being taken advantage of.

Now, I call myself the Head Goddess of The Wellness Universe, and my community and organization have gathered souls from around the world who make the world a better place. If you know me because of this, you probably cannot fathom reading what I just shared.

For you may know me as a confident, entrepreneurial, fairy-tale lifestyle living, happy, blessed woman who lives globally and has a generous heart, often being called 'too kind.'

The tool I share with you I often share with anyone I come across who I feel may need it. This visualization is not just for getting over a romantic break-up; it's for loss. When you give yourself to a person, project, or commitment that ends, sometimes your heart goes with it.

Your emotional investment is stronger than any other resource you can put into something.

You can make money back. You can get a new career. You can find a new partner. But your heart? You only have one.

My heart is the source and connection to my Goddess energy. To be a Goddess is to have a radiating, love-filled, wholly-owned, full heart. It is to be kind, compassionate, confident, empathetic, courageous, and creative. Being a good wife, friend, and leader requires my heart and love energy to be rooted in me.

# THE TOOL

In preparation for this visualization (takes about 20-40 minutes):

Emotionally, be ready to let go and purge.

Mentally, say goodbye.

Physically, be in a safe space that you consider your sanctuary.

Are you ready?

You will need (in order of importance):

- **A Quiet Space:** No distractions. This deep, healing, and life-shifting visualization requires your total focus and giving over to it.

- **A Dark Space:** The energy of my bedroom worked best for me. It is the place in the house that is my sanctuary and my energy. Conscious, subconscious, and unconscious live there. If you're traveling or away from your personal habitat, try to vibe with owning your energy wherever you happen to be.

- **A Candle:** To help you focus, setting your gaze on a flame helps to slip into a meditative state.

Let's begin.

I will share exactly what I did, and you are free to adapt to any version that resonates. Above all else, be gentle, but be truthful with releasing and purging all emotions connected with the loss.

I sat cross-legged on my bed. The lights were off. Only silence, that candle, and my emotions were in the room.

I inhaled and exhaled as I fixed my glance on the candle.

I recollected all of the emotional connections to the person, place, or thing (in this case, J) and let the tears flow.

I did not judge. I was saying goodbye.

Let the tears flow. Say your goodbyes.

Goodbye is a great place to start. It gives you finalization. YOU are in control of the final goodbye here. It can even be a "see you later" if this is a physical loss of a loved one, pet, etc.

Once I felt enough physical purging of tears, I closed my eyes.

I visualized a crystal-clear heart with an aurora borealis rainbow coating floating above my head.

It began to spin slowly.

I imagined putting words into that heart, and with each word, the heart began to glow.

'Worthy.' 'I love me.' 'Best friend.' 'Confident.' 'Trusting.' 'Grateful.' 'Forgiven.'

All of the words I believe about myself AND the words I wanted to own.

With each positive word the heart filled with light. It spins and spins and shines. Glowing brighter and brighter. Spinning faster and faster.

Glowing and radiating beams of white and golden light filling the room and filling me with a sense of readiness.

Once I have filled this floating heart with all of the significant and kind words that stream through my mind and body—as if they are downloading as knowings and needings and I finally feel complete—I (physically) reach up and grasp this heart gently, securely, and with all of my love, pull it down, and place it back into my chest.

I sat with hands over my heart.

I felt it. It's back inside of me.

Beating. Thanking me for being home again. Ready to serve me and to receive my respect, honor, and gratitude.

When I felt full and complete, I opened my eyes and blew out my candle.

This visualization was something that I needed, and I'm so grateful for having learned this tool. It course-corrected me. It sutured wounds.

It healed me.

May your heart beat within you with love, peace, courage, joy, compassion, and giving you all you need to be in your empowered Goddess energy as you journey through life.

May you be a beacon of inspiration and love for others.

May you own your truest version of *your* unique Goddess energy that empowers you to live your best life.


Blessings,

Anna

# CHAPTER 2

# A SELF-LOVE REVOLUTION

## THE PATH TO THE BEST RELATIONSHIP YOU'VE EVER HAD

Stephanie Bailey, CYT

## MY STORY

As I started to type, I felt my stomach churn with anguish. Could I hold the acid down, which I could feel inching its way up my throat? "Breathe," I kept telling myself, as I took a sip of water, then closed my eyes. *I've done this before, multiple times; why is this causing me so much stress?* This time was different. "Breathe, relax; you can do this." I opened my eyes, closed my laptop with only one word written, "Mom."

I was holding my truth, my story, deep inside, wearing me down as if I were carrying a heavy bag filled with stones—leaving remnants in various aspects of my life. My internal struggle of abandonment and not feeling worthy were smothering me, creating barriers around my life, especially my heart. The magnitude of love I should have had for myself instead translated into superficial love in many forms.

I gave myself plenty of reasons and excuses for why I didn't feel I deserved love, let alone the love I should have for myself. Abandonment was always at the forefront of my mind. Various times this dereliction would rear its powerful, ugly energy into my life.

I remember in elementary school, my teacher had everyone in class write a letter. These letters would be attached to balloons we each released in the air—hoping someone would find them and become our pen pal. My eyes lit up, and my smile expanded across my face—I thought I was going to explode. I knew who I was going to write. I had all hope in the world my balloon would find my perfect pen pal—my birth mom.

I put a lot of thought into my letter, expressing how much I wanted to meet her. I told my birth mom that it did not matter why she didn't want me. I told her how a good family adopted me, and now I had two brothers and one sister. I ended my letter telling her how much I loved her, my birthdate (so she knew it was me), my address (so she knew how to find me), and my name (so again, she knew it was me, her daughter).

The day I released my balloon, I jumped and danced around so much I couldn't contain my bladder. I remember closing my eyes as I held my special letter, giggling with pride—which was attached to a white string and yellow balloon—picturing my birth mom opening this and exhibiting the same joy.

Every day, for weeks, I waited for my letter from her to appear. My birth mom never wrote. Looking back, the odds of her finding my letter was one in maybe a trillion. However, the sadness and feelings of unworthiness filled my heart space expanding into my adult life.

Being adopted, I felt I had a shitty navigation system from conception. I was two and a half years of age and very different from the family who adopted me. My mother still reminds me, "Stephanie, you were a difficult child who was hard for me to understand and raise." Hearing these words, again and again, sank into my core—eventually becoming me—consuming me inwardly and spreading like an incurable forsaken virus.

Feeling "not good enough" became the theme song of my life and the catalyst for why I hopelessly sought love in all the wrong places, letting various toxic relationships enter my life along the way. I was desperately trying to overcompensate for the love I was missing within. In my mind, love was something obtained outwardly, not something which already existed inside me.

Opening my laptop again, I stared like a deer in the headlights at the only word I was able to muster, "Mom." A rush of insecurities swirled around like a familiar dark cloud from my childhood. *What is wrong with me?* Again, this was not the first letter I have ever written expressing my feelings. At this point in my life, I had mastered the art of writing letters and speaking my truth. But, this letter was different. This letter was significant for my extended healing and personal growth.

Looking at the word "Mom," my palms immediately became cold and sweaty. My body was restless and every muscle engaged with discomfort. I was letting my mind fill with doubt and worry. I was giving myself every reason in my head to close my laptop again and not proceed. *I'm forty-eight and still holding on to this emotional shit? You can go another thirty years without saying anything to her. There is nothing to gain by doing this. I don't want to hurt her feelings. I don't want to unleash feelings I have pushed down and bottled up just to become the victim again. What if my mom doesn't remember, and I feel like this was all in my head? Stop!*

I needed to let go of all the excuses and "what-ifs," remembering this was my journey to healing my wounds, which I had allowed to hold me back. Writing to my mom was a crucial and pivotal process in my journey to self-love.

I had to remind myself, *although this was not the first, this is one of the most important and impactful letters you will write in your life.*

When I was twenty-two years old, I wrote a letter to all the men who had molested me in various foster homes before adoption. I noted how the physical abuse I endured harmed my relationships with men (my subconscious tucked my abuse away). I wrote about my pain, feelings of unworthiness, and distrust with men. I told them how angry and disgusted I was for what they did to me—how could grown men do this to a child? I ended my letter by forgiving them.

After I finished writing, I burned that letter—releasing and giving this toxic energy to the Universe. I knew I would never know who those pedophiles were. However, I needed to remove the negative impact of this experience; I was letting it shape my life. Releasing these horrid thoughts and feelings from my body felt empowering. So why not do the same with the person who raised me? Why did the three letters, "Mom," on my laptop screen make me feel inadequate again?

Am I feeling inadequate because my mother is very strong-willed—something I have always admired and feared? Or is it because she has strong opinions on everything and everyone? Never afraid to tactfully or brashly express how she felt—through a look, hitting me, or cruel words.

Growing up, I constantly sought acceptance and validation from my mother. Unfortunately, our differences and hurdles kept us at arm's length for most of my life. But still, I admired how my mom embraced and fostered her independence. I felt her independence was her saving grace, especially when my dad died unexpectedly from a heart attack when I was twenty years old.

The emotional strength my mother embodies is a characteristic I learned and modeled from her. I also am a strong woman with strong opinions (but I refrain from judgment), and I don't need a man to define me. However, living up to my mother's expectations of who I was supposed to be—in her eyes—became exhausting. I felt like I was a hamster in a cage running on a wheel with no destination or purpose.

How could I ever be enough for any relationship when the relationship I had with my mom felt shallow? If I couldn't stop judging myself and questioning my decisions, how could I expect her to do the same? My mother had a unique way of reminding me of all I did wrong—with very little forgiveness; however, I chose to devour her judgment like a baby eating cake. I became weak-minded and was letting her opinions affect me. In truth, how could I expect her to forgive me if I couldn't forgive myself?

Forgiving myself did not mean I was okay with what happened, nor did forgiving her. Forgiving was to release the power I was bequeathing to all the relationships that negatively affected me—emotionally, spiritually, physically, and mentally—dimming my self-love and worthiness.

Writing about my feelings has also been an impactful tool regarding romantic connections I didn't get closure from after they ended. By writing, I created my closure. This tool also helped relationships with significant others where I felt there was half-listening and zero hearing. A letter can be read without interruption and reread to evaluate its part (if the ego allows it).

"Mom." As I continued to stare at these words on my laptop, I closed my eyes and started praying. *"Please God, give me the strength I need to share my truth to my mother, surrounded by your light and love, in Jesus's name I pray."*

When I opened my eyes, words started radiating out of my fingertips. As I recalled each event that impacted my life with my mom, tears flooded my eyes. Writing in itself was a release of the chains which bound my heart. I felt the strength of God as he wrapped his arms around me with love and protection. By completely trusting in his guidance, a massive piece of inner love I needed was able to emerge and triumph through writing this letter.

This letter I wrote to my mom was the first draft to eliminate all the toxicity manifesting in my mind, body, and overall love space. I needed to clear out the clutter of all the self-doubt, worthlessness, and self-deprecating lies left inside me. I typed until my hands were tired, my brain had no more to give, and my tears dried up. That night was the best sleep I had in a long time.

My work wasn't over since this was a letter I wanted (but not sure if I dared) to send. Days went by before I was emotionally ready to reread what I wrote—adjusting to having a more transparent, loving voice when I read it to myself.

Writing my mother was frightening yet self-serving, self-loving, and a heart-expanding experience. Having the strength to open my heart and share my story, my truth about my experiences from childhood through adult years was a necessary pain—she is my mother. We were brought into each other's lives by the grace of God, to learn and grow from our experiences—not hide or shrivel up. I never once had a feeling of regret that God chose my mom to raise me. I knew she loved me the best she could in my heart, with the tools she had from her own experiences and traumas—which were different from mine.

When I finished my letter, my stomach felt uneasy. The beating of my heart was faster than an Olympic sprinter as I pressed "Send." However, releasing this pain was a significant factor in repairing my inner brokenness.

I realized one crucial tool (out of many) in my self-love discovery: I would no longer let my past define my future, and writing about my feelings demolished the barrier around my heart space.

My true happiness has only resided in me. Letting go of caring what my mom thought was my driving force in sharing my story with her. I wrote not expecting or wanting a response back, which gave me the freedom to express what I needed to say.

After writing to my mom, my inner love expanded, becoming magnetic, attracting the man God has always wanted for me into my world.

Writing letters and releasing past hurt broke down barriers for me— freeing my heart and reconnecting my soul. Each person is different, each letter separate, and my choice to keep, burn, share or tear a letter differential.

I have gained a part of myself back with each letter I've written, mended my heart space, and uplifted my soul. Most importantly, this has created the path to the best and purest relationship I will ever experience—a deep, compassionate, healing, and unconditional love for myself.

# THE TOOL

There are multiple tools necessary for developing and embracing self-love. One method is writing to release the experiences and people who are holding your heart hostage.

Often we embed our traumatic experiences deep inside; an archaeologist would have a hard time finding them. Facing our past and sharing our truth can be very painful. Let's keep it real; what person in their right mind would want to unleash trauma they have barricaded—possibly for years or decades?

We must remind ourselves, keeping our painful emotions and experiences tucked inside is our love kryptonite. Often we do not realize this until our self-deprecating beliefs and behaviors emulsify how we can handle our challenging experiences or toxic relationships we choose, or the countless "failures" we endure.

By choosing to release any emotional, mental or physical power we have given to others, we gain a step towards regaining our self-love power back. This type of power represents self-confidence, self-worth, and inner strength to walk away from unhealthy relationships to cultivate a stronger, healthier, happier self with a magnitude of unwavering love—for you.

How do you know what to write to release? Listen to your inner voice. God is guiding you. Answers and guidance are always there if we pay attention. Whatever your emotional state is, embrace and accept so you can let go. Trust yourself.

Let's begin.

## 9 ESSENTIAL STEPS BEFORE WRITING:

1. Grab a pen and paper. Find a quiet space where you will not be interrupted or distracted.

2. Trust your intuition; this is your journey, no one else's.

3. Breathe. Again, sounds easy; however, even as a yoga teacher, I will forget to breathe. You are breathing to calm your mind, body and soul to create the clarity you need.

4. Tell yourself, "I am enough," repeatedly until you feel you are.

5. Take a moment to meditate or pray, asking for guidance.

6. Surround yourself with white light, love, and acceptance.

7. Let go of overthinking—trying to plan your exact words will hold you back from your truth.

8. Avoid insults and abusive language—sending a letter as this will only continue to block the love you seek within.

9. Release expectations for a specific outcome. You are writing for yourself to release barriers around your heart. Writing to get a reaction or response is counterproductive. The only person who owns the key to letting your spirit free is you.

Now you're ready.

Bring into your mind a person, people, or experiences that trigger overly protective barriers around you—mentally, emotionally, physically, spiritually—holding down your love from entirely radiating to its total capacity.

Write down the name(s) of anyone who has: diminished your worthiness, ignited feelings of emptiness, loneliness, heartache, loss, belittlement, unattractiveness, overweight, dumb, etc. Remind yourself, "I am in a safe place; God is guiding me."

Once you have these names down, reground with your breath. Emotions which appear can be intense—opening our inner vault is scary. I know this was the case for me. Breathe. You are not alone.

Write down these words: "Forgiveness does not happen overnight, nor does genuine lasting love I seek—both are ongoing journeys, leading me to self-discovery, abundant happiness, health, and the love I deserve." Say this several times before you begin writing.

When you're ready, write as if no one is reading. Write as if this is your last day on earth, and you finally get to share your story without criticism or the need for validation. Write everything and anything you can think of—this is possibly your first draft—let all your emotions out. Set yourself free.

Your goal on this first draft is to release all the pent-up pain, anger, fear, disappointment, frustration, sadness, defeat, confusion, insecurities, depression, loneliness, doubt, and stress. Grammar and spelling are not essential.

Write, cry, scream, freak out and write some more. Releasing your emotions on paper will feel like a self-induced exorcism. Amazing! You are getting all the bottled-up toxic energy out so your self-love can elevate.

There is great power in writing your truth. Releasing any negative energy you have been internalizing will regain the confidence you have lost. Writing a letter of release gives you the closure for yourself that you deserve, plus you don't have to worry about a silent treatment or feeling unheard because someone refuses to listen. Facing our traumas clears our emotional and mental clutter to allow space for happiness, health, wealth, abundance, and the love we deserve.

If you are choosing to share your letter—take the necessary time you need. This exercise might take multiple draft-rewriting until you feel confident and uplifted with your words.

After your letter is complete, close your eyes and reconnect with your breath. Whether this person is alive and able to be contacted or not will determine if you (and only you) decide to keep, burn, send, or maybe tear up this letter.

There is more power in not sending this letter, especially if you are vulnerable. Having been in an abusive, controlling, self-demolishing relationship can provoke harm again. Stop. If this is you, do not send your letter; instead, rejoice in burning it—this is as powerful.

Your biggest self-love tip to remember: you're not writing to get a response back; you're writing to let go so your heart can be free of harmful emotions and negative labels you have given yourself.

Remember, empowering your search towards finding love, one truth at a time, one letter at a time, one release at a time, will only strengthen you. Every step taken is one hurdle closer to having inner happiness and peace, surrounded by the love and positivity you now have created and deserve.

Developing all the tools for unconditional self-love takes work; however, I promise this effort is well worth it. Your inner love connection will be the most important and rewarding experience. The path you are creating is paving your journey in achieving the best and magnificent relationship you will ever have with yourself.

**Stephanie's** (aka Miss-Adventures) passion is advising, writing, and empowering women on dating, relationships, break-ups, being successfully, happily single, and most importantly, developing genuine self-love. Although the tools for developing love are not easy to obtain—nothing significant in life ever is—the rewards are endless. Her knowledge, experience, and expertise come from her own dating/relationship experiences, extensive self-discovery, and healing, along with her intuitive, empathic skills (given by God as a child). Stephanie finds her experiences help connect to her love clients on a deeper emotional level, which allows them to achieve their personal goals. Stephanie has been a love expert/coach for over twenty-five years with highly successful love results. Her approach is similar to a best friend, who is not afraid to hold one accountable for their actions and be their biggest cheerleader. She creates a judgment-free loving space for her clients and believes life should never be one big apology, but instead, lead by love, forgiveness, and trust within yourself. Stephanie has been a yoga teacher for over twelve years and a massage therapist for twenty-one years. Stephanie looks forward to helping empower women on their journey and guiding them on this new adventure to self-love.

"We can search a lifetime trying to find the love we need within others, but only search a moment when we realize the love we seek already exists inside us."

https://www.thewellnessuniverse.com/world-changers/stephaniebailey/

# CHAPTER 3

# FORGIVING MY MOLESTER

## HOW TO ACHIEVE MENTAL AND EMOTIONAL FREEDOM AFTER ANY TRAUMA

Donna Laitinen, Behavior Change Specialist

## MY STORY

Yes, I forgave my molester. I ask you to think out of the box now and stretch your comfort zone. This does not make me weak. This does not imply that I gave my power away. It's quite the opposite. I chose to do battle to reclaim my power!

Thirty-four years later, I'm honored to share how I got to a place of reconnection filled with self-love and worthiness of the good I desire.

I have fallen in love with this journey, and I'm literally watching my purpose take root. My intention of sharing the unfolding of my healing is to invite you to do the same. I'm helping others heal and healing myself in the process. I will hone it, master it, and share it!

I'm sharing the good, bad, and ugly of one component in my life, which led me to my spiritual awakening, knowing I have the freedom to choose.

*I am bringing you back to when I was 21.*

Where am I? I am at a college friend's house. The party is over. I enter a dark bedroom. One of my best friends is asleep in one of the twin beds. I get under the covers in the other twin bed and lay my head down to sleep. Next, I am sitting up, rigid as a steel pole, incapable of movement. The only movement was the beating of my racing heart. Confused and disheveled, I was in an unfamiliar room, my hands clutching the bedspread. It was lightweight. I could feel the embroidery and the raised nubbles that outlined the design on the bedspread. At that moment, I had my first flashback. I was a little girl. I was under an embroidered bedspread, and I wasn't alone. I could clearly see the designed embroidery of a cowboy riding a horse with the lasso rope in the air, the bedspread from my childhood home. Just like that, I remembered a moment from my childhood.

"Eruption" is the word that describes this intense irrational reality of a dream. Every hair follicle was raised, electrically charged with defensive energy as my inner being felt I was ready to remember. Doubt and uncertainty consumed me. I felt every cell inside my body collapse and deflate. The numbness and confusion took over. My heart felt heavy, like never before.

Was it real? Did this really happen? How could this happen? I could not shake the ugly sensations of feeling dirty. The memories of my past were now becoming my new reality. My body was responding to an invasion consuming me. I woke up my friend and said, "I think I was molested by my uncle when I was a little girl." She looked up at me with hungover bedhead and said, "Really? Wow, that's strange. Are you okay?" "I guess," I replied.

## I WAS DISCONNECTED FROM MY INNER CHILD.

Night after night for years, I found myself naturally lying with my hands across my chest with my legs and ankles crossed tightly. When I went to get out of bed, the unraveling of my wrapped self made it challenging to walk until my circulation flowed, allowing my muscles to let go of my protective defensive mechanisms.

As flashbacks revealed themselves, there were more questions and a need for answers. I remember saying to myself, "I refuse to play the victim role." Years later, I wrote a letter to my uncle and mailed it. Surprisingly to me, it was easy to write with clear intention, asking for answers. I felt empowered, bold, and productive. I was proud of myself for mailing the letter and scared for myself at the same time. In my mind, I took control of the situation by confronting my molester, magically expecting answers to my questions to *fix me*. It didn't quite work out that way, but there was some movement of my stuck, congested cells that kept me from letting the awe of life in.

My mind played tricks on me. My uncle now knew I was aware and looking for confirmation. I experienced illusions. One time, I was upstairs with two of my kids and a neighbor's son. I heard something downstairs and took the kids and hid behind a desk for an hour, thinking he was coming after me. I experienced illusions from my fear-based thinking and thoughts, unable to manage my emotions. My fear became my baseline behavior in life. Denial and unawareness of the dysfunction affected my ability to enjoy sexual intimacy, trust, and freedom to dance, walk, and speak, limiting me beyond my imagination! I would always settle by thinking something wasn't meant for me or that I wasn't smart enough. I never questioned why I felt or behaved this way or why I often felt like I didn't fit in. I was unaware that I was unaware until the inner work began.

As a child and adult, I felt a disconnect. I had more of an external connection of creating happiness in my life rather than an internal connection with myself. I was always looking for things externally that could make me feel happy. I did this to keep my feelings of unworthiness buried. I have learned *true* happiness can only come from self-love. My healing journey has been magical when I chose gratefulness instead of spite. There is no doubt in my mind the journey is just as important as the destination of introducing Donna to Donna in my wholeness. The self-compassion and authenticity for my fearless soul to be a light in the world have been the driving force to rise and thrive each day with a grateful attitude, making room to forgive myself and my uncle.

In 2018 I injured my back and couldn't walk. I was so angry I didn't recognize myself. *Who am I? Who is this miserable person?* My mind was restless and recycled all the unwanted moments of the past, especially at night. My body was defensive, rigid and full of aches and pains. It became evident that I was suffering mentally, physically, and spiritually and it wasn't only because of my back. I didn't know who Donna was anymore. The realization that I was a master at not allowing anyone, including myself, to see the real me was my wake-up call. I now know my back injury was the steppingstone to heal, recognize, and be inspired to take action. It allowed me the time for the awareness to reconnect to my inner being and higher power. I am now thankful for my back injury. The Universe stopped me. It was no coincidence.

I knew I needed help, and I turned to a higher power and asked for help, guidance, and unconditional love. There are many more tools I learned and developed to do the inner work to release the pain of my molester.

Since I was eight years old, my body physically held energy from this trauma on a cellular level, controlling me, and I wasn't even aware of its ripple effect. Over the years, every time those memories were triggered, I was unknowingly re-traumatized by someone's touch, words, and actions. My body became a defense shield. I was emotionally unavailable and unexpressive. I would always take things personally, immediately becoming defensive and reacting irrationally, often feeling regretful afterward.

As my healing progressed, I uncovered that the abuse occurred between eight and ten years old. It became evident I needed to release this energy congesting and limiting me. It affected me as a mother, daughter, and wife and hurt my relationships and encounters with others and in my careers.

In my early 50s, I was finally open and ready to reclaim, reinvent, and declare my life's path by introducing Donna to DONNA. Pain happens; suffering is optional. I did not know this. I embraced this knowledge and desired to be free from the prison I put myself in.

I made peace with my trauma by completely letting go of the toxic emotions with a clear intention to choose gratefulness instead of spite. I was open to find the flow, openly receive, and willingly give back.

As I dislodged the negative energy, I felt this light, like a chandelier. I could turn it up so bright to find a focus—with strength and conviction—to pursue my heart's desires by exploring my natural gifts. I found the source of energy that makes me feel alive and eager to start my day with purpose.

# THE TOOL

## PAIN TO PEACE

Feel free to let awe in. Are you ready for a mindset shift to flick the switch and release old traumatic energy imprisoning your body on a cellular level? Just like the muscle has memory, cells do too! For example, when you react irrationally in a situation, it often is due to someone triggering a traumatic memory. Someone pokes at that traumatic memory, and even if your conscious mind has forgotten or blocked those memories, your body remembers on a cellular level. It's like a knee-jerk reaction: you become defensive, anxious, angry, or guarded. This inability to manage your emotions becomes your blueprint.

Cells remember your memories and impact everything: the expression of your genes, the body's physical functioning, and of course, our actions, thoughts, and emotions. According to the CDC, "Childhood experiences, both positive and negative, have a tremendous impact on future violence, victimization and perpetration, and lifelong health and opportunity. As such, early experiences are an important health issue." Knowing this, you can begin the inner work to clear the harmful energy. You have the power to accept, recognize, control, and recondition your mind, and forgive. You have the power to resolve those memories so they no longer emotionally impact your life. When you think of that trauma, there will literally be no negative emotions attached. This is how you know you've cleared the unwanted emotions or memories of a trauma. This is the true magnificence of forgiveness and self-love.

First, know this, nothing will change until you change your mental conditioning. Second, you're ready and open to see through a different lens. Third, only *you* can decide to do the healing work. Fourth, surrender and have faith.

**Instead of** consistently reliving wounded memories, recycling regrets of the past, and continuing to embed the traumatic energy within you, ***try this way of thinking and acting instead:*** look within and have a dialog with yourself. For example, I forgive Donna back then. I was doing the best I could, given the circumstances. I have grown and expanded my awareness and wisdom over the years. I have compassion for Donna back then. Declare, "I let go, forgive, and forge ahead with a re-kindled spirit!"

**Instead of** living your life as a victim holding anger and resentment, which blocks feelings of gratitude, make a conscious decision to forgive. Gratitude is the gateway to forgiveness. Hang in there if you are not 100% with me. You can't feel grateful for your parents or others who have harmed you when you're still holding onto past anger and resentment about their abuse and neglect or still feeling hurt over betrayal, deceit, or abandonment. You cannot force yourself to feel grateful when intense negative feelings still exist, nor should you. You've been wounded. You can't deny it. Acknowledgment of the abuse or loss, guilt, remorse, or heartbreak—giving yourself permission to grieve—must happen first.

*Try this way of thinking and acting instead:* I'm taking back my power and declaring, "I am not a victim. *I am a victor!*" Knowledge is power, but taking action liberates emotional freedom. *Only* forgiveness can move you out of the victim stance and free you to move forward. Only *you* can come to the place where you want to forgive. In the forgiveness process, it is helpful to understand that *resentment is a cover* for underlying feelings that have never been expressed.

**Instead of** consistently asking questions like, "Why me? What's wrong with me? Who is to blame? Why does everything bad happen to me?" You're asking disempowering questions, continuing to feed your cells the negativity, keeping your energy trapped. You're asking the wrong questions.

*Try this way of thinking and acting instead:* What is the lesson in this situation? What is emerging in my life? What is my superpower or magic? What is my gift to share? What is my purpose? What is my source of happy energy? Why am I here on the planet? Meditate, reflect, and write daily in a journal about these questions. Once you ask yourself, the answers will start to come.

**Instead of** focusing on the hurricane and fueling the flames with negativity, which leaves no room for finding the solution. You're attracting more negative energy and chaos, sucking you into a category five hurricane, causing the most destruction. When you expect the worst, you will get the worst.

*Try this way of thinking and acting instead:* In any situation, always try to find the good in it. If you can't see it now, know that something good will come out of this situation. Know this situation has a purpose. Be open to the unexpected and expect something good to come out of this tragedy, abuse, or health issue. **Make it a habit,** and you'll feel some relief. Thinking and acting from your heart space automatically infuses positivity in every cell—every fiber and atom that makes up your body. Each time you practice this, you bring in refreshing, loving positive energy into your body and mind, dislodging and moving the trapped energy through you.

**Instead of** focusing on who is to blame, which keeps you in pain, *try this way of thinking:* allow yourself to be the observer and focus on what good has come from this situation. View it as a lesson to learn something. Ask yourself, what has this taught me? At some point, you realize your life experiences—the good, the bad, and the ugly—have made you the person you are today. Be thankful that you're not where you used to be in life. You've survived a lot, and it made you a better person. You will be the survival guide for others traveling this path. This is recognizing the gift in your suffering. Therefore, your suffering is redeemed in finding the blessing in the suffering. Pain happens. Suffering is optional.

## DO THE WORK OF FORGIVENESS.

This is when you recognize that you are responsible for your own thoughts, beliefs, and actions and that they're preventing you from living your best life. You now forgive yourself for those thoughts. You're asking forgiveness from yourself, others, or the universe.

- Write down on paper the names of people who have harmed you. Don't hold back.

- Maybe write it in the form of a letter to your abuser(s). State all the effects of the abuse/neglect and how it has impacted your life. Write in as much detail as possible.

- Write down all the things in your life for which you want to forgive *yourself.* Work on this for a couple of weeks. Let emotions arise. Your intention to clear will prompt this process.

- Build an outdoor fire or light a candle. If desired, add to the experience allowing for higher power guidance by bringing in candles, crystals, incense, and essential oils.

- Read out loud with feeling, with emotion with conviction. Place the paper in the fire and watch it burn.

- Visualize your list of forgiveness burning, disintegrating into energy particles, and floating up, up, and away. Visualize the Universe receiving and taking your forgiveness energy particles. Now the Universe knows you have made a resolution with yourself and those who have harmed you. The Universe absorbs your pain with non-judgment. The clearing has begun!

True forgiveness requires both attention and intention. It can be one of the most freeing sensations like an invisible weight has lifted. You're not forgetting; instead, by first acknowledging the wrongdoing, this allows you to sit with your feelings and hold space for these feelings. Ask for guidance from your higher power. Give your body permission to use your breath as a vehicle allowing your cells to release what doesn't service you. See the light, fireballs of light moving through you. Now, visualize your cells inflating, dancing freely in harmony and alignment with the peace you desire. Believe you deserve the good you desire. Ask for compassion to let go and forgive. Feel it. See it. Declare it. Hear it. Embrace it. Let your breath untie the knots in your body and mind with the intention to keep your heart open. Remember, where your thoughts go, your energy flows.

**Question:** How do you know you have cleared the emotional energy?

**Answer:** When you can visualize a specific scene from your abuse and not be emotional. You have cleared the negative energy from the past.

When you acknowledge the wrongdoing and forgive yourself for your thoughts over the abuse, you feel thankful for the lessons learned from the abuse and realize you are stronger light in this world because of your suffering.

I invite you to trust in the timing of your life and turn up the chandelier in you!

I chose to do battle to reclaim *my power* from my mental conditioning. Do you want to take back your power? I am a YES to making heart-to-heart connections and awakening compassion in our world through my commitment to serve others.

My name is **Donna Laitinen**; I help individuals ready to make a shift who want to reinvent, declare, and claim the life path their heart truly desires.

I do this by using my natural gift of rallying and inspiring people to ignite the spark of internal motivation through forward-vision thinking. My approach is based on behavior-changing and spiritual energy connections, in which I help people heal, recognize, and be inspired to take action.

I have created and continue to create energy healing systems, allowing for self-discovery, awareness, and consciousness to reconnect to our inner being and higher power.

## *Professional Experience*

- Behavior Change Specialist, Certified with the International Coaches Federation

- Meditation, Stress-Reduction and Relaxation Certified Coach, AAAISMA

- LiveStrong Certified Trainer, YMCA, working with cancer patients and cancer survivors.

- Yoga Certified

- Personal Fitness Trainer, Certified with American Council on Exercise

- Associates Degree in Exercise Science

- Reiki Healing

- Volunteer, as a Meditation/Relaxation/Stress-Reduction coach for Autism Support Groups.

### My Coaching Services:

Creative Energy Thinking * Cultivating inner beliefs and outer actions into alignment * Transform hesitation, fear, and doubt into boldness, trust, and confidence * Meditation/Relaxation * Visualization/Manifestation * Raising Vibration * Empowering sacred fulfillment * Self-Love * Inner Peace * Forgiveness * Creating life-changing Rituals * Harmony & Balance between masculine and feminine energies * Expansion of Consciousness *

www.thewellnessuniverse.com/world-changers/donnalaitinen/

# CHAPTER 4

# REFRAMING THOUGHTS

## HOW TO BREAK FREE OF HARMFUL BELIEFS AND FOSTER SELF-LOVE

Stacey Wharton, MSW, BSW

## MY STORY

I was seated in a twelfth-floor study room like I normally did weekday mornings in grad school. As I sipped my coffee, occasionally glancing out the window at the view of the city, I felt particularly at ease. Around me was a very special group of women; each of them supportive, empowering, and badass in their own way.

My mind wandered, as it often did. Unhelpful thoughts flowed in and out of my head, a reminder of my long-lasting struggle with self-image and self-love. I realized that my thoughts and beliefs had become more intense and harmful since the development of my eating disorder and the various experiences of assault I encountered (physical, sexual, psychological). I felt stuck in a negative, endless spiral.

*I am fat. I am not beautiful. I am worthless. I need to change all that is wrong with me. I need to be better. This keeps happening. Something must be wrong with me. It's my fault. I should've reacted differently. I am broken. Why me? What a sad and ugly truth.*

And then, in the blink of an eye, I was back in the present moment. As we sat around sharing and validating each other, something shifted inside of me.

Hearing the gender-specific experiences of those other ladies, one after another, helped me to deconstruct the things I believed for so long. *I'm not alone anymore. We are in this together.* This particular day was the beginning of my quest to break free of the harmful beliefs that were consuming me and compromising my health. *I can do this!*

I came to understand that the distress I experienced didn't originate from a fault of mine, but was instead a result of the difficult events that happened in my life, the social context I was living in, and the messages I received about who and what I was supposed to be.

And with understanding, came feelings of confidence that enabled me to identify the things I wanted to work on. It was important for me to be more loving and nurturing to myself, and I knew I needed to shift my mindset to accomplish this.

The thing about thoughts is that you can learn to work *with* them rather than against them. Though it may be exhausting, it is possible to challenge and reframe your thinking habits, simultaneously empowering and liberating you.

Like many others, I have endured and suffered the consequences of gender-based expectations and violence. I was fortunate to have a network of unconditional support and love, and yet, I still struggled. We need to do better for our girls and sisters. We can empower each other on a micro-level by sharing information, changing the dialogue, challenging harmful messages, being kind, and fostering love.

# THE TOOL

## REFRAMING THOUGHTS

The world is continuously bombarding us with messages, norms, and expectations (explicit and subliminal). They are transmitted through social media, news, academia, social interaction, radio, television, advertisements, and other methods of communication. Unfortunately, these messages are not always in our best interest.

Our minds and bodies continuously absorb this information, whether we are aware of it or not, creating background noise. In addition to the background noise are thoughts that are more prominent in our day-to-day life. An example would be thoughts regarding all the tasks on your to-do list.

For some people, the abundance of information coupled with a tendency to think a lot can be overwhelming. If you have ever thought to yourself, *I can't turn it off; my head is spinning, I can't relax, there is too much to do,* you are not alone!

Research has shown that our thoughts, emotions, and behaviors are connected. This is crucial because it means our perception of things influences how we experience them. If you are always thinking of worst-case scenarios, situations that made you upset, painful memories, to-do lists, or injustices of the world, you will experience that on a physical and emotional level because your body will be flooded with stress hormones. This may lead you to feel anxious, tense, or physically unwell. And in response, you may avoid things, become withdrawn, or get stuck in habits that are unhelpful for you.

If you think you aren't good, skinny, or pretty enough, you will likely internalize this message and believe it to be true. The more you think it, the more you believe it. The more you believe it, the more likely you are to act on it.

This reality has left many girls and women at the mercy of the diet culture, the beauty industry, and the media, resulting in eating disorders, body dysmorphia, and many other challenges.

These channels of information often target specific groups, and skillfully at that, by sending out the message that girls and women need to look and be a certain way. They are then able to capitalize on the insecurities and harmful beliefs that result from those messages by selling products or procedures to "help" people meet those expectations.

To break free of harmful beliefs and make space for kind, nurturing, and loving ones, you must first learn to **recognize** what is happening in your mind.

You can start by asking yourself the following questions:

- What specific thoughts are present for me (right now)?
- What was I thinking earlier today, yesterday, this past week (and so on)?
- What occupies my mind when I try to relax or go to sleep?
- What types of thoughts come to mind when I think of or describe myself?
- Do I have kind and loving thoughts about myself?

This can be a difficult and triggering task, so take the time you need. Once you have a better understanding of your thoughts, you will be able to identify the ones that are beneficial to your health and well-being and those that are harmful.

The goal of **reframing** is to take any unhelpful thought you may have and frame it in a way that serves you better. Start by writing down a thought you would like to change. Next, write down everything you can think of to challenge that thought. Here is an example:

- I am fat. → I am not fat.
- I am fat. → I have fat.
- I am fat. → I am beautiful.
- I am fat. → My size does not define my worth.
- I am fat. → What other people think or say about me belongs to them.

This exercise requires that you be honest with yourself. If you are trying to convince yourself of something that does not feel true to you, your efforts to reframe unhelpful thoughts and beliefs may be thwarted.

In this sense, telling yourself, "I am not fat," when you do not believe that to be the case, would be ineffective. Instead, consider a reframe more in line with your perception.

- I am fat. → I am not where I want to be with regards to my body image/weight.

Here are a few additional examples:

- There is a positive in every bad situation. → I may feel differently about this at some point, but right now, I do not see any positives.
- I am not good enough. → I am feeling insecure about my self-worth.
- I am a failure. → I did not reach my goal, and I feel (insert emotion) about it.
- Something bad is going to happen. → There is always a chance that something bad will happen, but that doesn't mean it will.

## VALIDATING STATEMENTS

It can be helpful to add "this is something I can work on", "and that's okay", "I will get through this", or any other validating statement you find empowering to your reframed thoughts.

- There is a positive in every bad situation. → I may feel differently about this at some point, but right now, I do not see any positives, **and that's okay.**
- I am not good enough. → I am feeling insecure about my self-worth; however, **this is something I can work on.**
- I am fat. → I am not where I want to be with regards to my body image/weight; however, **that's okay because this is something I can work on.**
- I am a failure. → I did not reach my goal, and I feel discouraged; however, **I will get through this.**
- Something bad is going to happen. → There is always a chance that something bad will happen, but that doesn't mean it will. **I have gotten through difficult moments before, and I can do it again.**

## GRATITUDE

Gratitude is another great tool to help you reframe thoughts because it can co-exist with adversity. This means that you can be struggling and be grateful at the same time.

I have found gratitude to be particularly powerful when it comes to body image.

- I am fat. → I am not where I want to be with regards to my body image, but I am grateful to have a body that keeps me strong and healthy.
- My stretch marks make me less attractive/beautiful. → I feel insecure about my stretch marks; however, I am grateful to have had the opportunity to bear a child and give life.
- Having a child ruined my body. → I feel insecure about my body at times; however, I am amazed at how my body healed and recovered after birthing a human.

Once you are more comfortable with the practice of reframing, you can start to tackle some of the more profound beliefs you have about yourself.

- I hate myself. → There are parts of me that I would like to work on, and I will get there.
- I hate myself. → There are parts of me that I would like to work on, however, I do like/love (X, Y, Z) about myself.
- I hate myself. → I do not love myself the way I want to, but that's okay because this is something I can work on.
- I hate myself. → I am doing the best I can to work on myself. Hopefully, with time and effort, loving myself will come easier for me.

You will notice that many of your thoughts are automatic and negative. Consequently, you may have to reframe over and over and over again. Though this practice requires continuous effort, it does become easier with time. Most importantly, keep it simple. Your new thoughts don't need to be elaborate or complicated; what matters is that they resonate with you. The rest will come.

*"A reframe is not about telling yourself that your fear is wrong. Reframes are about finding another way to look at the possibilities of your life."*

– Rebecca K. Sampson

## CHOOSING LIBERATION AND SELF-LOVE

I am hopeful that this chapter empowers you to embark on a path to liberation and self-love or to move forward on this path if you have already started. By practicing reframing, you are enabling yourself to change the impact of harmful messages, one thought at a time. When you change the message, you change the belief. When you change the belief, you flourish.

Remember to be realistic, loving, and true to yourself.

*"If a problem can't be solved within the frame it was conceived, the solution lies in reframing the problem."*

– Brian McGreevy

**Stacey Wharton** is a social worker providing mental health services in a health care setting. She is passionate about helping others work through challenges and adversity to improve their emotional health, well-being, and quality of life.

Outside of her practice, Stacey aims to empower others by sharing wellness information, tools, and resources on social media.

Stacey has earned a bachelor's degree and a master's degree in social work and has several years of experience working in child welfare, youth and adult mental health, and education. She has also taught an introductory-level social service course at a local college.

Stacey lives in Ontario, Canada, with her husband and son and enjoys spending time with loved ones, reading, going for walks, and traveling.

For more information about Stacey, please visit:

https://www.thewellnessuniverse.com/world-changers/staceywhartonstruykmswrsw/

# CHAPTER 5

# THE LEGACY JOURNAL

## STORY KEEPING FOR THE ONES YOU LOVE

Patricia A. Talbot, Ed.D.

## MY STORY

Story keeping, storytelling, and story-making are central to our lives as human beings. We naturally collect the surprising, touching, and traumatic moments that happen to us and store them in our memory banks for later reference, sometimes consciously and sometimes not.

Often, we retell those moments as memories to help us stay connected to our earlier selves or connected to others through shared experiences. When we assign special meaning to such moments, they become deeply ingrained and take on significance as important life lessons no matter how brief the moment or unnoticed by those around us.

*The Legacy Journal* will help you keep better track of such moments and put them to intentional use in your life and the lives of those you love. What follows are a few such moments, memories, and the corresponding lessons, from my own recent life as a grandmother.

## MOMENTS

I. "Now you know."

I whispered these words into my son's ear as I pulled him into a tight embrace.

After hours of waiting through the night and most of the following day, Jamie rushed into the waiting room to announce the birth of his long-anticipated son. His face was flushed, and his eyes were tired, but his smile shined with a combination of pride and visible relief.

*Now you know what it's like to feel love for a child of your own.*

II. *An Angel's Kiss.*

I entered the room to see my daughter-in-law sitting up in bed looking vibrant as always with my tiny but healthy grandson, Jacob, curled upon her chest. The first thing I noticed was a small brown birthmark in the shape of a heart on his fuzzy little shoulder.

*It looks just like an angel's kiss.*

III. "T is for Talbot."

Jacob traces his finger over the letters carved into the stone on the walking path near our home, memorializing the life of his great grandfather.

"T is for Talbot."

He dutifully repeats the lines fed to him as he smacks the cold marble with the palms of his 18-month-old hands.

*So glad I captured that on video.*

IV. "I've gotta get back and play with my sticks!"

We're taking one last ride on the paddleboat before heading home from the lake. Jacob suddenly pops up out of his seat between his two sisters with a sense of urgency.

"We've gotta hurry!"

"What for?"

"I've gotta get back in time to play with my sticks!"

*Oh! How I love this boy!*

IV. "I believe in you, GoGo!"

Playing Putt-Putt golf at almost seven, Jacob encourages me as I step up to take my shot toward the hole.

"I believe in you, GoGo! I believe in you!"

*How incredible is that? My grandson believes in me.*

## MEMORIES

I. "Now you know."

I had waited through most of the night and a long day with my husband, our other adult son, and my daughter-in-law's parents in anticipation of the arrival of our first grandson.

Jacob came into the world already loved by so many who had shared the ups and downs of this young couple wanting and waiting for their children to come along.

*Oh, Jacob, we've been waiting so long for you.*

II. *An Angel's Kiss.*

"When I came into the room, I saw your little body curled up on your Mama's chest. The first thing I noticed was the little brown birthmark on your left shoulder where the angels had kissed you and reminded you how many people were waiting to love you here on Earth."

Jacob giggles in delight every time I tell of the moment I first met him. It's a story I often retell at bedtime before we continue the ritual by recounting the names of all the people who love him and were waiting for him to arrive.

"Grandpa and GoGo, Gigi and Grandfather, Uncle Jon, Uncle Joseph, Aunt Marin, Uncle Samuel, Uncle Peter, Papa, Ninny…"

III. "T is for Talbot."

Since that first time, whenever we walk past the memorial, I stop and replay the video of Jacob tracing the letters. The act of doing so has become a ritual connecting him to a great grandfather he never met but who would have delighted in his every move the same way he did with Jacob's father and his father's father.

*Let us never forget.*

IV. "I've gotta get back and play with my sticks!"

For now, it's the grownups who love to tell and retell this one. Jacob doesn't yet get the joke, and we don't want to make him self-conscious about this simple joy as he revels in simplicity during complex modern times.

*Yes, Jacob, enjoy those sticks as long as you will.*

V. "I believe in you, GoGo!"

No doubt about it, I perform better because of Jacob's encouragement.

*I hope I will always be worthy of your belief in me.*

## MEANING

I. "Now you know."

From this moment forward, these young parents will know what it feels like to love a child of their own. Now, they understand what I mean when I say the words.

"When you stub your toe, my stomach hurts."

Parental love is a love that never wavers and never dies no matter what happens from this point forward.

II. *An Angel's Kiss*

You were loved long before you were born. You will be loved all the days of your life and far beyond it.

III. "T is for Talbot"

You come from people who mattered to the world. It's important to carry them with you in all that you do. You matter to the world, too.

IV. "I've gotta play with my sticks."

The fun does not have to come from expensive toys or structured activities. Some of the best things in life come from nature and the freedom to explore within it. Fallen branches and bits of driftwood easily become the tools of imaginative play when children are left to their own creative devices.

V. "I believe in you, GoGo!"

These words from my grandson were welcome and unexpected at that moment from one so young. Encouraging other people is an act of love and generosity. We are never too young or too old to give and receive reassurance and support.

## ROLE SWAPPING

Jacob's encouragement at that moment reminded me of another memory from more than a decade earlier. It was the moment when I first felt my role swap from caregiver to the receiving end of such care in a single instant.

I was riding with my son in the open ocean on the back of one of those "personal water crafts" (like a motorcycle for the water). Overcome with a panic caused by the speed and unrest of the rolling sea around us; I began to tremble and cry. Despite his youthful desire to keep going, Jamie sensed my discomfort and turned the vehicle around, slowly heading safely back to shore. All the while, he assured me that I would be okay.

He was right. I was okay. I was then also moved by a poignant shift in my perceived role and a new reality.

At that moment, my son and I switched places. He became the leader, and I, the follower. I looked at him with new eyes as I relinquished control with the recognition that he was now the capable young man we had raised him to be. What came next for him would be out of my hands.

## STORIES

Moments like this become the stories of our lives as we repeat them and assign meaning to them, so they become locked in our memories, ready for the next retelling. The more we conjure them up and the more we share them with others, the more powerful their influence is in our lives and our relationships.

This cycle of story keeping, storytelling, and story-making is deeply aligned with the cycle of human life. When we hold on to moments of the past, tell them again as memories in the present, and give them meaning that can influence our actions in the future, we are literally writing the stories of our lives for ourselves and for posterity. The repetition of the cycle is essential to our development and crucial to our journeys if we are to reach our fullest potential as ones who understand our places within a complex and interconnected universe.

As a mother and a grandmother, I have come to understand the important role I can play in keeping this cycle alive for those I love most.

## AGOGO AMAYI

My grandchildren (now three of them!) call me "GoGo." It's a name I chose as a symbol of my intention to stay "on the go" with them as I grow older and they grow even more energetic. The name is also a nod to my many friends in Malawi, a small country in sub-Saharan Africa, where I traveled many times to study abroad with university students planning to be teachers.

In Malawi, the Chichewa term "Agogo Amayi" means "Grandmother" in English. Malawians often shorten the name to "Agogo" when referring to their own beloved grandmothers or those who fill a grandmotherly role in their lives.

Grandmothers the world over, who are fortunate to be a part of their grandchildren's lives, have a special opportunity to become the story keepers, storytellers, and story makers for their families and those they love. Those who are not biological grandmothers may step into the role of "Agogo" by noticing and nurturing the stories of those they hold dear within their chosen family of neighbors, friends, and colleagues.

To capture the spirit and intention of these "elder goddesses" for the purposes of the book, I will use the term "Agogo" to identify the feminine elders who capture the moments, retell them as memories and assign a deeper meaning to teach life lessons worth passing down (or around). By capturing the moments, retelling those moments as memories, and assigning meaning to them in the retelling, feminine elders take the opportunity to share a deep connection along with important life lessons that will live on long after they are gone.

Agogo is not always biologically connected to those she serves as story keeper, storyteller, and story maker. My own mother and grandmother figures included biological family members like my Mama, my Grandma Ayres, and my Aunt Ethel, as well as special neighbors and family friends collected through life by my parents. These adopted grandmothers included Mama Eva (my grandfather's second wife), Lilly May (my Aunt Ethel's boarder and friend), Aunt Rose, and Miss Annie (both older women friends my mother claimed for us as we moved from place to place during my growing up years). Each of these elder women in my life conjures memories of stories like how I watched soap operas in the afternoons snuggled up close to my grandma. How Aunt Ethel took us to her dress shop to pick out something special every time we visited, how Lilly May acted like she was part of the family, and how Miss Annie made ugly dolls out of apple cores. Even the briefest of memories connects me to lessons around big ideas about togetherness, self-confidence, and creativity.

All these female elders in my life were sources of love, support, wisdom, and the keepers of the stories that gave my life structure and helped me create meaning and a feeling of connectedness to family (both biological and claimed), to life lessons, and to my history.

As family elders who have lived for a while, those in the role of Agogo are in a position to fulfill a special role as keepers of life's moments, reminders of life's memories, and makers of meaning. When we embrace the role of story keeper, storyteller, and story maker, we are giving great gifts by preserving life's precious moments, keeping memories alive, but perhaps most importantly, helping those we love to assimilate meaningful moments into an understanding of their own life story and their own potential for goodness.

The more surprising the moment, the greater the opportunity for transformation. When something unexpected or unusual happens, it gives us the moment's pause we need to notice and commit it to memory. It may even tell us, "This is worth writing down." When we take the time to do so, we greatly enhance the chance that we will commit the moment to memory which allows the possibility that we might access it for retelling at a later time. When we assign a lesson or a moral to the moment, we claim an even greater opportunity to use it as a tool for passing along a meaningful legacy.

# THE TOOL

## THE LEGACY JOURNAL

When you embrace the role of Agogo as story keeper, storyteller, and story maker, you give one of the greatest gifts of love possible to the people in your life. Whether those you gift with moments, memories, and meaning are family members, friends, or new acquaintances, they will be surprised and delighted by the small things you notice and retell with affection and notes of wisdom learned from shared experiences.

In Matthew Dicks's book *Story Worthy*, the author describes a daily practice he calls "Homework for Life," in which he recommends keeping track of the most "story-worthy" moment in each and every day on a simple spreadsheet. I have no affection for spreadsheets as I find them cold and uninviting, but the act of creating a daily "homework" practice of taking five minutes at the end of every day to jot down the most story-worthy moment is one I've adopted with the use of a simple notebook I've come to call my "Legacy Journal."

Like "Homework for Life," *The Legacy Journal* encourages a brief and regular practice of story keeping for later reference and use when, where and however the occasion arises.

By taking five minutes at the end of each day to capture just one story-worthy moment with enough detail that the moment can become a memory along with any deeper meaning it might carry, you will have a wealth of stories you can pull out and use when storytelling and story making are in order.

Start your own Legacy Journal in the form that suits you best. A spreadsheet, a beautiful notebook, or a file on your computer will all work if the form pleases you enough to revisit it often. I've created both a fillable version and a printable version you can access through the link in my bio that follows.

The journal can be duplicated as many times as you like for the years to come. You might also duplicate the file to create a separate *Legacy Journal* for each of your own loved ones individually. I prefer to keep one journal going and make sure to make a note of the person most involved at the top of the page, so they are easy to find if I'm looking for a story about a specific beloved one for a special occasion.

If you choose to make your own *Legacy Journal*, you'll want to make sure to jot the date along with the name of the main "character(s)" on each page for easy retrieval. Who will enjoy the retelling of this moment the most?

Include the labels "Moment," "Memory," and "Meaning" down the left-hand side of the page and jot just enough detail for you to easily recall your intentions when the time comes.

Remember your notes under "moments" are about story keeping. You are recording what was said, seen, or heard that caused you to take notice that something "story-worthy" was happening.

Under "memories," you'll add additional details that help you give more context to the story so that it can be retold more fully. The retelling of significant moments keeps them alive for those you love.

Under "meaning," you'll note any lesson, moral, or message the memory brings up for you that's worth holding on to. If the moment was noticeable enough for you to take a pause, there is almost always a lesson there, even if it is as generic as "Life is full of surprises!".

Your *Legacy Journal* can grow indefinitely. When the occasions arise that call for storytelling—bedtimes, mealtimes, birthdays, graduations, weddings, or funerals, you will have a wealth of stories at the ready to tell and retell aloud or in writing.

When you become Agogo (the moment keeper) in your most treasured relationships, you will fulfill one of the most time-honored roles of the feminine elder—creating a legacy for those you love and leaving a legacy for yourself. Children, grandchildren, friends, neighbors, and colleagues treasure the retelling of stories where they are the central characters and are surprised to have forgotten moments brought back to them in a way that shows how they were noticed and how they matter in the story of life.

Storytelling is a uniquely human endeavor. It is the way we learn and the way we teach. It is the way we create community, family, and a shared history. By claiming the identity of Agogo, wise women connect with the deeper meaning and purpose of their own lives and help those around them to do the same.

Access your printable or fillable copy of *The Legacy Journal* at https://www.thewellnessuniverse.com/world-changers/patriciatalbot/

**Dr. Patti Talbot** is the Founder and CEO of Blue Roads Education Group. She helps professional women cultivate new skills, refocus their talents, and develop the mindset to change the world on their own terms so they can create a more equitable, inclusive, and healthful world for everyone.

As a public educator in PreK through graduate education for more than thirty-five years, Patti's been a part of the growth journey for people of all ages and stages of life. By focusing on the four big ideas inherent in the company mantra, Homegrown Solutions for a Patchwork World, she now helps clients honor their roots and transform the way they show up and work with diverse others in courageous action.

Patti's signature programs are available through Blue Roads Changemaker YOU Academy. Clients are encouraged to begin their Changemaker Journey with the foundational Changemaker YOU course introducing the sixteen attributes all changemakers have in common. Strengths and needs are assessed for participants as they relate to their individual calling to create social and environmental changes.

Upon completing the short Changemaker YOU course, participants can work with Patti to develop a program specifically designed to help them meet their goals as changemakers supported by a mastermind-style community of learners called The Changemaker Circle.

Access *The Legacy Journal* and learn more about Changemaker YOU at https://www.thewellnessuniverse.com/world-changers/patriciatalbot/

# CHAPTER 6

# EMPOWERING YOU!

## STEPPING OUT OF FEAR AND CHOOSING LOVE IN 5 STEPS

Debbie Prediger

## MY STORY

Oh, the headaches, how they'd wake me up in the middle of the night; the throbbing pressure was unbearable. I was so good at ignoring the pain, pretending I was okay and pushing through it. Even in my sleep, I could feel the sharp stabbing through my head and shoulders with numbness moving down my back.

The doctors couldn't find any reason for the pain. I had so many tests and procedures trying to find answers and the tests always came back clear. "We can't find anything wrong, Mrs. Prediger." And although that should have been a relief, it wasn't. There was something wrong, but what could it be?

I was so tired of doctors telling me to take pain medication to mask the symptoms. In fact, one of the doctors asked me what I was taking for pain and how often. When I replied I wasn't taking anything, he slammed down the big file he had on me and said, "Well, then, you're not in enough pain." That was the end of that appointment. That experience knocked me backward, and I started to believe, *maybe it wasn't that bad; maybe I should just take medication and minimize the pain*. Looking back, I can say thank goodness that when I tried to take painkillers, I would get dizzy, nauseous, and then throw up. *I'd rather have the pain*, I said to myself. Even today, I hear Tony Robbins say, "Life isn't happening to you. It's happening for you." This is definitely how I see it looking back at that pivotal moment.

For years I lived like this, nothing worked, and I was too exhausted to keep searching for a doctor to give me the answers I was seeking. What was wrong with my body at the core? Not just the headaches but what was causing them? The last test I had was for a brain tumor, and the one before that suggested I had multiple sclerosis. I was so sick of feeling sick and tired. Enough was enough; I had to figure this out myself.

That's when I discovered energy work. It all sounded a bit crazy to me, but what did I have to lose? One healer led me to another, and I started to find relief from the constant pressure in my head, the dizziness, and the numbness in my neck, back, and legs, which was better too.

I was shocked. *Could it be so simple as my body was just out of alignment and energy couldn't flow? Why didn't the healthcare system have a way of testing for this and treating it?* I felt confused and frustrated and started to question the healthcare system I'd been a part of my entire life. It just didn't make sense to me that with all those tests and procedures, they couldn't find anything wrong or bring me relief. Yet for the next six months, I was free of pain, the light came back in my eyes, and I could sleep again. Little by little, I eventually started to feel the numbness come back. At first, it wasn't painful, but over time it felt just as bad.

*Time for a body tune-up and alignment, or was there still something blocking the energy flow*, were questions I asked myself. And soon, I found myself obsessed with learning from energy teachers such as Donna Eden, author of *Energy Medicine*, Dr. Sue Morter author of *The Energy Codes*, and everything I could read on Chinese Medicine, pranic healing and eventually Bruce Lipton's book: *The Biology of Belief*.

I continued to follow the clues about energy fields, the charkas, and how our thoughts create our reality through our emotions. Emotions are meant to be energy in motion, and when it's not in motion, it has become stuck in your body, causing pain, discomfort, and even dis-ease. I started to ask questions like, "Does the pain I am experiencing correspond to an emotion?" Something I'd heard people say resonated with me, and I had an inner knowing to go deeper with these questions, to keep searching. I could feel myself getting closer, and I woke up excited to learn, on a quest to find answers following my own intuition and inner knowing of what was real and what would lead nowhere.

I discovered essential oils, and at first, even though I was interested in learning more about them, I had a belief I couldn't use them because smells made me nauseous, and my headaches would return. Perfumes, cleaners, and laundry soap affected me instantly, and I avoided the cleaning supply aisle in the stores due to the overwhelming smells. Something about the essential oils kept pulling at me, and one day I read an article about the frequency of certain essential oils. *What is frequency?* I remember asking myself. Here's what I found: the Emotional Vibration Analysis Frequency Chart measures every person on this planet. We are all vibrating at a very subtle hertz frequency rate. Following my gut, I knew there was more I needed to know, so I researched who was the expert in these topics of vibration, frequency, our thoughts, emotional resiliency, and the heart-brain connection.

Wow, now I was fired up. Did you know that you can raise your frequency just by using an essential oil? Our thoughts are energy, and they are also on a frequency scale. In fact, we can't find a solution to a problem if we don't raise our consciousness because the answer isn't on the same frequency as the problem. It was all so fascinating, and it totally resonated with me. I paid close attention to where I was on the frequency scale. I was feeling all the emotions now that I'd stopped running from them.

Guilt and shame are a 20 on the scale. Apathy and anger are a 150. Jealousy, regret, and courage are 200. Acceptance: 350. Love: 400. Joy is 540. And peace: 600. I was now on a mission to raise my vibration to 'love' (or above) as my new normal. The scale helped me understand or visualize how far I need to raise my frequency to be where I intentionally choose to be. Discovering that we can choose our emotions? Wow, now that was freeing, empowering, and exciting!

My goal was acceptance, joy, and peace. I thought I was always in the frequency of love because I loved others so much; however, what was missing was the love of self. Self with a capital "S," the purest form of love, unconditional love, and acceptance there is. The definition I found when I searched Google is "True self-love is: The commitment to objectively know myself as I am, to fully experience life as it comes to me, and to honor my potential by continually seeking ways to grow."

This means to me that we are on a quest to discover who we are at a soul level and to continue to align, grow, and constantly become more of who we were created to be.

Using essential oils to raise my frequency was the start of the quest or journey, but like everything else I did, I wanted to learn more. Why were some brands more powerful than others, why did some brands give me headaches, and others were pure bliss? I found Carolyn L Mein's *Releasing Emotional Patterns with Essential Oils* book, and that's when everything seemed to click—my years being a nurse, discovering how the human body was meant to work. I noticed where people experienced the pain or discomfort corresponding to the emotion they were either experiencing or running away from. The more I learned, the more questions I had; thank goodness there were lots of places to find answers.

I returned to those books from Dr. Sue Morton and Donna Eden, Joe Dispenza, and Bruce Lipton; sure enough, the answers were there. I had missed them the first time.

I always had a heightened awareness, able to follow the clues like breadcrumbs; it was like the path lit up for me to find the answers. I would hear inner whispers, words, phrases, and even knew things I didn't remember knowing. These abilities or gifts seemed to come alive again when I started to use the essential oils, and I could see solutions and answers to every struggle. I was quick to decide and knew the answers intuitively.

I was now doing energy healing and wellness consulting using essential oils in all of my sessions.

In these sessions, I used a device to perform a bio-investigation of the human body in a process known as bio-communication. In short, it asks your body questions and records the responses in the form of impulses it receives. I'd give the 30-plus page report to my clients, and they would purchase the supplement or essential oil that the device suggested.

Many of the clients wanted more than just me using the device to test them and hand over the 30-plus page report. They wanted me to explain how their liver had anything to do with the anger they were feeling or the worry that would just overtake them. I was always interested in learning why the body was showing the sign or symptoms. Healthy bodies are in balance and don't have pain, illness, or disease. What was the root problem?

I started to teach classes on essential oils and basic struggles I saw in many of my clients, such as lack of sleep, exhaustion, overwhelm, self-doubt and worry, feeling of nothingness, lack of hope or purpose.

From those classes, I was asked to do individual consults to help them understand what their report meant and connect the dots to the possible cause. I'm not allowed to diagnose or prescribe medications, nor did I have any intention of doing so, but these people were confused about what the reports even meant and where to start on a total health plan, so I offered a service that was filling a gap in the healthcare system.

Clients that came to me for wellness advice soon realized I was different and that I was helping them on all levels of health and wellness. Emotionally they were stronger, they slept better, their energy levels were higher, and their thoughts were more positive as they recognized the good in situations. My intuition continued to get stronger, and I often would hear my client's worries or objections before they spoke them out loud. This is where the next pivot point in the way I served my clients and myself happened.

Over time, and through many healing modalities, training, and teachers, I learned to master the energy field. I learned we have an emotional energy body as well as a physical body and that channeling higher wisdom was a gift that I could use.

Today I know we have all the answers inside of us. In fact, everything we need is already in us; we've just forgotten that important fact. We've been taught to seek answers outside of us, that help comes from others, or a pill, or a thing.

I help people remember just how powerful you are. Your thoughts, your imagination, and the vision you create in your mind is the most powerful tool of all, and it's free to every single person on Earth.

I empower people to remember their dreams, their wisdom and hear the whispers of that inner truth.

Sounds easy on paper, but old habits and patterns are driving the bus, especially when we are in fight-or-flight reaction mode.

The Signature Empowering You reset works on quickly resetting your triggered response as well as that electrical zap of fear, anger, hopelessness you feel in your body.

Releasing these unwanted emotions before they get trapped in your body, causing deeper issues such as pain, discomfort, or dis-ease, is important to break free from the physical and emotional pain that builds over time. Running from our emotions never works; we continue to pile thoughts, emotions, limiting beliefs in our body until it screams at us to release them.

# THE TOOL

Imagine this; your kids are fighting, hitting, and screeching at each other in the middle of the grocery store. You're trying desperately just to get your groceries and go home. Breathing deeply, you ask them one more time to please be nice as you pay and then leave the store. Thank goodness you will soon be home, and your husband can help you unload the groceries and watch the kids for a bit while you unwind before dinner.

As you take the groceries from the cart to put into the car, the bag breaks, groceries go everywhere, the cart moves and scratches the side of the car, the kids are still screaming, and you fall to your knees right there in the parking lot sobbing.

The kids come to see what's wrong; they pick up the food on the ground and tell you. "It's okay, mommy, we will help. It will be okay." Meanwhile, your brain is telling you things like, *you're such a loser, no wonder your kids misbehave you're a terrible mother, no one else has all these things happen to them, am I being punished by God, what is wrong with me, why does everything happen to me?* It is definitely time for a 60-second reset.

## EMPOWERING YOU 60-SECOND RESET

**Step 1.** Acknowledge the experience that has triggered your emotion.

**Step 2.** Name, and feel the emotion

**Step 3.** Identify where in your body you feel it

**Step 4.** Use a blend of essential oils I call the release blend to unlock the limbic system. (Recipe: one drop of Stress Away, one drop of frankincense, one drop of lavender.) Placing one drop of the mixture above into the palm of your hand, rub palms together, and then tent your hands over your mouth/nose.

**Step 5.** Breathe deeply and slowly into that memory, into the place in your body you feel the emotion for 60 seconds until you feel it shift, lose its emotional charge, or changes perspective.

It is highly suggested to journal what you saw, felt, heard, and knew to be true after the 60-second reset. This can be repeated as often as you desire, and if you are feeling anxious constantly, I highly suggest a full session designed to help you get out of your own way and let go of the emotions stuck in your body. It's time, and they are telling you to pay attention.

Check-in with yourself; maybe this reaction is a deeper triggered reaction you've touched on in a fight-or-flight response, and it needs another layer of the reset or a full Empowering You Release session.

**Debbie Prediger** spent a lifetime in healthcare as a natural caregiver that started before the age of ten, taking care of the family's meals, laundry, and day-to-day household chores. Her heart, however, was always outside in the field with her horses and other farm animals. Later she realized she could communicate with animals.

At age 14, Debbie was a candy stripper, a volunteer nurse's aide at a hospital 45 minutes away, and as soon as she graduated from high school, she started full-time working in the nursing home of that same hospital.

Debbie's dream of being a nurse started when she was just 6 or 7, and she spent a year in the hospital away from family, first in the hospital 45 minutes from her parents and then in the city hospital 3 ½ hours away from anyone.

Lonely, afraid, and very confused Debbie found comfort sitting on the knees of the kind nurses that worked there. She felt special, loved, and no longer alone. From that day forward, she has been on a mission to make sure others felt the same way. Unconditionally loved, worthy, and surrounded by kindness.

Over time Debbie became the person people called on to help when someone was sick, and the caregivers needed a break before they dropped from exhaustion. This brought many opportunities to hold the hands of the dying as well as those left behind. Something she felt extremely blessed and honored to be able to do.

Extraordinary gifts appeared, evolved, her sixth sense got stronger, louder, and bolder with each of these opportunities. Today Debbie proudly uses all of this wisdom to empower other healers, visionaries, world-changers, and people that are passionate about leading from their hearts and making the world a better place for all of mankind.

You can connect with Debbie Prediger through her WU profile page: https://www.thewellnessuniverse.com/world-changers/debbieprediger/

# CHAPTER 7

# THE ART OF JAZZ LIVING

## OVERCOMING CHALLENGES
## WITH GRACE, EASE & JOY

Leah Skurdal, Intuitive Wellness Guide, Ancestral Energy Healer

## MY STORY

Full transparency here: I admit to being a little afraid of fully embodying the goddess in me.

Part of my hesitancy comes from the religious tradition I grew up with that glorifies the masculine and diminishes the feminine. In some contexts, it's heretical to imagine that the one masculine God could have a feminine side. Throughout history, heretics have been brutally tortured and murdered for beliefs outside the established system. The residue of patriarchal programming clings like plaque in my arteries and veins. It's a little scary to share views beyond the dominant paradigm but, I tend to push the boundaries.

The one God of all people—whatever name you give Divine Love—has many facets, expressions, and religions. Multiple gods and goddesses represent aspects of the one God of all creation. I use a deck of goddess divination cards for clarity. Each goddess card represents an aspect of The One that is helpful to examine more deeply when she shows up.

I brought my deck of goddess cards along when I visited my father as he first became ill. Holding the cards to my heart, I prayed, *Divine Love, I align with the highest good. I request a goddess to help clarify this situation.* Closing my eyes, I drew the card of Kali, the goddess of endings and new beginnings. I understood that my father was dying, and this was the beginning of the end. *Thank you, Divine Love expressed as Kali.* My dear father's health continued to decline until he died a year later. Knowing it was the beginning of the end helped me prepare so I could better serve my family during the transition.

On the one hand, I feel whole as I embrace the feminine-yin aspects as well as the masculine-yang aspects of The One God. On the other hand, my personality resonates more easily with the expansive yang energy of growing, expressing, giving. I thrive during the waxing full moon phase. I often feel uncomfortable during the waning moon phase as the moon's light decreases. I often resist the contractive yin energy of allowing, grieving, and receiving.

What do you resonate with more easily? Expansion, expression, and giving? Or contraction, listening, and receiving? Maybe you easily flow between the two expressions.

Let's take a deeper look at the sacred marriage of Divine Feminine and Divine Masculine energy.

## EITHER/OR VS. BOTH/AND

Humans experience life through duality and contrast: masculine/feminine, giving/receiving, light/dark, exhale/inhale, expressing/listening; I don't like this and I do like that. The viewpoint of duality is the three-dimensional world of either/or.

We also live in a quantum world of both/and. Quantum physicists have proven energy can exist simultaneously as both a wave and a particle. Our attention influences the energetic expression—mind-blowing concepts to our limited thinking. While we easily recognize that you or I can be *both* a spouse *and* a child, we might struggle to accept that *two seemingly opposing viewpoints can both be true at the same time.*

One of my struggles with either/or thinking is valuing one aspect of the Divine over another. Historically, cultures have uplifted the masculine over the feminine, resulting in the oppression of women. I can get stuck thinking in limited human terms of victim-perpetrator consciousness. I hesitate to embrace the rise of the Divine Feminine if it means overpowering the Divine Masculine. Too often in history, the victim has become the oppressor.

I notice this tendency in myself. When I'm aware, I notice how often I victimize myself or respond from victim mode. My husband asks, "Did you put away the X?" If I'm not mindful, I might interpret the question as criticism and step into victim consciousness. My interpretation (which might not be my husband's interpretation) goes like this: *I feel criticized. I don't want to feel like a victim. I choose to feel powerful by criticizing you.* I shoot back angrily and defiantly, "No. I'll get to it after I take care of Y and Z." I stepped unnecessarily into perpetrator mode—and the victim-perpetrator cycle continues. *The old paradigm of **power over others** is the established way much of the world works and the result of either/or thinking.

*The new paradigm of **power with others** includes the balance of masculine and feminine power—which starts within the individual balancing masculine and feminine energy within themself. Are you receiving as much as you're giving? Are you listening as much as you're expressing? ***Are you resting as much as you're rushing? Both/and.***

The sacred marriage of Divine Feminine and Divine Masculine is represented by the figure eight infinity symbol ∞ —one flowing gracefully into the other. Where the two flows meet, the shared power births the Divine child—the third path—better than either individual expression. The third path lifts up and out of duality into an upward spiral of evolutionary expression. *Creativity. Innovation. Intuitive insight.*

One way to embrace the third path in oneself is through *The Art of Jazz Living*. Following the third path and practicing *The Art of Jazz Living* creates a sacred space where you can meet challenges with grace, ease, and joy.

The Art of Jazz Living is a concept I developed a couple of decades ago that grew naturally from the jazz cooking classes I taught. Some people prefer the familiarity and consistency of following a classical music score or a cookbook recipe. Real-life is more like jazz music—the blending of classical tones with Afro-Latin rhythms infused with the spontaneity of improvisation. You might not have all the ingredients you want, so you get creative and improvise.

Yep. Sometimes life does get messy, and you have an epic fail. Mastery in The Art of Jazz Living requires the vulnerability to fail and the moxie to succeed despite the challenges. I agree with Stephen McCranie's observation: "The master has failed more times than the beginner has even tried." Practicing The Art of Jazz Living with curiosity and light-heartedness gives us space to innovate and find new solutions. The world could use some improv about now.

*I invite you to play with applying the principles of jazz living to your life and see what new possibilities emerge.*

# THE TOOL

## PRINCIPLES OF JAZZ LIVING

The Five Principles of Jazz Living come from principles of jazz music; they aren't the only principles of jazz, and they're not exclusive to jazz music. These five principles—which cross religious, spiritual, and cultural traditions—can be useful in navigating the complexity of the current predicaments we face in America and in the world. Jazz music is a uniquely American contribution to the world music stage. America is poised to make another unique contribution to the world stage by embracing a third path beyond duality. The Art of Jazz Living provides an inspirational, dynamic and energetic tool for approaching life's challenges—one that may help the future of our grandchildren.

## APPLY FRESH PRINCIPLES TO LIFE

The Art of Jazz Living includes skills of flexibility, adaptability, teamwork, listening, and emotional intelligence—attractive skills that add value to many areas of life. Integrating the jazz living approach into your life can help you respond to the complex challenges of daily living with more graciousness and integrity of body, emotions, mind, and spirit.

Spiritual principles of jazz living:

1. Find the **rhythm,** keep a steady beat. Practice body awareness.

2. Find the inner flow. **Connect** to your natural state of inner well-being.

3. Listen for the **groove**. Let go and allow Divine Love to uplift you.

4. Individual **voice**. Shine when it's your turn. Improvise. Take a risk.

5. **Collaborate**. Harmonize. Let others shine.

The energy pattern flows downward – inward – upward – outward – around.

Imagine one of those days. You come back from a stressful meeting between the board of directors and volunteers; the kid hit a guard rail and dented the car; you realize your employer lied to you; the dog pooped on the carpet; you spilled salad dressing on the shirt you were planning to wear. Add two more items, and you want to hide in the closet with a package of cookies and a bottle of wine.

You have what it takes to handle the next crisis and get your groove back so you can navigate complexity and uncertainty from your place of centeredness and inner well-being. Try practicing these steps every day to build your inner spiritual core muscles.

*Rhythm.* Practice body awareness. When you are aware of your inner ecosystem, you can settle your sympathetic nervous system. You aren't stuck in a fight-flight-freeze reactive stress response. Instead, you use your body awareness tools to stay grounded and present at that moment.

Notice what is going on in your body. What emotions are present? Where in your body are you feeling an emotion? Find ten minutes to yourself, put on music, and move. Fast or slow. Just move your body. If you only have five minutes in a bathroom stall, that's a start. Breathe into your belly. If you can get outside in nature, hug a tree, breathe fresh air, take a walk or run. Hug your fur, baby. Do a yoga video on YouTube. My daily practice of yoga, weightlifting, and body-soul movement keeps me feeling grounded and anchored in my body.

*How do you find your rhythm and grounding?*

*Reconnect.* Toggle inward to awareness of the Divine within as you toggle between two computer screens. You might use breathwork, prayer, meditation, exercise, guided imagery, or whatever works for you to reconnect to your creative inner wisdom. The Divine is both outside of you and within you.

Imagine breathing through your heart as if you have a nose in the center of your chest. Find something beautiful or something you appreciate. Imagine that behind your physical heart in front of your spine, you can step through a doorway inward to your soul and through soul into the loving embrace of God the infinite, Divine Love—whatever name you give the transcendent.

Pause a moment to get out of your head and into your heart when you're at a stoplight, in a meeting, or at a soccer game. Toggle from your head to your heart and inward to your natural state of inner well-being.

You can find a guided meditation to reconnect to your natural state of inner well-being on my WU profile page.

https://www.thewellnessuniverse.com/world-changers/leahskurdal/

***Listen for the groove.*** Listen to your heart's wisdom for inspiration. Feel into the upward spiral and be carried on your breath—inward, upward, outward, downward, around.

Where do you find your groove? Exercise, cooking, gardening, nature, artistic expressions, prayer, meditation?

Some meditation disciplines refer to an inner smile, an upturn of your inner energy. Reconnecting to my inner well-being when I'm off track feels like an updraft as if a breeze has lifted a leaf into the air. I allow myself to ride the feeling of being uplifted and carried on the wings of love.

Imagine how you *feel* hearing your favorite song. Don't get wrapped in your mind trying to figure it out. The groove is in your heart—not your mind. Tap into your intuition by opening your heart. Try an inner smile—even a little one.

There are appropriate times to embrace sadness. Singing the blues is part of the human condition. Process the feelings. Then, allow the energy to keep moving through without getting stuck and entangled. You don't need to disconnect from Divine Love.

Connect inward and listen with the ears of your heart for the next right steps. What's the feel, the essence, of what you want to create? Experience harmonious interactions with loved ones? Feel appreciated at your workplace? Feel radiant health and vitality? If you focus on the essence, let go of control and allow the greater good to fill in the details, it might turn out better than you imagined. What inspiration wants to birth through you?

**Shine your individual voice.** When we're aligned with inspiration and our natural state of inner well-being, the music of our lives takes on magical qualities. Take a risk and improvise to make something fresh and generative at that moment.

One day, I walked into a new client's room to offer a 15-minute massage and energy healing. "What do you need today?" I asked the back of her head as she lay face down on the massage table. "I have a migraine, and everything hurts," she replied. I placed my hands on her back between her shoulder blades. Her energy felt chaotic. I worked to smooth out her energy field while massaging her frizzled head, neck, and shoulder muscles. By the end of the session, her energy felt calmer and less chaotic.

An intuitive clarity welled up in my heart and jumped from my heart out my mouth. "You have something bigger to do with your life!" I shared. "Your container is way too small!" Startled, she responded, "You're the third person to tell me that lately." I had never met this woman. I only saw the back of her head and wouldn't be able to identify her. Within fifteen minutes, I had read her energy and shared a valuable insight that confirmed the message she needed to hear. I may have changed the trajectory of her life by sharing what welled up in my heart. Sometimes, my intuitive hits surprise me. I'm getting used to trusting them.

Speak the truth in your heart with inner spiritual authority so others can be blessed. That doesn't mean dominating the conversation or hammering someone with your opinions. When improvisation becomes self-indulgent, it can become uninteresting and annoying. Think of an ego-based person who talks incessantly.

Can you listen with the ears of your heart to what the other person needs at the time? Ask your heart wisdom, *what would you love to do?* Share your interpretation in a way that adds beauty and harmony. Or not. Step forward with compassion and show up as the best you have to offer at that moment. Or not. Some days our best is better than other days. If what you offer doesn't land as you wished, step back, ground, reconnect inward, listen, try again.

Take space—make space. Notice when it's time to step back and allow others to shine and practice flowing between leadership and followership.

***Collaborate***. Jazz musicians perform at their peak when they're all in the groove or 'group flow.' In jazz bands, the individual expressions blend and flow from one player to the other in a joyful and playful dance. Jazz Living embraces the paradox of both/and—individual expression aligning with the oneness of shared truth, creating a collective space of WE.

Imagine two overlapping circles. One circle is your space. One circle is my space. Where the two circles overlap is the shared "we" space. When we bring curiosity to understand another's perspective into "we" space, we can come up with new innovative solutions. Different beliefs and perspectives can coexist harmoniously when supporting an individual's dignity, acceptance, and belonging.

Have you had any experience of group flow when ideas clicked and the team worked together as a whole? Sports teams find the group groove and win championships. Work teams synergistically combine skill sets to manage stellar projects. Theatrical groups come together on opening night for magical performances. I was in a therapy group that bonded so well we hated to end the program.

How can you maintain your own rhythm, flow, groove, and voice while allowing others to share their unique talents? Can you listen with curiosity for what you might learn from another perspective? Can you integrate your truth and another's truth for joint meaning-making of shared truth?

## PRACTICING THE ART OF JAZZ LIVING

The Art of Jazz Living is a fusion of classical and improv—blending what you know with something new to handle challenges with the ingredients on hand. You don't always have the luxury of a five-star retreat center or a weekend cabin retreat to refresh and renew.

How can you use what you have on hand to push the reset button? Start with the sacred marriage of Divine Feminine and Divine Masculine within yourself. You are, we each are, part of the Divine unfolding, evolving through our unique expressions. What will Divine Love express through you? An intuitive insight, creativity, beauty, harmony, freedom, a fresh perspective.

Give yourself sacred time and space to get grounded and be present with what is. Note the missing ingredients and acknowledge the ingredients on hand with gratitude. Tune inward to your natural state of inner well-being for guidance. Listen for inspiration. Take space to shine and make space for others to shine. Bend the notes—blend the flavors. Find the flow of what wants to be expressed uniquely through you. The essence of Jazz Living is to play the song in your heart with all you've got and allow the music of life to express through you.

**Leah Skurdal** is an Intuitive Wellness Guide, Ancestral Energy Healer, workshop facilitator, inspirational speaker, and best-selling author. Leah guides people to navigate stress and nurture their bodies by reconnecting to their intuitive inner wisdom. Her transformational workshops and courses awaken the healer within each person to intuit what serves the expression of their innate well-being.

Leah Skurdal is a core blogger on The Wellness Universe platform, a contributing author to *The Wellness Universe Guide to Complete Self Care: 25 Tools to Achieve Anything*, a contributing author to *The Ancestors Within: Discover and Connect With Your Ancient Origins*, and author of *Seeking Serenity: How to Find Your Inner Calm and Joy*.

Leah has spoken at the Parliament for World Religions, The Women and Spirituality Conference, the Complementary & Alternative Medicine Club, and many spiritual centers, business women's organizations, and other venues. Leah co-hosted the Global Summit for Transformational Educators through the Diamond Kaleidoscope Initiative.

You can connect with Leah Skurdal through her WU profile page: https://www.thewellnessuniverse.com/world-changers/leahskurdal/

# CHAPTER 8

# GO TO BED LIKE A GODDESS!

## HOW ONE NIGHTLY AFFIRMATION CAN SPARK GRATITUDE AND CHANGE YOUR LIFE

Tina Plantillas, Spiritual Life Coach, and RYT

## MY STORY

I couldn't believe I was standing in a puddle of my blood, with only a tee shirt and panties on, surrounded by strangers as I closed my eyes and tried to remember to breathe.

I felt a horrific pain in my stomach, like a punch to the gut. I looked down and saw I had cuts all over my body. *What the fuck just happened ?!* My stomach and my legs looked like I had been involved in some sort of brutal knife fight. I could not believe my eyes. In a panic, I hobbled through shards of glass, cutting the bottom of my feet, making my way just inside the doorway to scream for help.

As I called for help, I assessed my body and saw a large piece of glass sticking out of my hip. My body was hot and tense. My husband, Will, was running towards me, pulling up his pants rushing from the bathroom. "What happened!?" He exclaimed. I tell him, "A glass bottle exploded in my hand when I picked it up," as I was crying. He is trying to get a look at this large fragment protruding from my hip.

I'm looking to him to try and read his face and reaction to see how bad this is. He stays calm. He is the calmest in tense situations, so this scared me because I looked to him to indicate how I should react. I tried to remember to breathe as my body started to get weaker.

At this point, our daughter, Jazmyne, comes in, still rubbing her eyes from just waking up, and asks, "What is going on?" She starts to approach and can see how bad the situation is. While her dad is kneeling to get a closer look, I'm purposely trying not to look, as I can feel the blood dripping out of my body. Looking to see if he should pull it out, Jazmyne and I both exclaim, "NO! We don't think you should pull it out." I told him we had seen one too many Grey's Anatomy episodes to know—DO NOT PULL IT OUT. "Call 911, Jazmyne!" he yelled as the blood flow continued to pool on the floor around my feet.

As Jaz called 911, Will was holding a towel around the area. He asked her to bring me a long tee-shirt before the first responders arrived since I was half-naked due to the weekly weigh-in. Within minutes they pulled up. So thankful to have a fire station just around the corner!

I stood there trembling, vulnerable, bleeding, scared, and half-naked, surrounded by what felt like a dozen first responders evaluating me. Okay, I may be being dramatic, but when you are standing there bleeding with the "suns out, buns out," then even a few can feel like an audience.

First responders observed my blood pressure dropping, and I was whisked away by ambulance to the nearest hospital. I was lying on the gurney when all of a sudden, I started shaking and feeling a crazy amount of pain through my right leg. I asked the EMT next to me what was happening. She said the adrenaline from the initial shock is probably starting to wear off, so now I may be experiencing the pain. Holy shit, was she right. My body had never experienced this before. *What is happening? Am I going to make it to the hospital? Is this the end for me?*

I arrive at the hospital and get taken to an emergency room to be assessed. Doctors hovered over every inch of my body. They were doing an ultrasound of my stomach as a white-haired man with big blue eyes approached my face and stared into my eyes so deeply I felt a chill in my soul. He introduced himself as a chaplain. *Why is there a chaplain here? Oh my god, I am going to die?* I know he was there to comfort me, but at this moment, it just sent me into a panic as tears were streaming down my face.

I then felt a horrific pain as I screamed, "Oh my god, what the fuck was that?' I heard a man's voice say, "They pulled out the glass." The jolt down the right side of my leg gave me the feeling that it was on fire and being electrocuted at the same time. My eyes felt as though they were about to bulge out of their sockets.

From there, a CT Scan determined I had more glass lodged in my leg not visible by the naked eye. I needed emergency surgery to remove the remaining glass and stitch up the rest of the damage.

It turns out the piece of glass that was stuck in my hip was millimeters from my femoral artery! I am so thankful we didn't attempt to remove it ourselves and that it was not any closer, or I literally could have bled out and died right there in my entryway.

I got sent home the same day after surgery with just a prescription for pain pills. I asked, "Okay, so what do I do next? I can barely walk. I need help getting up and down." The answer was a generic, "Rest for a week, don't use stairs, etc." I was in so much pain, not to mention that my right leg was numb in some areas!

The following year placed me on a journey to heal the daily pain and discomfort I endured. In an attempt to heal, I saw many professionals and tried several modalities such as physical therapy, massage therapy, electrons plus therapy, stimulation, cupping, scraping, etc.

The physical recovery process was painful, but the hardest part was the mental recovery process. I went through a deep depression for months after this accident. It was the strangest thing to me, almost as if I were witnessing myself from the outside looking in. I was so disconnected from myself.

We owned a business at this time, and I was unable to work for a while. When I did go back, I only had the energy to go to work, come home, and return to lay in bed.

Laying in bed even started to feel like a chore. My body was heavy, and it was uncomfortable to move and find enjoyable positions to lay. I didn't have an appetite, making it difficult to find the energy to get up and move around. I would be up all night, unable to sleep. I tried many natural supplements to sleep. I experienced plenty of "why me" moments during those nights of restlessness.

I would cry because I felt lost and did not know what to do next or how my life would unfold from here. These scars were deep, they were bright red, and they made me look like a victim. What would people think if they saw them since they are perfectly framed around my bikini area? *Will I have to wear long shorts to the pool now?* I was so self-conscious of the hot pink, deep scars that remained.

It was an incredibly difficult period. I knew what was wrong, and I simply could not snap out of it. All I could see were these gross scars and a severe lack of mobility. I could not wrap my head around how or why it happened and what it was trying to teach me.

I felt it was difficult, but I had to find a way to find small wins in my day because I had no other ideas on what to do. I got creative. I had to start hyping myself up for even the smallest win. I would accomplish a task as small as "tidying up" and tell myself, "Yes, Tina, good job!"

I was so grateful I was able to get up and move a little bit more. One thing every day that I could say I accomplished. After a while, I started to notice I would have these little conversations with myself like, "Hey, this is so great you did this, this, and this today. I am so proud for doing that— you are amazing!" It became a practice for me, and I will teach it to you too!

I realized I was missing a significant foundation of my yoga practice: self-compassion and love for myself, mind, body, and spirit. Which is something I have spent so much time on in the past. *How have I lost this connection to myself once again?* Luckily for me, I have been there before, and this was all too familiar.

Before I started practicing yoga in 2010, I had no clue about a mind-body connection. No clue how it would feel or even how it could feel! I felt insecure about my body for some reason. I'm assuming it was from the pressure of being a woman and merely existing. There is a constant pressure to be beautiful, but not in your own way. "Be a lady, but don't be sexy. Have a perfect body. But not too thin or you'll look anorexic. And not too thick—you're getting fat." When I look back, I wish I didn't care about other people's opinions so much.

Once I started to be more consistent with my "good job" affirmations, I turned my praises to my body. Turning my thoughts into my feelings. *How did I feel in my body today? What did my body get me through? How could I thank my body instead of criticizing it?*

Even with all my scars, I can still love my body. And most days, my nightly affirmation is simply, "Thank you body, good job. You got me through this day. I love you."

Today outside opinion doesn't matter to me. It's my body, my rules. I love my body so much, and I love it for me and no one else. It's the most personal relationship I will have in my life, and I am only concerned with what makes me happy when I look in the mirror.

I learned that it was the power within me to turn it around. Instead of giving my power away to the circumstance, I was able to turn my focus to me and what I could control—my thoughts. You are the key to it all. You never need to look outside of yourself to find validation. You can be your hype person and own your inner Goddess.

# THE TOOL

Not everyone goes through something as traumatic as I described in my story, but many are overwhelmed right now. The weight of the world alone could cause one anxiety.

I had to start with small wins. They were small, but they were still worthy. This is a way to begin the practice of building yourself up. Keep showing up each night to tell yourself you did a good job and mean it! Keep building on your list each day. You are slowly changing your mindset to a level of gratitude. Keep this practice up and notice how your life changes.

It is quite simple, and for a good reason. When life gets crazy sometimes, we just need a bite-size action item that is so simple and easy to remember and is always with us.

At the end of your night, right before you are about to go to sleep, close your eyes and repeat the following. "Your name or Goddess nickname, you did a good job!"

This is the perfect moment to praise yourself with positive affirmations. Give yourself kudos for something you crushed today. Heck yeah, go for it! Feel free to add additional affirmations and go for as long as you possibly can. Build yourself up, Goddess! Never feel bad about empowering yourself. It is always within you.

If you are not feeling it, and you are saying something to yourself such as, "I suck. I didn't do anything worthy of saying a good job about," at this very moment, guess what? You paused. You took a moment of reflection. You showed up. Now you can start to ask yourself why is it you are feeling this way. The more you do this, the more you question your feelings towards yourself. In doing this, you are building inner trust. You are reminding yourself to check in each day and nurturing this very personal relationship with yourself. Keep showing up.

This is the moment of reflection where you have the choice to find the good in each day. Sometimes we do not give ourselves enough credit for all that we do. We see everything as "expected" without seeing all the good that we do for ourselves and the good we do for others that most of the time go unnoticed.

We all have our own stories. Maybe you are a stay-at-home mom, have a full-time corporate career, or are in the midst of finding your own soul's purpose. All of those things can drive a lot of pressure. Constantly feeling that we aren't doing enough. We should be doing more, giving more, just being "more." With this nagging voice in the back of our heads, it is easy to see why we have lost connection to just allowing ourselves to appreciate all that we do accomplish.

We need to make time to appreciate ourselves. Celebrate the little things, because some days that is all we got! We keep going; we keep showing up. Continuing to believe that tomorrow is another day, and we choose how we want to live our lives. Do we want to keep feeling how we have been feeling, or are we ready to embrace our inner power and inner Goddess?

What I learned the most from this experience was how to stretch my love. Stretch my compassion for myself and my body as it healed, remembering that I am the one who holds that power. As I reflected at the end of each day, I realized more and more what a powerful soul I am. You have this power. We all have this power. Once we realize that it all starts and ends with us and that we are the thoughts we choose, we can begin to shift to an attitude of gratitude. This is one of the greatest gifts you can give yourself. You can start this shift with this one simple tool and embrace your inner Goddess each day.

**Tina Plantillas** is a Certified Spiritual Life Coach, Yoga and Meditation Teacher, Movement facilitator, and Commercial Credit Corporate extraordinaire.

Tina's curiosity for self-improvement started at a young age, always picking up a self-help book from the book store. In exploration to find a way to get into better shape, she found yoga in 2010, unexpectedly discovering the mind-body connection that would change her life.

Tina obtained her 200-hour Yoga Teacher Training certification in 2012 and began guiding amateur and professional athletes, bringing her relaxation techniques to high-level corporate employees, and facilitating movement events at the Phoenix Art Museum.

Her empathic soul has lead her on a journey of service. Whether that involves guiding a mindful yoga class to corporate associates or coaching clients through the struggle of trying to find their soul's purpose. Tina believes that to be truly happy, one must be open and connect to their highest self.

Tina's goal in life is to serve with love and help others learn to love themselves on a deeper level. She helps her clients find joy to create a life that feels aligned with their souls. Her passion is assisting clients to be kind, patient, and compassionate to themselves and others.

https://www.thewellnessuniverse.com/world-changers/tinaplantillas/

# CHAPTER 9

# A SPIRITUAL SOLUTION TO LOW SELF-ESTEEM

## RECLAIMING YOUR INNER GODDESS THROUGH THE PRINCIPLES

Del Adey-Jones, Principles Practitioner

Do you suffer from low self-esteem? Are you tired of settling for crumbs in all areas of your life? Do you stay in relationships where you feel disrespected and emotionally abused? I get it. That was me before I came across a new paradigm in spiritual psychology known as the 3 Principles. Before I explain what the 3 Principles are and how they changed my life beyond anything I could ever have imagined, I would like to begin by sharing my story.

## MY STORY

I was born in 1959 in a pious and puritanical chapel-going community in an idyllic part of the United Kingdom, known as North Wales. However, my childhood was not ideal, and my mother was neither pious nor puritanical. She was not your typical June Cleaver type of housewife. Instead, she was a maverick who danced to the beat of her own drum. I was the product of an eight-year affair she had with my father, a married man who lived in the nearby village with his wife and two daughters.

One of my earliest and most impactful memories was when a stranger came to our home when I was four years old.

"Keep your hands off my husband," she pleaded.

I was sitting on the top of the two steps that separated our kitchen from our sitting room. I could feel the pain of a chipped ceramic tile digging into the back of my chubby bare legs, but I dared not move.

The smell of burnt toast from breakfast lingered in the air. The embers of the coal fire crackled in the fireplace. The morning sunlight shone through the kitchen window illuminating the anguish etched on the woman's face.

Her short-cropped brown hair framed her tear-stained cheeks. She wore a floral cotton housedress under a grey wool cardigan. Her slim legs were encased in tan nylons and sensible shoes. She was pretty in an understated sort of way. But no match for my mother.

My mother stood before her, proud and unflinching. Her folded arms rested in defiance against her heavily pregnant belly. Her jet-black hair was quaffed in the bouffant style of the times. The arch of her penciled eyebrows framed her violet eyes. She was known as the *Welsh Elizabeth Taylor*, and she didn't disappoint.

"Get her away from me," the woman snapped as I reached out to comfort her.

At that moment, I remember thinking to myself, my mother and I must have done something terrible to upset this poor woman so much. I didn't understand the intricacy of what was going on, but I knew enough to feel an overwhelming sense of shame. I decided at that moment this meant I was bad, and I should never have been born.

Once I turned five years old, I attended the local village primary school with my father's *real* children, as I thought of them. That's where I learned the words "illegitimate" and "bastard." Not just from the other children but from the teachers too. Their obvious contempt and disapproval were palatable. In my innocent young mind, I thought that being illegitimate meant that I wasn't as legitimate as others; therefore, I didn't deserve the same love and respect.

Believe it or not, I never met my father. He would visit my mother once a week late at night while my siblings and I were asleep. At the time, my mother ran a Bed & Breakfast out of our tiny Welsh cottage while she and my siblings and I slept in separate little trailers in our backyard. I shared a trailer with my older sister. We were given strict instructions not to go anywhere near my mother's trailer on the nights my father would visit.

The highlight of attending the local village school was that I would often see my father dressed in his navy-blue mechanics overalls, standing on the front doorstep of his terrace house. He was handsome, blue-eyed, with tousled sandy brown hair. I would stare in his direction in hopes that our eyes would meet, and he couldn't help but fall in love with me. Our eyes never met. Once at school, I would play in the yard near the front gates, convinced that if I just spun around fast enough, I would see him sneaking a peek at me through the chain-link fence. He was never there.

In my innocence, I thought all fathers must love their children, so his rejection of me must mean I wasn't good enough to be loved. I felt that he would want to claim me as his child if I had been pretty enough, good enough, skinny enough, or clever enough. His abandonment cemented my low self-esteem and made me feel that I wasn't worthy of being loved by him or anyone else. He was the first of a long list of narcissistic men who would play a pivotal role in my life.

As if life wasn't hard enough, my mother, with no emotional or financial help from my father, found herself in desperate need of money to support us. The bed and breakfast business was seasonal, and she needed to find something else to do to provide a more stable income. During that time, the UK government decided to shut down the enormous mental institutions and pay private citizens to take care of the mentally disabled people in their homes. So, my mother decided to convert our little Welsh cottage into an after-care home for the mentally disabled. By the time I was nine years old, she'd saved enough money to rent a massive old mansion and expand the business.

To say my mother was overwhelmed and overwrought was an understatement. She was often at her wit's end between taking care of fifty mentally disabled residents and trying to raise seven children single-handedly. She was in survival mode and would often lose her temper both emotionally and physically. While she lived in separate quarters, my siblings and I lived amongst the residents. I took this to mean that she didn't care about me. There were no locks on our doors, no privacy, and no safety. Imagine, "One flew over the Cuckoo's Nest," and you've got the picture.

I was a frightened, scared, and unhappy child who grew into a fearful, timid, and sad teenager. Like many fatherless girls, I grew up looking for validation from any man that would pay me attention. As you can imagine, I attracted some unscrupulous men willing to pay me the attention I craved, just not in the way I needed. By the time I reached twenty, I was contemplating leaving the planet. I didn't feel I had the skills necessary to survive life.

Luckily for me, at the age of twenty-one, I went on holiday to California and never left. During my visit, I discovered a metaphysical bookshop called The Bodhi Tree. It was a lovely old cottage, barely visible from the street, hidden by large trees and foliage. Inside was a network of tiny rooms linked together. Each room had bookshelves and tables piled high with every conceivable book one could imagine on spirituality and self-improvement. I felt like a kid in a candy store. As I meandered from room to room, I discovered more hidden treasures. Desperate to make sense of my tumultuous childhood, I devoured everything I could get my hands on.

That was the beginning of my 30-plus year search to find the answers for which I was looking. In addition to my years in conventional therapy, I studied everything from Buddhism to Hinduism and Kabbalah to Kundalini Yoga. I sweltered in sweat lodges and drank Ayahuasca in the desert. I participated in dozens of workshops, from "Healing the Shame that Binds" to "Reclaiming Your Shadow." I must have spent hundreds of thousands of dollars over those years trying to fix myself and find the confidence that seemed to elude me.

Despite all the work I had done and all the money I spent, I still felt broken and inferior. I was always on the lookout for the next best thing to improve myself and rid myself of my low self-esteem. I had a library full of self-improvement books that could rival the self-help section of Barnes and Noble. Like Band-Aids, my walls were plastered with certificates and qualifications I gained in hopes of covering the gaping wounds of my insecurities.

My chronic low self-esteem had me settling for crumbs in all areas of my life. I stayed in emotionally abusive relationships long past their expiry date. I was a people pleaser who pretended to be needless and wantless so as not to bother anyone. I hid in the wings of life, afraid of being found out, criticized, and ridiculed.

On the outside, I looked confident and capable, while on the inside, I lived with the constant chatter of negative self-talk. Despite my inner demons, I managed to carve out a career as a costume designer and artist. My crowning glory was getting married and the birth of my two beautiful sons. For a while there, I thought I'd made it.

Fast forward to 2009. As the Universe has the habit of doing, I found the answer to my years of suffering from low self-esteem during one of the most painful periods of my life. My *dark night of the soul* came when I discovered that my marriage of eighteen years wasn't what I had thought it was. Against my will, I found myself amid a whirlwind of painful discoveries and humiliating revelations. My marriage was ending, and the fantasy of providing my children with the stable two-parent family I had wished for as a child was unraveling around me.

The answer to my problems came while I was returning home to California after visiting my sister in Spain. The two and a half-hour flight from Barcelona to London had been excruciating. My mind was in overdrive with painful memories of the past and fear of what my future would look like as a fifty-year-old divorced mother of two young sons. I was exhausted and in a state of panic, not knowing how to escape the incessant horror show playing out in my head. My thoughts were driving me mad.

As my plane landed in Heathrow, my anxiety mounted to the point of a full-blown anxiety attack. Somehow, I managed to disembark the aircraft. Then, desperate for something to calm me down, I headed for the airport bookshop. I was standing in the self-help aisle, searching the shelves for the latest book that would provide me with the magic pill, when it happened. A book jumped off the shelf and knocked me on the head.

Well, maybe that's a slight exaggeration. Let's just say the title of the book figuratively knocked me on the head. The black letters "Stop Thinking. . .Start Living" jumped off the yellow book cover and caught my eye. *This is precisely what I need*, I thought to myself. I bought the book and barely made it to the gate to board my next plane home.

I didn't take my usual nap on that portion of the journey. Instead, I read that book from cover to cover. It was life-changing, and not because it shared tools and tricks to improve myself, become a better person, be more confident, or be less riddled with insecurity. On the contrary, the book seemed to suggest that I was perfect just as I was. Nothing broken, nothing lacking. Apparently, I'd been a Goddess all this time; I just didn't know it!

# THE TOOL

The tool I would like to share with you is a new paradigm in spiritual psychology known as The Principles. The Principles are a description, not a prescription. They describe the system behind how we humans experience life. The following is a brief overview of the teachings of The Principles.

## WE ARE SPIRITUAL BEINGS HAVING A HUMAN EXPERIENCE

The Principles teach us we are *spiritual beings having a human experience*, and as such, we are all Gods and Goddesses at our essence. We all emanate from the same spiritual energy that creates all living things. Regardless of the environment we grew up in, the circumstances of our birth, the color of our skin, and our socio-economic status, we are all equal, *which* means that none of us is *more than* or *less than* anyone else. Of course, we might appear different in the physical world of form, but we are all the same at our spiritual essence. Understanding this one aspect of the Principles was pivotal in helping me overcome my feelings of inferiority. Feelings of lack and comparison come from the personal mind, full of insecure thoughts and negative chatter. However, when I settle into my true spiritual nature, ideas of less than and not good enough melt away.

## WE LIVE IN AN INSIDE-OUT WORLD

The Principles teach us that we live in an *inside-out world*, not an outside-in world. In our culture, we've been raised to believe that the way we feel directly results from our circumstances or the people in our lives. The truth is our experience of life comes via our thinking about our circumstances and the people in our lives, not directly from the outside world itself. Every second of every day, we are living in the feeling of our thinking. Once I saw this, I felt more empowered and less of a victim of my circumstances or toxic people in my life. I recognized that I was in charge of how I experienced my life. Nothing or nobody could make me feel anything without my permission.

## WE ARE NOT OUR THOUGHTS

The 3 Principles teach us that human beings have anywhere from 60,000 to 100,000 thoughts a day. These thoughts are nothing but energy running through us. They are not personal to us. They are not informing us about who we are. They are up for grabs by anyone. Unfortunately, many of the thoughts we have about ourselves have been with us our whole lives. They are so familiar we believe they are telling us about who we are. We have no power over which thoughts pop into our heads. However, we can control which thoughts we want to indulge in or where we choose to place our attention. Understanding this helped me see that I didn't need to believe or disidentify with my insecure thoughts.

Furthermore, I didn't need to change my thoughts. All I needed to do was change my relationship to my thinking. So instead of fighting my insecure thoughts, I ignored them. Before long, they lost their intensity and stopped showing up.

## INNATE WISDOM

Each of us is born with innate wisdom. It is an integral part of us. Our wisdom is specific to us. It guides us every moment of every day. It is always available and always has our back. Life becomes so much easier when we take our hands off the wheel and let our inner wisdom guide us. When I learned to tune out the constant chatter of my insecure thoughts, I heard my inner wisdom. Following the gentle guidance of my wisdom has been liberating.

## INNATE WELLBEING.

Each of us is born with the gift of innate wellbeing. Innate wellbeing is our default setting. Regardless of our circumstances, states of mind, or moods, we bounce back to our innate wellbeing when we are not focusing on our negative thinking. I am no longer afraid of my low moods or feelings of anxiety and depression. I know that no matter what I am going through, I will return to my natural state of wellbeing in time.

## INNATE RESILIENCE

Each of us is created with innate resilience. It doesn't matter what has happened to us in life; we can never be broken or damaged at our core, our spiritual essence, our inner goddess. Therefore, there is no need to fix ourselves. We may get bumped and bruised, but we are resilient. Knowing that I was never damaged was very helpful as someone who suffered from abuse of all kinds. Was I impacted by what happened to me? Yes. Was I permanently damaged by what happened to me? No.

## SEPARATE REALITIES

The Principles teach us that each one of us is living in our separate reality—our individual thought-created-Universe. Someone else's behavior has nothing to do with us; it has to do with their thinking and level of consciousness at the moment. This was so helpful to me when I needed to forgive the people who hurt and abused me. I stopped trying to understand why they did what they did. I saw that it wasn't personal. They were doing the best they could, given their thinking and level of consciousness at the time.

## LIVING IN THE PRESENT MOMENT.

Lastly, The Principles teach us to live in the present moment. We feel fear and anxiety when we listen to our insecure thoughts about the past or the future. We have no control over the past. It's gone, over, and done with. We cannot change it. And the future is an illusion. The only thing we have is the present moment. When we live in the present moment, we are connected to the truth of who we are at our essence, divine Gods and Goddesses.

If you are interested in learning more about The Principles, please reach out to me at

https://www.thewellnessuniverse.com/world-changers/deladey-jones/

**Del Adey-Jones** is a Principles Practitioner, Teacher, Author, Youtuber, Blogger, and host of "Insightful Conversations" and "Secrets of a Life Gone Right." She is also the founder of *The Way Out of Codependency and Narcissistic Abuse......through understanding The Principles.*

Del's passion is helping people find freedom from the debilitating condition of Codependency and Narcissistic Abuse. Thanks to her unconventional and dysfunctional childhood growing up in the UK, and her personal challenges, including divorce and raising children as a single parent, her work is informed by the empathy gained from real-life experience and her deeper studies of Spirituality and Psychology.

Using her down-to-earth, relatable approach to coaching and her commitment to creating a safe space to explore the Inside Out Understanding, she continues to serve a wide range of clients worldwide.

# CHAPTER 10

# LET GO OF THE HOT COAL

## LEARN HOW TO FORGIVE YOURSELF AND OTHERS WITH EASE

Lolita Guarin, Stress Management Expert

## MY STORY

I could hear a commotion outside the door, my dog excited, jumping up and down, wagging his tail, barking impatiently, hurrying someone up to come in. The door should be open by now, but all I hear is the key looking for the lock, circling around, scratching the door.

I looked at the clock, and my heart jumped. The time of day my dad came home would predict what kind of state he was in. If he came home at 3 pm, that meant he was sober. If he came around 7 pm, he was too drunk to argue and went right to bed. If he didn't show up by 9 pm, that meant he wouldn't be coming home at all that night.

*But it's 4 pm, which means you'll have no idea what state he's in.* I knew for sure that he wouldn't be drunk enough to go to bed. That meant, depending on his mood, he could be very happy, making jokes, talking for two hours, or just annoyed with me, yelling, banging the table with his fist, and violent.

I don't wait until he finds the lock; I rush to the door to open it for him. He stumbles in, and my dog is so excited to see him. I serve him dinner. He eats slowly, murmuring some story that I must listen to. Most of the time, I have no idea what he's talking about, but I can't leave the kitchen, or he will get angry that nobody is listening to him. He pauses as he chews and looks through the window into the distance like he's thinking about something very important, then agrees with himself nodding his head. I watch him eat. And if I am lucky that day, he'll go to sleep before my mom comes back home from work. If not, I will need to hear them arguing about him being drunk again, but then at least I can leave the kitchen and listen to them from my room until my dog escorts my dad to bed.

Having an alcoholic father was not a novelty in Lithuania, where I'm from. Many people's fathers and mothers drink often. It was not easy to survive in the Soviet Union, but we all did the best we could. Every day brought uncertainty. I hated to go home after school, fretting about waiting on my dad to come home. Sometimes I had to swallow the embarrassment and fetch him from the street where he had passed out drunk, and sometimes I would watch him breaking things, fearing for my life. Many times, I would have a conversation, acting like all was well and laughing at his jokes. He never hit me, but all the time, I felt terrified. That's how I grew up, in constant fear.

As I'm telling you this, remembering those days, my heart clenches, and it's hard for me to breathe. The last time I saw my dad drunk was twenty years ago, and we are not in Lithuania anymore, but it sure feels like yesterday. When I was a kid, I promised myself I would leave home, take my mom with me, and never talk to my dad again when I grew up. I would never look back. I was wrong. My dad is still in my life. But now, he is sober.

For many years, I felt anger towards my dad for causing me and my mom to suffer. And at the same time, I was angry at myself that I couldn't do anything to change things. I couldn't even stand up for myself. I felt betrayed by the person who should be watching over me, who should support me, protect me, and make me feel safe. But my dad was the terror in the house. I have no idea what people mean by saying someone is "Daddy's girl."

How do you forgive those that hurt you? How do you forgive yourself for letting them hurt you? I'm sure you've heard before that holding on to anger towards another is like holding a hot coal in your hands, hoping that the other person's hands will burn. But in the end, you're the one who gets burned. You're still holding on while the other person lives their life as if nothing happened.

Forgiveness is a complicated process where someone who has been hurt chooses to release themselves from the hurt and resentment towards the person who hurt them. Many resist forgiveness because it feels like if we forgive, we let the wrongdoer's behavior be justified or accepted. That is why I couldn't forgive my father for a very long time. It would make me very angry to think about the pain he caused my mother and me.

When I started the journey of healing my soul, I read many books about self-development, trying to understand what was wrong with me. *How come other people can be happy and I can't? Why am I feeling fearful all the time and I can't relax? Why do I have such low self-esteem and can't finish things?*

I remember one day I was reading a book about how to run a business, and the author mentioned in her story how she struggled with anger, guilt, and low self-esteem due to being an adult child of an alcoholic. The concept was very new to me. I immediately picked up a book on that topic that she had recommended and finished it within days. I couldn't believe my own eyes. I was reading about myself! Suddenly I understood that there was nothing "wrong with me." I'm not a freak, not a cracked saucer in a perfect set. I realized I'd experienced childhood trauma, as many of us have. The reality is that it is nearly impossible to live on this planet and never experience traumas. Some can be big, some can be small, but they are still there. The key is to learn from them, grow from them, and not be broken by them.

As I was reading about how children who are experiencing trauma adjust to survive, I learned that some grow up being adaptive by changing their behavior, healing. Some become very resilient and narcissistic to survive. And some just break, can't handle the pain, and turn to different substances and destructive behaviors to run away from pain and try to numb their emotions. And since nobody ever taught them how to deal with those emotions and pain, they keep hurting themselves and others on their path.

And that is when it hit me, why my dad was an alcoholic. It was not by choice. He didn't wake up one day and say to himself, "I will be an alcoholic and hurt the people that I love the most because that is fun!" I realized that his own family emotionally abandoned him from an early age.

They always disapproved of him and made him feel incompetent, no matter how good he tried to be. He was always given the least attention and had to take care of the younger siblings. His parents gave attention and support to the younger siblings and not to him since he was "managing on his own."

All children need safety, support, and nourishment. And not all children get it because I believe all families are dysfunctional in their own ways. And so it goes, from generation to generation. Many grow up feeling lonely and abandoned and then have and raise their own children while feeling like isolated and misunderstood toddlers inside. And since nobody ever taught them how to deal with emotions and process the trauma, they can't teach healing processes to their children.

Our analytical mind assigns meaning to everything to explain the world and feel safe. We can interpret someone's behavior as against us, but in the same way, we can explain that behavior as something that has nothing to do with us. As soon as we stop thinking of hurt as something personal done to us, we can move on. But, of course, it is challenging to do that when we try to forgive the person responsible for nurturing and protecting us in the first place. The only way to move on is to recognize what happened, accept it, reframe it, understand it and forgive.

I made a decision that day to forgive myself and my father. I understood that he wasn't hurting me and my mother on purpose. He just didn't know how to handle his pain. It's your turn now. I am inviting you to be courageous and release the hot coal you are still holding. It is time.

# THE TOOL

I want to share a tool with you that will help you release the anger that keeps on burning inside your heart, keeping you away from peace and freedom. It might be a straightforward tool or very difficult to implement. It all depends on you. And remember, to forgive doesn't mean to forget or approve of that kind of behavior. Don't get intimidated by the process. Try a few times if you don't get enough courage to do it all at once. Be patient with yourself. Give yourself time and move forward one day at a time. Trust me. It will be worth it. But like any tool, the key to success is in using it.

1. **Acknowledge the feelings.** Allow yourself to feel the pain, the suffering, the hurt, the anger, despair, disappointment. Permit yourself to feel what comes up. It can be challenging to face that due to the hurt that you buried inside. The pain can be still fresh as an open wound or old like an ugly infected scar. It takes courage to face it, so give yourself credit. Remember, what you resist, persists.

   The hardest part is recognizing and facing the anger, hurt, and all those feelings you want to run away from. So you must stay with yourself, by your side, honoring your feelings because there is nothing worse than to abandon yourself at the moment when you need your support the most, as you were abandoned by the people who are supposed to take care of you. You might even feel guilty that you feel angry at those who hurt you, especially if they're family members or people close to you. You might even feel it is a virtue to sacrifice yourself and your well-being for others, but it doesn't give you peace; you feel violated, abandoned, and mistreated.

   Find a place and time where you won't be disturbed, create a safe space for yourself, and just be. If you don't feel like being by yourself, then ask your friend who you trust to be with you through the process, someone who you can talk to, call on, or write.

2. **Name your feelings.** Take time to take a piece of paper, a notebook, or your diary and write how that person who hurt you makes you feel. This is the time to face your feelings and name them. For example, write: "I feel angry, disappointed, etc..." It's been proven that acknowledged and named negative emotions become less painful because they become separate from you. They are not a part of you that can hurt you or control you anymore.

   Write the letter and get all your feelings out and place it in an envelope. Imagine sending the envelope. If you feel good about it, you're welcome to send that letter to the person who hurt you, so they read and see how that made you feel. If you don't feel comfortable with the person reading it, you even can throw it in the trash or safely burn it to "send it."

   If you don't feel like writing a letter, you can imagine talking to the person. Close your eyes and see the person coming to the room where you are. If you feel comfortable, imagine them sitting in front of you. Tell them how you feel. If you can talk out loud, do that. Talk as long as you want to, yell, shout, bang a hand on the table, let it all out, just make sure you don't hurt yourself or others in the process.

3. **See it from the other point of view.** Any situation can have a different meaning if seen from a different perspective. Get into the other person's shoes by trying to figure out the reasoning behind their behavior. It might be difficult but try. I remember a great story about a driver that stopped behind another car at an intersection. As the green light came on, the first car wasn't moving forward. More than that, the woman came out of the driver's seat, opened the passenger seat in the back, and started looking for something. The driver behind her got very annoyed and started shouting at a woman to move. As it turned out, her toddler in the back seat started choking, so she jumped out of the car to help him. Everyone would have done the same thing if that was their child. The driver felt stupid for yelling at her after he found out the truth.

   Most of our behavior is based on self-preservation and survival, even if it hurts others. Ask yourself: what's their reality? What kind of family did they grow up in? What circumstances made them behave in a way that hurt you? I believe that only hurt people hurt others because they don't know how to handle their pain. So, by hurting others, they feel in control of the situation, especially if they feel no control over their surroundings. Many don't even know they are hurting someone. Many soothe themselves with alcohol, drugs, or destructive behavior. Remember, we handle the situation the way we know how to. Much of the behaviors we learn from family members, and the behavior lasts from one generation to the next.

4. **Let it go.** You might be so hurt that you can't explain why the person would hurt you that way, but you still can decide to forgive them because you are ready to move on. That is the time to write again. You can write by hand or type on your computer. Write another letter of forgiveness to yourself for being hurt, ashamed of your feelings, and not being there for you. Remember, you did the best you could with what you knew and what you could do.

   Write the last letter to the other person for hurting you. Make a decision and intention to forgive them and let it go. If you started this process not by writing but by talking with the person in your imagination, you could continue the process by talking to them. Imagine telling them that you forgive them and letting them and yourself go free. Imagine that person leaving the room.

**Lolita Guarin** is a passionate author, empowering speaker, and trustworthy coach for busy professionals and adult children of addicts. She is a licensed and certified Stress Management and Life Coach, author of the book "Crush Stress While You Work" and "Stress Management for Adult Children of Alcoholics. " Lolita has been featured as a guest on the "Ask Dr. Nandi Show" and many podcasts.

She is a founder of Be Amazing You who provides coaching and online courses to lower burnout and increase energy and well-being. To teach stress management, Lolita has organized and facilitated online and in-person workshops for groups and individuals. She also teaches stress management in the workplace one company at a time by speaking. In addition, she founded a membership for continued support to those who have suffered childhood trauma due to an addicted parent and others who suffer from burnout, low energy, and stress.

Lolita has dealt with stress and tried many stress-release techniques over the years as a busy professional and childhood trauma survivor. After her health deteriorated due to stress, one night, she ended up in the emergency room. Lolita didn't want to medicate herself, so she went on a quest to find a solution that consisted of natural remedies and practices. Managing stress without medication became her priority.

And now, after years of researching stress relief techniques, attending workshops, coaching, and practicing on her own, she found that there is a better and natural way to battle stress than go on chronically depleted. And it starts with recognizing and healing childhood trauma as a precursor to how we deal with stress in general, which became one of the teaching pillars to managing stress.

To find more info about Lolita go to
https://www.thewellnessuniverse.com/world-changers/lolitaguarin/

# CHAPTER 11

# SUDDENLY SINGLE

## HOW TO BECOME "ME"
## AFTER BEING "WE" FOR SO LONG

Carrie Hopkins-Doubts, MA, PCC

## MY STORY

I've had a profound desire to belong to the people I care about ever since I was a child. That has also translated into a deep need for an intimate partnership.

I love being married. I've done it twice now. And, now, I'm suddenly single again, at a stage of my life where I never expected to be alone.

I have not lived alone in over 40 years. Even after my divorce, over 14 years ago, I lived with my daughter. Then I married my second husband, and we started a beautiful life together that lasted over 15 wonderful years. This chapter of my life ended abruptly with his death only five months ago.

I hate living alone.

My work as a life coach helping people through loss and major life transitions has equipped me very well to navigate through the grief, anxiety, loneliness, and sadness that I feel every day. I don't like feeling this way any more than anyone does. I heard myself say yesterday (to myself - right? -

because there isn't anyone here to say it to), "I'm tired of feeling angry and sad all the time."

I'm working on finding my "me" after being a "we" for such a big part of my life.

Tom and I had plans. Now those plans are tossed on the scrap heap as I'm working to create plans of my own that will address the questions that face everyone after a serious "rug-being-pulled-out-from-under-you" experience.

*Who am I? What do I want?* And, the even more daunting question: *Why am I still here?*

These are hard questions to wrestle with, especially when grieving.

Grief, a subject I know a lot about, has now grabbed my full attention. It's personal now. If you're going through a divorce, breakup, or the death of your spouse or partner, you're likely to be experiencing grief as well.

## SOME POSSIBLE EXPERIENCES OF GRIEF

Dealing with loss creates stress on all levels: physical, mental, emotional, social, and spiritual. You may be experiencing some or all of the challenges listed below. As you're reading through this section, circle those that apply to you now.

**Physical:** trouble sleeping, low energy, muscle aches and pains, immune suppression, weight gain/loss, heart palpitations. Then there's the stress of the legal and financial issues you face when suddenly you're widowed or divorced.

**Mental:** initial denial, disorganized thinking, difficulty concentrating, irrational thoughts, regrets, the judgment of self and others.

**Emotional:** initial shock and numbness, emotional flooding, sadness, anger, anxiety/fearfulness, guilt, sense of helplessness and hopelessness, longing or yearning for the past.

**Social:** isolation and withdrawal, avoiding crowds/gatherings, being "dropped" by friends or family, lack of understanding or support from others, difficulties with holidays/anniversaries, loneliness.

**Spiritual:** a crisis of faith, feeling of abandonment, anger at God, deep questioning *why*, loss of meaning/purpose, feeling unworthy of love.

Yep. I'm checking a lot of the boxes right now. How about you? What are you experiencing as you're going through this grief? Are you, like me, trying to figure out how to be a "me" after being a "we" for so long?

## ADJUSTMENTS YOU MUST MAKE

Your world gets turned upside down when you lose a partner. There are external, internal, and spiritual adjustments you'll need to make in order to be your best "me" after losing your mate.

a. **External adjustments** – Living daily without your partner. Life changes dramatically when a person who has been an integral part of your life is no longer there. You may need to go out and get a job, sell your home, move to another city, learn new skills that your partner used to handle, become a single parent, and so on. Life changes like these can seem overwhelming, especially when they come all at once.

   What's helpful is to be open and flexible to change, being gentle and patient with yourself while you are learning new skills, and celebrating your successes along the way.

b. **Internal adjustments** – Creating a new identity out of your loss. Women who have their sense of self-tied into their role as a wife may find this adjustment challenging. Ultimately it can be transformative and deeply healing. The question, *Who am I now?* really comes into the forefront and demands an answer.

   What's helpful is to examine your values and priorities, let go of patterns in consciousness that contribute to and perpetuate self-victimization, and to explore courageously the additional questions of *What do I want?* and *What skills and strengths do I have that will help me move forward?*

c. **Spiritual adjustments** – Loss of a partner can deeply shake your faith in God/The Universe, leaving you feeling vulnerable and abandoned. It often brings forward the deep question, *Why am I here, and what is my purpose?*

   What's helpful is to continue to ask for Spirit's assistance and be willing to explore these questions, patiently listening to your inner wisdom for your answers.

**What I know to be true now: I know that I'm going through an** *experience* **of loss and grief, and that's not who I am. That's not "me."** **Same for you. Grief is not who you are.**

## LETTING GO OF "WE"

We all long to belong. To someone. To be special to someone. A wedding ring is a symbol of that belonging.

When you are divorcing, it's clear when it's time to take off your wedding ring. For some, it's when the intention to separate has been shared, and the marriage is being dismantled. For others, it's when the divorce decree is complete. And, taking off your ring may or may not be easy to do. It's an important sign that you're ready to let go of being a "we."

For widows, it's not so clear. Choosing when to take off your wedding ring is a very individual decision. Some women leave it on indefinitely as a sign of their enduring attachment and still think of themselves as married. Some wait until they feel ready to embrace a new relationship.

I was attending a meditation retreat and heard my inner voice speaking to me. *You are not married now. It's time to take off your ring because it is anchoring you to the past. Time to let go.* With tears streaming down my face, I reached over and took off my ring and put it in my purse.

I can't tell you how vulnerable I felt after that! I felt naked and alone. I no longer belonged to anyone. It was just me. And, a very kind man (an angel, really) gave me a big hug and let me cry on his shoulder to remind me I wasn't alone.

**My heart hurt, yet I knew it was time to face the reality of being single again.**

## WHY IS IT SO HARD TO BE "ME"?

Your pain is real, and it can feel relentless at times. It's easy to feel victimized and complain about your ex or your loss, to say it's so unfair. You sort through the memories, replaying events and conversations in your head. You vent your anger, frustration, disappointment, hurt, confusion, sorrow to everyone who will listen. You hear yourself creating a history of your past that makes you look good to protect yourself from what you think is the secret truth about you:

- No one will ever want me again
- There's something wrong with me
- I'm not enough
- I'm too old, too heavy, too set in my ways, too _____ (fill in the blank) to be attractive to another person.

The biggest lie you tell yourself is that you are unlovable or unworthy of being happy.

You have not discovered the real truth about yourself. Not yet.

Your heart has been broken by your attempts at finding the love you've been searching for in other people, things, experiences. The responsibilities you've shouldered feel like burdens, and you carry them with resentment. You feel all alone.

You are angry. You feel that the one who should have loved you, been there for you, wasn't. You protect your heart from ever getting hurt again with a wall, separating you from everything and everyone.

You have doubts. So many doubts that eat at your heart and make you afraid of your life.

These are all illusions.

Do you want to know the truth about yourself?

You are perfect as you are. You are made of love, and so you don't need to search for it outside yourself. You don't need to be doing the "right" things to prove you are worthy. You are worthy. Your life is precious. Everyone else's life is precious, too. All life is precious.

You have heard this before. But have you ever lived from this level of truth?

## WHAT TO REMEMBER WHEN BECOMING "ME"

**My invitation to you is to start living in the truth that you are as God created you. You are a divine being having a human experience. You are capable, resourceful, creative, and whole, just as you are. You don't need to be fixed. You don't need to protect your fragile ego. You are meant to live a courageous, soulful, open-hearted life.**

When you know this, you will arrive at the moment of your death with no regrets.

If you are not living this way. understand that your life is now in session. It's happening to you now, and now is the time to make the adjustments in the way you approach your life to align it more fully with your values and your purpose.

It's time to embrace being a "me," with all your flaws, complications, wounds, and blemishes that you think are holding you back.

You've tried living the other way, waiting for life to give you what you want, waiting to be ready to go big, waiting for the "right" person to love, waiting until you get in shape and lose those 15 pounds, waiting for the right time just to be you.

Your life is now in session. It's not going to wait for you to start living.

# THE TOOL

## MEETING YOUR FUTURE SELF

Quantum physics is discovering that time and space can be very fluid when we look at them in terms of energy. We are able to experience multiple fields of time and space just by opening our awareness to them.

What if you were able to experience your future self in the present moment? Not only that but your *ideal* future self? The *future you* has some wisdom to share with you (the "now" you) about how to create your ideal future. You can trust her.

Communicating with your future self is a tool that I use with my clients. The reasons this can be powerful is based on these premises:

- You are a multi-dimensional being, able to access information from the quantum field of possibilities that are not limited to this space and time.

- Your head intelligence is not the only source of information, nor is it your best source of answers for the deep questions you face now.

- You possess the answers to your deepest questions and can access them through your heart and body intelligence.

- You can learn from your future as well as from your past.

- You can avoid the negative consequences of your "default future" by consciously deciding who you choose to be now in service to your ideal future.

It's easier to access your innate wisdom when you let go of the stories you are telling yourself about your situation. Your stories may have truth to them, and they may not. However, they are part of the known past and what you think is the predictable future. Doing this exercise bypasses the head and gets you into the heart.

## THE STEPS

*I've recorded this exercise for you so you can be guided through it (rather than trying to read the steps and do them at the same time.) To download the audio recording I created just for you, click here:*
https://www.thewellnessuniverse.com/world-changers/carriedoubts/

1. Make sure you are in a private, quiet space where you won't be interrupted.

2. Have a paper or journal and something to write with.

3. Take some time to center yourself and set your intention to fully experience this exercise in service to the maximum value for you. You might write down your intention in your notes.

4. Stand up in your space – making sure you have plenty of room to move around.

5. Close your eyes.

6. Bring to mind a situation that you are dealing with that is causing you worry, anxiety, hurt, or any other emotional disturbance. Just allow yourself to experience it fully without it needing to be any different than it is, just for right now.

7. Ask yourself, *What is it that I'd rather be experiencing than this? What is it I'd like to move into?*

8. Open your eyes and choose a spot in your space that represents what you'd like to move into. This is a time - one year into your future where this situation/challenge has been handled successfully, and you're experiencing more of what you want.

9. When you are ready, walk over to that space and step into it.

10. As you arrive into this space, one year into your future, you'll notice you are different. You are your future self, the one who is living one year into the future. Your situation/challenge has been handled.

11. Get a sense of what's here. If it helps, you can close your eyes. Just feel into what it's like to be free of the feelings, thoughts, and behaviors that have been holding you back. You've successfully navigated beyond that, and you are living the life you want to live.

12. What do you notice? What does it look like from here? What does it feel like from here? What's the energy you sense from here? Check-in with your body. What is it feeling? Just breathe into all of that. Give it a word or two to describe what's here for you one year in your future.

13. Now that you are fully here in this reality, what does your future self have to share with you about how she got here? (Turn to face the spot in the room where the "now" you had been standing.) Let yourself speak to yourself from the heart.

14. When you feel this is complete, move back to your original spot in your space – the place you were standing in when the exercise began.

15. What did you discover? Take this time to write some notes in your journal/paper. What do you know about your situation that you didn't know before this exercise?

16. Based on what you learned, what steps do you see yourself taking in the next six months to start moving into that desired future state for yourself? What needs to be your focus for these next six months? Write these down.

17. Who do you choose to be in order to make this possible? What qualities do you need to embrace fully to take these steps?

18. Zooming in, what steps do you have for yourself for the next thirty days? Write these down as well.

19. Write down one step to take over the next seven days. And what do you need to focus on in the next twenty-four hours to make that happen?

20. Take the time to acknowledge and appreciate yourself – and your future self – for being here for you.

Here's a poem to soothe your heart and bring you a moment of peace:

*Acceptance untangles the tentacles of judgment*
*While sacrificed attachments burn hot.*
*The seemingly endless fuel of concerns ends with a ceremony.*
*Allowing throws a coming-out party for freedom.*
*Home is not far now.*
*Love steps forward and claims us for its own.*
*Never lost or misplaced, just with us – while we were.*
*Who we are is answered by whose we are.*
*God's embrace is joy without limits.*
*We are divine and living in infinity.*

~M.D.

**Carrie Hopkins-Doubts**, MA, PCC, is a Spiritual Resilience Coach supporting people through major life transitions. She founded Life's Next Chapter Coaching in 2012 and is a Co-founder and contributor to her newest company, Hero Within, with fellow coach and friend Mauricio Acevedo.

Carrie earned a Master of Arts in Spiritual Psychology with an Emphasis in Consciousness, Health, and Healing, from the University of Santa Monica (USM) in 1998 and a Master of Science in Spiritual Science from Peace Theological Seminary in 2003. She served as the Director of Education at USM for 20 years.

After studying Psychology, she received her professional coaching certification from the Institute for Professional Excellence in Coaching (iPEC). She is a Certified Grief Counselor by the American Academy of Grief Counseling. Carrie holds the Professional Certified Coach (PCC) credential with International Coaching Federation (ICF) with certifications in Mentor Coaching, Relationship and Divorce Coaching, and Transformational Presence Coaching.

Carrie works with men and women experiencing transition, whether in relationships, career, health, or spirituality. She works to engage her clients in discovering and embracing purpose and meaning in their lives, utilizing a potential-based coaching philosophy.

Working with individuals and groups, Carrie helps people reconnect with their hearts, reclaim their power, and re-align with their purpose to create their life's next chapter. She has created a nine-month program, Rebuilding Your Life After Loss. Her newest group coaching program, Finding Your Hero Within, is for men who are struggling with mid-life crises to help them embark on their hero's journey and live into their purpose.

She has written numerous articles on grief, divorce, and transition and is a contributing author for the Huffington Post, The Wellness Universe, SimpleReminders, and Connected Women Magazine.

To connect with Carrie, use the following link:
https://www.thewellnessuniverse.com/world-changers/carriedoubts/

# CHAPTER 12

# THROUGH THE FIRE

## HOW TO KEEP MOVING FORWARD

Pat Bell

According to Greek mythology, "The Phoenix is a long-lived, immortal bird that cyclically regenerates itself. It obtains new life by rising from the ashes of its predecessor."

## MY STORY

The ghost of trauma can continuously haunt its victims if not dealt with properly. It can occur in many forms and can be the result of more than one life-defining moment or event. For example, many school-age children are emotionally traumatized as a result of ongoing bullying by their peers. Additionally, divorce, death of a loved one, childhood abuse, emotional abuse, and prolonged illness; can all alter one emotionally and spiritually, causing underlying trauma and feelings of hopelessness.

I met Hannah a few moments after birth. The sun was warm and billowy clouds nearly covered the oceanic blueness of the sky. She only cried for a moment. I came to understand later that she wasn't a crier. She preferred to explore her surroundings, and she loved to draw. Hannah is my second-born daughter.

Hannah had a perfect Apgar score. She hit all of her infant milestones early. She never wanted to be confined to highchairs or playpens. She started to climb out of her crib before the age of one. Clearly, we had an adventurous soul on our hands. She was strong, active, and independent. Her eyes always danced with the excitement of discovering another adventure.

Then one morning, at two years old, Hannah's face and arms became covered with red hives. I was alarmed, so we took her to the emergency room to be examined. Consequently, the doctors discovered that she had a number of food allergies; peanut, dairy, and soy. She was given an epi-pen for the peanut allergy.

As she grew older, she loved to ride her bike, play with her dolls, and hang out with her siblings. Hannah was a straight-A student and at the top of her class. School was a breeze for her. All of her teachers loved her and respected the effort that she always put forth completing their assignments. Surely, a future filled with adventure and monumental achievements lie ahead for our Hannah, but then. . .

"Mom, can you pick me up from school? My stomach is hurting really bad."

"Can you go to the nurse's office and lie down until I can pick you up?"

For the next few years, these phone calls and texts would happen on a regular basis. But a year before I started to receive these phone calls from her, I noticed that she began to sleep longer. She was becoming tired, less talkative, and weary. My once energetic child would lie down when she came home from school. She would ask me to wake her up earlier in the mornings so she could complete homework assignments. I didn't know at the time how much her request back then would become a testament to who she was until much later.

The other kids didn't understand why all of a sudden she was feeling unwell and needed to go home early every day. How could they understand? We didn't either. During seventh and eigth grade Hannah's health declined rapidly. She was no longer the active girl we knew. She spoke of stomach pains daily, and newfound brain fog enveloped her. She was evaluated by one of the best hospitals in Texas. She was tested, poked, and prodded. But still, no exact diagnosis except food allergies. In the meantime, school was becoming more of a physical and emotional struggle for Hannah.

Unfortunately, Hannah's classmates began to bully her. What others are not capable of understanding, they begin to abhor. Not only did this illness take away her health, but it was also isolating. Hannah has always been a very high achiever and meticulous about her work. She loved to draw pictures, and prior to her falling ill, her goal was to attend an arts university and major in fashion design.

But the day she graduated middle school was just another burdensome moment for her to get through. She looked beautiful in her teal blue dress. Her hair was curled and flowed down her back. But as her mother, I could feel the heaviness of this mystery illness on her face and her spirit. She graduated with honors, hugged her friends goodbye. Many of them she had known for over eight years and most she would probably never cross paths with again.

Hannah was accepted into a prestigious high school. Upon graduating high school, she could have earned her associate's degree and would be ahead of the college game. The day she was interviewed by the high school's representative, Hannah wasn't feeling well. The representative greeted her enthusiastically, "It's so nice to meet you; we are glad to have you here!" Hannah smiled back warily. At the end of the interview, Hannah told the representative that she had not been feeling well. Hannah was concerned that she would not be able to keep up with the fast-paced curriculum. The representative tried to ease her fears and told her that she would be fine. Of course, she was speaking solely based on Hannah's classroom performance. She was not aware of the war that Hannah's body was waging against her.

Beaming with pride, we knew that this would be a great opportunity for her under any other circumstances. Therefore, like any proud mother, I encouraged her during summer break as we continued to seek answers from healthcare professionals. Still, we could not find a definitive diagnosis for Hannah's symptoms. She was losing weight and fatigued to the point of being bed-bound. She had unexplained body aches, migraines, stomach pain, and brain fog. I grew more concerned about my daughter's future.

"Mom, I don't think I feel well enough to attend the school." The pain on her face and the sadness in her eyes stopped me in my tracks for a moment. Although, her declaration didn't exactly take me by surprise. As summer progressed, I could see she was feeling worse and turning more within herself, not knowing what the next day would bring.

"Hannah, are you sure?" I asked. "This is a great opportunity. All of your hard work has paid off."

"Yes, mom, I'm sure. I can't do it right now. Can we try homeschooling, until I feel better or the doctors find out what is wrong with me?"

I agreed because I knew in my heart that this was the last option she would have chosen for herself.

Over the course of the next few years, there would be numerous doctors appointments and tests. We prayed a lot. There were many tears seen and unseen. Hannah got used to feeling unwell. We all took on this uncertain new normal. Sometimes she'd be too tired to dress or put on her shoes for doctor's appointments. Therefore, her brother and I would help her. I can vividly remember her brother kneeling down to tie her shoelaces. The same younger brother she guarded and protected when they were very young. Watching her suffer tore at our spirit and made us question everything. Hannah had done nothing to deserve this horrible illness that inhabited her body. Although my son has never complained, I know that Hannah's illness has been difficult for him too.

"Mom, I don't think I will be here much longer."

I hear her words. But no mother wants to hear those words. No mother wants to see her child suffer at all. But, when the suffering comes, we must do all that we can to bear the unbearable. Hannah's head is down, her shoulders drooped. Her eyes are far away, as if she's staring in the distance toward a kinder, gentler place. Surely, in her heart, she's already left us and perhaps, even made peace with her parting. I hate these days. On these days, she doesn't say much. It seems that even words are too heavy and burdensome to utter.

So, I pray. I pray with all that I am that my daughter's life is spared, and we both get through this day in order to fight this monster another day. Whatever that means. Indeed, ghost fighting is treacherous, but we have grown accustomed to war with the invisible enemy.

*Father, please let Hannah live. Please return her health and her strength. Please give her back her life. I know in my heart that her burden has been much too heavy. I question my heart, my motives. Is it selfish of me to want to keep my child here with her family at any cost? I bargain, and I plead with God, even offering to trade my life for her's. What mother wouldn't freely give her life for her child's if such a bargain could indeed be rendered?*

Hannah has been sick for over half of her young life. After over a decade of doctors we still do not have any clear answers for her overall health problems.

Yes, she has food allergies and some environmental allergies. A rheumatologist once diagnosed her with "symptoms" of fibromyalgia. However, we feel like something has been missed; therefore, we continue to seek answers. Hannah continues to fight for her mental and physical wellness. As anyone who has experienced prolonged illness knows, it weighs heavy on every aspect of your being. She has become her own best advocate. We are immersing her body with as many healthy minerals, vitamins, and nutrients that we can. We feel that something in Hannah's environment caused her body to shift from healthy to illness. Therefore, there must be a way to reverse or reset her health by flooding her body with as many organic nutrients as humanly possible. In the meantime, we are continuing to see doctors and explore all medically healing and diagnostic avenues.

Hannah has become a great soldier in this fight. She has taken the lead in finding alternative solutions to heal herself from within. She still struggles daily. She still feels very unwell. She still has those bad days. She has missed out on a lot due to her illness, physical pain, and chronic fatigue. Her life has been much different from other healthy young women her age. But, she refuses to quit or give up. Giving up isn't an option. She still has her dreams. She still wants to attend university. She is still the best big sister to her younger brother. Her brother will be graduating from college soon. She has supported him all through her illness as best she can. If the cards were aligned just so, Hannah would have graduated first, and with honors, I am sure of that. But, her hand was dealt a bit differently. So, she continues to fight for a better, more just hand. Those who love her and support her on this journey, well, we fight too and won't give up.

The lack of empathy from family, friends, and strangers can traumatize the soul and the psyche of someone suffering from prolonged illness. I dream of a world where there is more empathy towards those who are fighting illnesses in their bodies or their minds. It is difficult enough, having to deal with chronic illness and pain. Societal apathy and isolation can make the quest for healing almost insurmountable. Hence, let's try to approach others with empathy and kindness, as many are fighting battles that can not be seen with the naked eye.

# THE TOOL

## HOW TO KEEP MOVING FORWARD

There are a number of tools that can be used as we experience some of the unexpected challenges of life, whether we are ready or not. As a family, we continue to seek answers for Hannah's undiagnosed illness. The last decade has been grueling, traumatizing, and painful, both mentally and physically. In spite of the ongoing challenges, we have managed to keep moving forward, and so can you.

I read a quote that perfectly sums up the last ten years of my family's lives, "*If you are going through hell, why stop there?*" Yes, why stop when you are in the midst of the fire when your goal is to not perish in flames but to feel the calming breeze of freedom and wholeness on the other side? No matter how hard things become, keep going. Cry, plead for healing, curse, and shake your fist to the heavens. But, keep going. I'm certain you will never be made whole if you lose hope and give in to despair. "*If you really want to be made whole, then get up!*" Author Unknown.

Hannah faces her mighty dragon every day.

Your suffering has caused trauma and scarring. It's the scarring of the soul and mind where eyes can not reach. Face it, but do not allow the trauma to wound you mortally. Even on your most trying and difficult days, choose to step out of the fog. When your energy is drained, and you feel like you can no longer bear the pain, choose to help someone, no matter how small of a gesture it may be. As I am writing this, Hannah is helping her younger brother with his tie. It's career day at the university. Students are required to wear a suit and tie. Thus, Hannah took it upon herself to find a YouTube instructional video to help her with the process. It turned out nicely! Is she still in pain daily? Yes. Does the pain sometimes cause her to moan out loud? Yes, but occasionally, she summons the strength and the courage to step outside of the pain and help her family where help is needed. Then, she rests. Although, it's hard for her to sleep deeply due to the pain.

Stay positive and find joy everywhere that you can. I have always tried to keep a positive mindset in all things. It's how I've managed to get through the challenges that life will often bring. I never imagined that I would have a child with health issues. One never imagines these difficulties. But, when they come, you must figure out a way to handle them with strength, compassion, and joy. Yes, joy. Even in the midst of suffering, as you walk through a traumatizing event, joy can still be found.

I have become the accidental clown in my family. I never really knew I was funny. Most of the things that I do which cause people to laugh are quite accidental. I've learned that humor can be healing. At the very least, it causes you to forget your current situation for a few moments. It may even interrupt pain receptors in the brain momentarily. I like to sing out loud. Granted, I am no Mariah Carey. However, when I hit the high notes, Hannah immediately laughs. "I don't know what you're laughing at. That was good." Then, I laugh too.

Imagine this, being asked by your grandson to make a rap video. Was I up to the task? Well, of course I was, because it would make Hannah laugh, and she adores her nephew. Now, she didn't know that I'd be rapping along to Eminem's "Lose Yourself." But, what the heck. I gave it a shot. I started bobbing my head back and forth and recording for my grandson. I glanced behind me and asked, "Hannah do you see this?" She started laughing, "Yes, I see it." I also use different accents sometimes. She always exclaims, "Mom, that's really bad." However, I think I'm pretty good at imitating different accents. The main purpose of the silliness is to get her to laugh, at least for a moment, to take her mind off the pain in her body.

Choose to become your own best advocate concerning your illness. Research your illness. There is a host of information right at your fingertips. The internet is a great resource, and it's free. Additionally, explore therapy as a means of helping you to deal with the emotional effects of coping with long-term illness. I know you may feel that your body has turned against you, and the suffering has produced a level of emotional trauma that you never knew you would be forced to face. Use the moments where you feel the pain is bearable, and become defiant! You do not know how strong you can be until you have no other choice. My faith has taught me not to get comfortable with the unacceptable. Do not accept that trauma, sickness, or suffering is your lot in life.

If possible, indulge in a hobby that brings you joy and brings you alive. Yes, even with everything else that you are experiencing in your life, any moment of joy can be the thread that keeps you connected to hope. Read poetry, learn a new skill or listen to music. Both can calm your spirit and the sadness in your mind. Hannah

loves to listen to K-pop music. She saw her favorite group SHINee in concert four

years ago. This brought her so much joy! For a few moments, listening to their music helps her to forget about the pain in her body and the suffering that she's enduring.

Surround yourself with people who love and support you, if you can, someone who will walk this journey of healing with you even in your darkest moments of pain and suffering. A loving support system will intercede for you when you feel that your journey has become too difficult for you to continue it alone. A support system is vital when you are healing through trauma and long-term illness.

This chapter is about having the strength to move forward in the middle of the struggle. If you quit or give up in the middle of the struggle, you will miss the miracle awaiting you. You can choose to fight. Hannah wakes up each day, and she fights to heal her body. Hannah will defy the odds. You can defy the odds too.

**Pat Bell** is a certified English As A Second Language teacher and a serial entrepreneur. She also invests in real estate and the stock market.

She is in the research stage of founding an educational healing-based company. She has been published in four poetry anthologies to date. She is on a spiritual journey of healing that will benefit all whom she encounters.

https://www.thewellnessuniverse.com/world-changers/patbell/

# CHAPTER 13

# THE RAINBOW WATERFALL

## CLEAR NEGATIVE ENERGY
## IN TWO MINUTES

Angela Orora Medway-Smith, Cariad Spiritual,
The Life & Soul Alignment Coach

## MY STORY

*'You've seen my descent, now watch my rising.'*

–Rumi

I am Angela Orora, a spiritual channel, coach, and teacher; I am a survivor of abandonment, bereavement, betrayal, rape, domestic violence, depression, and baby loss.

Like you, I'm a divine being having a human experience, a spark of the Divine in human form, a goddess or god, capable of creating miracles and moving mountains.

Death has always been part of my life. I was raised in a small Welsh fishing village in a family of strong women with four generations living under the same roof. By the time I was fifteen years old, four close family members and a school friend had passed over.

A born psychic and empath, I saw and talked to spirit people, and when I told my mother and grandmother, I was made to feel that it was perfectly normal although not to be talked about; people wouldn't understand. Later, in my twenties, I began a life-long journey of spiritual study and trained as a spiritual healer and professional intuitive.

I began to understand the cycle of life and rebirth and the journey of the soul. This knowledge has saved my life. Let me tell you how.

All my dreams came true when I married my darling husband. I was 31, and we'd both had great careers and previously traveled the world before we met. We were madly in love, ready to settle down and raise a big family. We were overjoyed when I fell pregnant on our honeymoon. I was fit, ate a balanced healthy diet, and blossomed. I felt a deep love and connection to my growing baby, and after the first trimester, we started thinking of names and decorating the nursery. Everything was perfect.

At about fourteen weeks, I started bleeding and took to my bed for a fortnight; then everything settled down. Panic over.

It was at the twenty-week scan they called in the consultant. Our baby boy's brain had not developed. Numb, frozen, I watched from the ceiling, outside my body as my husband held me. They told us he would be stillborn, and I needed to go through labor to deliver him. Sent home to return the following day, I sat up all night finishing crocheting his cot blanket; it was needed for his coffin now.

A forty-hour labor followed; we were frightened and alone when he was born. No midwife came. It was ten minutes before they came for him, our precious Thomas, born sleeping.

They brought him back to us, freshly washed and wrapped cozily in his blanket, dark hair, the image of his father. The nurse wept. Still numb and frozen, I continued watching from the ceiling.

We buried him in a baby cemetery; I had no idea such a thing existed. Hundreds and hundreds of babies. Lost dreams. Hearts ripped out—rivers of tears.

For weeks I sat in the dark, not able to face anybody, my poor grieving husband a go-between to the outside world. Desolate, I searched for answers. Why? This was a time before the internet, so I quizzed my doctor, consultants, and obstetrician, searched the library, talked to health workers.

The answers I got horrified me. Our baby's death from anencephaly was preventable. The link between Neural Tube Defects (NTDs) and folic acid had been established over thirty years earlier, before I was born! I should have known about this! Why didn't I know about this?

I learned that in the USA, flour is fortified with folic acid to help prevent NTDs, not so in the UK! Our government's promises years earlier of prioritizing this information hadn't materialized. Thomas and ten other babies had been stillborn in just my hospital that year because they'd broken this promise. This needed to stop, and I rose from this dark pit of depression to pour all my love and pain into making it happen.

I enlisted support from my genetic consultant and started to campaign. Boxes of posters, leaflets, and envelopes were piled six feet tall, filling my dining room. Every night after work, my husband and I stuffed and labeled envelopes. We mailed them out to surgeries and pharmacies across Wales. I shouted from the rooftops, spoke on local radio, told our story in newspapers, anything to stop this happening to others. Finally, I persuaded a member of Parliament to ask a series of embarrassing questions directly to the British Prime Minister.

Success! Within weeks of my questions, £3 million was allocated for a three-year information campaign across the UK to encourage women to take folic acid for three months pre-conceptually, and I was asked to be part of the professional dissemination group in Wales. Still working full time, I took holidays to make the hundred-mile round trip to monthly meetings, helped formulate and deliver a campaign across Wales, I kept talking to the media, keeping the momentum going that I'd created from my kitchen table.

I enlisted obstetricians to collate statistics, and at the end of the three years, there were only five NTD related stillbirths in my local hospital rather than eleven. This pattern was replicated around the country, with a reduction on average of six fewer unnecessary baby deaths multiplied by over five hundred UK maternity units. Three thousand fewer stillbirths, six thousand fewer grieving parents in that one year.

This figure has continued to fall now that the UK has eventually mandated fortification of flour with folic acid. My baby's short life in 1994 started this, preventing the loss of over eighty thousand babies in the UK.

Those three years were tough. More challenges were faced and overcome. I fought for new procedures to support women who face stillbirth after labor, better training for radiographers who have to deliver devastating news, pre-natal bereavement support groups for dads as well as mums. I didn't want anybody to experience what we'd gone through.

It turned out that I could get pregnant incredibly easily, but my genes and my body didn't create a safe place for my babies to grow. Three years after our marriage, as well as having a genetic predisposition of having another baby with an NTD, I'd been diagnosed with antiphospholipid syndrome, juvenile diabetes, asthma, and thyroid issues. During this time, five more angel babies had blessed our lives.

My spiritual belief and understanding of the soul, spirit, and our purpose on this Earth kept me sane. I believe that every person who chooses to come to this Earth chooses how long they stay before they arrive. My six angel babies didn't need to stay here for a long time to follow their soul's path. Hard as it was, heartbroken and grieving, I found comfort in this: my truth.

Before our fourth wedding anniversary, our son Matthew, our *gift from God* (as his name means), was born. He was a month early and had difficulty breathing, and I was very sick. On his third birthday, we brought his baby sister Caitlin home from the hospital; she was seven weeks early, and we'd both been very, very sick.

My husband and I decided not to tell the wider family about our pregnancies; it was easier that way. They hurt for us, so it spared them. It was hard enough that friends and neighbors crossed the street instead of talking to us because they didn't know what to say when we had to bury another baby.

So, it was with a joyful heart that I rang around to tell our family our news. I rang my lovely psychic medium cousin. She gave me the news that filled my soul with joy. *Ten days earlier, my grandmother had come to her with a baby girl lying still in her arms; around them were three little boys and three little girls, my angel babies. Nodding and smiling, my grandmother had said, "she'll be fine."*

At this time, our new daughter was on a ventilator as she'd burst one of her lungs. My cousin had rung our home, and there'd been no answer, and had waited for us to call so she could pass on this message.

Since then, when I need reassurance, as we all do, my angel babies and other family members who have passed come to me and to other medium friends with messages. I feel truly blessed.

You see, death is not the end. I view it as going home. I believe we come to this planet with a job to do, and to see our beautiful world; this rollercoaster of life with all its joy and pain, challenges and victories is a 'school.' The challenges we face, how we respond, that's what helps us grow and learn. I've learned many, many lessons and emerged differently!

It's time that this story is told again. It's a testament, like many other stories of rising from despair, that one person can make a big difference. Anybody. You just have to decide to do it.

Developing your soul connection isn't rocket science; it's very simple, and it can all start with taking responsibility for yourself, for your own energy, and with it your own destiny.

The Rainbow Waterfall is the tool where you can begin this journey.

We are all-powerful divine beings made in the image of the Creator, goddesses, and gods; take control of your energy and remember that!

# THE TOOL

*'I am not this hair, I am not this skin, I am the soul that lives within.'*

– Rumi

You are not simply flesh, bone and blood. Your spirit, the aspect of your soul that has decided to incarnate on this planet at this time, resides in your physical body. You also have an energy body, a finely balanced electro-magnetic field both in and outside your body.

In simple terms, your energy body is made up of seven main energy centers or chakras which many people 'see' clairvoyantly as the colors of the rainbow. You are connected to the Creator, the Divine, through a chakra above your head and through it to your Crown chakra. A central energy channel runs along your spine linking your seven main chakras, and other energy meridians flow throughout your body. You also have an egg-shaped 'aura' around your body made up of several different energetic layers, like the layers of an onion.

You don't need all this information to use this tool. Still, it's helpful to have this basic understanding of the chakra colors (the rainbow colors, red, orange, yellow, green, blue, indigo and violet) and your egg-shaped aura that surrounds you.

When we absorb negative energy, are stressed, or have a physical or emotional injury, it affects the energy body first. If left unchecked, this imbalance can manifest in physical problems and 'dis-ease.' So, cleansing and recharging your personal energy field can prevent future problems and help stress and anxiety.

All energy is neutral. It is we humans who program it, and we can shift, re-program, and replenish our energy body when we know how. That's how The Rainbow Waterfall works. I've used this exercise for over 35 years and passed it on to hundreds of students and clients worldwide (it's available as a free audio download on my Cariad Spiritual website.)

*It's helpful to do this visualization in a shower for the first time so that your body records the physical feeling of the water, but it's not essential. Our minds are incredibly powerful.*

So, let's begin. I'm going to lead you on a visualization that you can use anytime, anywhere, to clear negative energy, recharge, and protect your energy system that you can distill into two minutes.

Welcome to The Rainbow Waterfall.

Close your eyes, set the intention that you want to cleanse, clear, refresh, replenish and protect your physical and energy body and remove any negative or stuck energy that does not serve you.

Visualize stepping onto a big flat stone underneath a tropical waterfall. The water that runs off the stone returns to the earth to be recycled.

As you stand beneath, the water droplets magically change color. Stand under each color for as long as you need.

The first color that washes over you begins to clear your Root Chakra, the energy center at the base of your spine that stabilizes you. It's every shade of red, from deep ruby red to the brightest crimson. Feel the color-charged water move over your physical body and through your energy system, removing sludge, removing any stuck or negative energy. Breathe in the color, feel the color energy moving through your lungs, into your blood, your muscles and bone, into every cell in your body. Feel it move through your energy meridians, clearing any blockages. Visualize any negative or stuck energy you've been holding onto being returned to the earth to be recycled, re-purposed, reborn.

After a while, the droplets change color to orange, cleansing your Sacral Chakra, the center of creativity in the middle of your belly. All shades of orange flow from the palest peach to zingy fresh tangerine. As before feeling the color-charged water moving over your physical body and through your energy system. Breathe in the color and feel the color energy moving through your lungs, into every cell in your body, and through your energy meridians. Once more, visualizing any negative or stuck energy you've been holding returning into the earth.

Next, the Solar Plexus, the energy center just above your tummy button, is cleansed. The water droplets become yellows and golds, cleansing fear, anxiety, negativity. Wash it away, breathe it away and return it to the earth.

The droplets change color to green. The glorious emerald green of the Heart Chakra, the place you store emotional pain, dulling your shining heart. Allow the color to cleanse and clear; send this intention with each breath you take, cleansing your physical and energetic body, returning emotional pain and tears to the earth.

Sky blue droplets begin to pour in next, cleansing your Throat Chakra, your center of communication, often blocked when you don't speak your truth. The colored water and your breath cleanse, deeply shifting stuck energy from unsaid words, returning it to the Earth.

Your Third Eye needs indigo colored-water to help you see more clearly, allow these indigo droplets to pour over, breathe the color deeply, return any negative or stuck energy to the earth for recycling.

Finally, violet, the last rainbow color, these vibrant violet droplets pour over you, drenching you in the highest vibration of the color spectrum, cleansing your Crown Chakra, the chakra at the top of your head that opens you to higher states of consciousness. Allow the color to do its work. Breathe

the color deep into your lungs and allow it to fill your whole being. Feel it wash over you, all negative and stuck energy being returned to the earth.

*(Note. if you're actually in the shower, complete this section while soaping and shampooing and the next part while you rinse off.)*

The colors of the water droplets have cleansed and cleared, healed, and harmonized your entire energy system, so now we're going to recharge, renew and replenish!

The water droplets change to brilliant white, water infused with the brightest white light from the Creator starts to pour over your body, it starts to move deep into your body through your breath and in through your Crown Chakra. As you stand in this stream of divine light, it starts to fill every part of your being.

Feel it fill your toes, your feet, ankles, lower legs, knees, and thighs. Imagine your body tingling as it fills with divine light, charging up like a battery as the energized water floods through your energy system, filling buttocks, hips, waist, and chest, pouring down your arms into your hands and fingers. It fills your throat, your head. Breathing deeply as you move this energy through your lungs. Your body is now completely filled. It starts to pour over you, starting to fill every layer of your energetic being so that you GLOW! Stand under this stream of divine light-infused water as long as you need to feel fully recharged and replenished.

When you feel it's time to step out, as you wrap your towel around you, it's time to create a layer of protection. Very simply visualize an egg-shaped bubble around you. On the outside of it, place a colored layer of silver/platinum; it can be as light as gossamer or as heavy as a can of silver paint, depending on how you feel (external negative energy will reflect off this.)

Now, finally, pick a color. The first one can come into your head and fill your bubble with it; it's the color you need today. Be intuitive if you need more than one color, then just visualize them swirling together around you.

You can use this tool to start your day, freshen up after work or, at any time.

Nip to the restroom, as you wash your hands, bring down The Rainbow Waterfall using rainbow-colored droplets, dry your hands and bring down the recharging, replenishing divine light. Shrug your shoulders to refresh your bubble and bring in the color you need. Two minutes.

Kids love this visualization; I get them to use the Cloak of Invisibility from Harry Potter as their protective layer.

Use The Rainbow Waterfall to take control of and protect your own energy and change your life. You are a goddess, a god, a spark of the Divine in human form. Remember that.

**Angela Medway-Smith** is a spiritual channel, teacher, healer, and coach from Wales. Her business is called Cariad Spiritual.

Cariad is a Welsh term of endearment derived from *caru* – to love. It reflects who she is, a spiritual being who works from the heart with love. Holistic healing is her passion. Over the years, she's set up healing clinics, created spiritual festivals and holistic events, raising money for children and baby charities, as well as supporting hundreds of healers on their path with classes and training, and giving thousands of clients worldwide guidance from spirit.

Angela helped found Divine Energy International, a worldwide membership non-profit for energy healers, offering support, training, and many other benefits to our tribe of brave healers. Its vision is *a world where energy healing is for all.* She's on a mission! Changing the world one person at a time.

Angela works both in-person and online spreading the light at workshops, festivals, and retreats all over the world.

She devotes her life to awakening Divine Souls like you to their potential. She believes that we all have the ability to transform, to emerge from the chrysalis of this human life, to be the butterfly, and soar, developing a deep connection to our soul, aligning with our true destiny. She has developed many different tools in her 35+ years of a spiritual journey to support you to achieve this.

Angela is also incredibly blessed to be a direct channel to the Angelic Realm and Ascended Masters and has channeled a book on the Divine Rays called 'The Book of Many Colours' to help people connect to their souls path through these amazing vibrations.

Angela offers spiritual consultations, Life & Soul Alignment Coaching, healing, healer training, and Sacred Energy Therapeutics.
https://www.thewellnessuniverse.com/world-changers/angelamedway-smith/

# CHAPTER 14

# HOW YOU CAN BE A GRITTY GODDESS

## CLAIM YOUR INHERITANCE, AND LIVE A LIFE YOU LOVE

Dr. Pamela Poston

## MY STORY

### EDITH

Ellen ran from the house and screams she heard coming from her mother's bedroom. All she could think about was getting to her father at the coal mine. Edith discovered her younger sister Ellen was missing and she raced off to find her. As she ran through the cemetery, her heart was pounding so budly in her ears she could hardly think. She prayed, "Please, God," she prayed, "let her be ok."

Edith's job was to watch her younger sister as her mother was giving birth. The tiny house was filled with the midwife and female relatives tasked with helping to bring this new baby into the world. Edith became distracted for just a few minutes, but long enough for her little sister to run for the comfort of her father's arms.

The shortest way to the coal mine was through the cemetery and along the train tracks.

As the railroad tracks came into view, Edith's blood ran cold. She could see a tiny figure on the tracks and behind her, the specter of a train plodding its way toward the figure. A guttural cry struggled from Edith's throat as she sprinted toward her sister. Urgency fueled her as she reached Ellen, whose foot was lodged in the ties of the tracks. Ellen sat paralyzed with fear. Edith worked feverishly to free her foot, stripping the sock and shoe off the child. She moved the foot back and forth, releasing tension little by little. She could feel the vibrations of the black engine on the iron tracks, hear the bellowing whistle pierce the air, and smell the acrid black smoke from the stack.

Alerted to disaster, the engineer slowed the train, breaking as hard as he could. Finally Edith freed Ellen, throwing her from the tracks, but before she could jump, one of her legs succumbed to the knife hard steel of the train wheel. No one remembers how Edith got to the hospital. The doctor tried saving her leg, but there was too much damage. They amputated it at the knee.

My great-grandmother Edith White married Alex Braddock in 1911 at the age of 22. She bore nine children. One, Henry George, died in infancy. Stiff upper-lipped, my English great grandmother baked half a dozen pies every Saturday on her coal stove that gleamed with polish. Her lace curtains over sparkling windows were visual perfection, each pleat tucked just so and attached to the windows with tiny pins. Every Sunday, Edith walked to church no matter the weather, all eight children following like ducklings. The weight of her wooden leg tied with heavy leather straps around her waist must have been burdensome for the slim, barely five-foot-tall Edith. Strangers wouldn't know the leg covered with a heavy cotton stocking and graced with a sensible shoe was not flesh and blood. Never complaining, doing what all other mothers and wives did, Edith accepted her body and filled her life with children, love of home, faith, and family. Edith had grit.

## MILDRED

Mildred didn't know what was happening. She kept fainting, feeling the heavy yolk of exhaustion most days. Taking care of her Russian-speaking mother-in-law, who had dementia, parents, one of whom was disabled and diabetic, three adolescent girls, and keeping a home during the depression took its toll. The family called it a "nervous breakdown." Doctors wanted to give her electric shock therapy, the treatment of choice in those days for "nervous" conditions. She refused. Why would she want electricity coursing through her head when all she needed was rest and nobody to need anything from her?

Doctors and the family's fear overruled her choice and voice. She had the therapy. It must have been terrifying lying there in that cold white room, getting ready for the shocks. I think it was a consciousness of spirit that filled Mildred's brain as the anxious depression subsided. Once she became a Christian at the tiny Nazarene church she and her husband Ben helped build, she was all in. Religion and her faith became her passion and purpose in life. Leaning on faith, Mildred decided to make caring for others her mission. She believed God's instruction was to become a servant to others. A pillar of the church, she would go to the sick and shut-in with cloth-covered baskets of food, bringing prayer and comfort to those in need.

Whenever I spent the night as a child, I would hear her praying for others from my room. A chant-like cadence to her prayers drew me in though I couldn't hear the words. Whenever I think of my grandmother, I think of nurturance. She showed her love with delicious food, warmth, quiet determination, compassion, and faith.

While sitting beside her bed when she was dying, I watched her go through the motions of feeding herself as if she were at a banquet or one of her bountiful picnics. Maybe she learned that nurturing the self was also part of God's plan. Mildred had grit.

## MARCELLA

Marcella cried when she saw the holes in her only maternity dress. It was silk, and the insects at the submarine base in Key West, where she and my father lived, made a feast of the fabric. Pregnant and alone because her husband was on sea duty, Marcella muffled her sobs in the pillow. The baby was weeks late, and she was swollen, uncomfortable, and on bed rest. Her mother was miles away, and there was no one else. She prayed for strength. Feeling sympathy for the young mother-to-be, the nurses took up a collection for a new dress. Their kindness was proof of her belief that God would take care of every need. For as long as she could remember, her faith provided strength in the most challenging times.

Marcella met my father, Jack, in ninth grade. They fell in love and were married at 18. He joined the navy, so they packed up their wits and determination and moved from their small coal-mining town in Western Pennsylvania, far away from her close-knit family. After the Korean war, my father enrolled in college to become an electrical engineer. Marcella was the unsung heroine at his side, working two jobs and caring for two small children. She always did what she had to do for her family.

Decades later, when my father was diagnosed with mesothelioma, Marcella rarely left his side. Each night she crawled into bed beside his deteriorating body and gently touched his arm, letting him know she was there for whatever he needed. As his condition became worse, she kept vigil over him even though the stress of caregiving and premature grief took a toll on her health.

He died in the early hours of the morning, 11 months after diagnosis. We called the ambulance to transport his body to the hospital, and Marcella left the room as it arrived. When she walked back into the bedroom she held a pair of pressed khaki pants and a crisp, fresh shirt. Through my tears, I watched her wash his face and comb his hair. Casting aside the hospital gown he'd been wearing, she lovingly dressed him. Kissing him on the forehead, she was satisfied. "Okay," she said, to the attendants, "You can take him now." Marcella stood in the doorway as they carried him down the steps to the ambulance. I heard her whisper, "Goodbye honey, I'll see you again." Marcella had grit.

## GRIT

What is grit, and why is it a goddess-like characteristic? Goddesses have represented beauty, love, sexuality, motherhood, creativity, courage, fertility, and ferocity. Webster's online dictionary defines grit as firmness of mind, invincible spirit; unyielding courage; fortitude. These characteristics interface with many of those possessed by the goddesses listed in myth and literature. For example, the courageous Mesopotamian goddess, Innana, to her peril, went to the underworld to rescue her sister Ereshkigal, recounted in a poem, *The Descent of Innana*. Empanada (Panda) was the Roman goddess of asylum, charity, and hospitality. Her temple on Capitoline Hill was where food was distributed to those in need. Greek goddess, Aphrodite, was the goddess of love and beauty, responsible for overseeing marriage. It's fair to argue that the goddesses listed above possessed grit, as did my ancestors, Edith, Mildred, and Marcella. All three lived with passion, purpose, and perseverance. They were the gritty goddesses in my life.

# THE TOOL

Do we inherit characteristics like courage, faith, and the capacity for love from our ancestors? Some scientists say we're not only what our parents ate, but also what our grandparents ate. Following this trail, it turns out that aside from food, it is essential for the healthy development of future generations whether we smoke, move frequently, or even think positively. All these actions influence the changes in our epigenome. DNA is not our destiny, though it does play an enormous role in shaping it. Epigenetics acknowledges that your behaviors and environment can cause changes that effect the way your genes work. So, we're the sum of our genetic blueprint influenced by our life experiences.

## EXERCISE:

**Step 1.** Write a letter of gratitude to your ancestors, mentors, or those you admire. If you don't know their story, interview those who knew them well.

Thank them for the gifts (characteristics) that have inspired you.

Example:

Dear Edith, Mildred, and Marcella,

This thank you note lets you know how much I appreciate the gifts you've passed on to me. Your courage, selflessness, giving nature, nurturance, limitless capacity for love, faith, and unwavering devotion are all part of my goddess inheritance. I claim these gifts as my blueprint for living life to the fullest.

With gratitude and love,

Pamela

**Step 2:** Circle all the gifts that hold positive energy for you. Now, write them in the table.

Next, think of at least five strengths you possess. If you can't think of five, ask people who know you well. List them below.

_____

_____

_____

_____

_____

Examples:

| My Ancestors' Attributes: | My Strengths: |
|---|---|
| Courage | Tenacity |
| Selflessness | Enthusiasm |
| Faith | Curiosity |
| Nurturance | Creativity |
| Limitless capacity for love | Caring |

Combine these ancestral attributes and personal strengths to create your goddess avatar. Let these characteristics influence and inform your behavior and actions. Check-in with yourself from time to time to be sure you are leading your life with your best attributes. Now, get ready to add grit as a way of creating your gritty goddess life.

**Step 3.** The elements of grit: The three P's: passion, purpose, and persistence.

Author Angela Duckworth, the author of *Grit*, defines it as passion and sustained persistence applied toward long-term achievement, with no particular concern for rewards or recognition along the way. It is a combination of resilience, ambition, and self-control in the pursuit of goals (purpose).

### 3A. Passion:

*"Follow your Heart but Take Your Brain with You."*
*And don't forget your gut.*

– Alfred Adler

Sometimes we find ourselves bound by expectations, our own and other's, of debt, fear, or salary that seems too good to leave even if we are miserable. We feel stuck and are just "going through the motions." We keep trying to think our way out of "stuckness." However, passion is about heart energy, and we need to let the brain in our heart lead. This fist-shaped organ contains more than 39 million neurons. Though not as many as the 86 billion neurons in the head brain, the heart's superpower is energy. The largest electromagnetic field in the body generates from the heart. It sends as many messages to the head brain as it receives. Scientists who study energy cardiology have discovered that your heart creates thinking hormones like those made in the head brain. Leading with heart energy can ignite our desire for change.

What about your gut? Your gut-brain consists of two nerve centers with approximately 100 million neurons. The gut-brain processes information as we sleep. The gut produces 70 percent of the stress hormone cortisol, released to regulate metabolism, control blood pressure, and help form memories. Seventy percent of serotonin, the neurotransmitter responsible for thinking clearly, is produced in the gut. When you learn to listen to all three brains, you become deeply engaged. This engagement state lets you apply passion to everything you do, at home, at work, and in life.

In this exercise, we will get in touch with all three brains. We will open our minds, kick start the energetic field of our hearts, and get in touch with our bodies.

**Exercise:** Get into a comfortable seated position. Close your eyes and take three breaths, breathe in for four, hold for seven, and blow out slowly as if through a straw for eight. Now, breathe normally into your heart space. Visualize yourself the last time you were doing something you love. You might have even lost track of time while doing this thing. Notice where you were, the sights, the smells, sounds, textures, etc. Are there others around you, or are you alone? Get in touch with how you are feeling. Is there excitement, joy, fear, anticipation, contentment? Scan your body from head to toe. Are there places you feel blocked? Breathe into those places. Place one hand on your heart and one on your belly. Breathe into both those spaces. Notice how your body is feeling. Rest in this energy for a few minutes, just taking in the surroundings, the emotions, and allowing the energy to surround you and even emanate out toward the world. Now see yourself realizing it's time to stop what you're doing. On the count of five, four, three, two, one, come slowly back to this place in time.

Take a moment to orient yourself to the room.

Now write what you saw and experienced. Use these guiding questions.

What was the thing you were doing?

Why were you doing it?

Where were you while you were doing this thing?

Who was there?

When were you doing it?

How did your body feel while you were doing it?

How did you feel when you had to stop doing it?

*(Go to my link for an audio version of this exercise)*

Write what you think your passion or passions might be:

_____, _____,

_____

Applying passion to whatever you do will lead you to a fuller, more satisfying life.

You can create the habit of doing the tasks in your life with passion, no matter how mundane or challenging. Over time you will discover what you love.

**3B. Purpose:**

*"My mission in life is not merely to survive but to thrive; and to do so with some passion, some compassion, some humor, and some style."*

– Maya Angelou

## WRITE YOUR MISSION STATEMENT

**Exercise:** My mission in life is to _____ , and to do so with passion. To achieve my mission, I will use my inherited characteristics of (Chart 1)

_____ , _____,_____.

My strengths (from Chart 1) _____ ,

_____ , _____ ,

are tools I will use to accomplish this.

**3C. Persistence:**

*"We are what we repeatedly do.*
*Excellence, then, is not an act but a habit."*

– Aristotle

**Exercise:**

1. Write, I'll be happy when _____ , _____ ,

_____

_____ .

Now take the piece of paper and do any of the following:

- Tear it in pieces.
- Shred-it.

- Flush it (only if you have written it on toilet paper).
- Burn it (outside).

    It's essential to get rid of I'll be happy when thinking because it's a limiting belief. Limiting beliefs keep us in survival mode, preventing us from thriving.

2. Build new habits and make them part of your lifestyle change. One way to approach this is to practice habit stacking, attaching a new behavior to something you already do. Habit stacking allows you to create a set of simple rules that guide your behavior and plan which action should come next. Once comfortable, you can generate habit stacks for whenever the situation is appropriate.

    The formula is:

    After I [CURRENT HABIT], I will [NEW HABIT].

    Clear, James. Atomic Habits (p. 79).

**Exercise:** Write out several habit stacks that you feel would be beneficial.

**Example:**

After cleaning up the dinner dishes, I will take a walk.

According to Clear (pp.79-80), the 1st Law of Behavior Change is to make behavior change cues obvious.

- Cut bad habits off at the source by removing exposure to cues that lead to those habits.
- Make cues of good habits obvious in your environment. Over time, your habits become associated with the context surrounding the behavior.

**Example:** Clean out the old cues. Get rid of the cigarettes, throw away lighters, ashtrays, or anything that cues you to smoke. If you smoke in a specific place after dinner, changing the context by changing the place you relax, a different room, or a different chair while enjoying a piece of cinnamon candy. Place a bowl of cinnamon candy beside a new chair. Another desirable habit would be taking a walk after dinner, so putting your walking shoes or your dog's leash on a hook by the door will cue you to walk. Be creative. You'll discover obvious cues and ways to rearrange your old environment.

My challenge to you is to claim your true gifts and strengths and extinguish limiting beliefs. My hope for you is that you'll learn to approach life as a gritty goddess with passion, purpose and persevere toward living a life you love.

Angela Duckworth explains Grit is the key to success and .... https://qz.com/work/1233940/angela-duckworth-explains-grit-is-the-key-to-success-and-self-confidence/

Clear, James. Atomic Habits (p. 79-80). Penguin Publishing Group. Kindle Edition.

Habit Stacking: How to Build New Habits by Taking .... https://jamesclear.com/habit-stacking

Epigenetics – something that we do not have in our genes .... https://fundacjabirn.pl/en/2019/02/19/epigenetics-something-that-we-do-not-have-in-our-genes-and-we-can-still-pass-on-to-our-children/

**Dr. Pamela Poston** is a Transpersonal Psychologist and Licensed Clinical Mental Health Counselor. She has practiced for 20 years in Charlotte, NC. While working with clients during those 20 years, she has met many gritty goddesses. Pamela describes gritty goddesses as those who show up for life. They get knocked down and get up to try again. They make mistakes and learn a better way. One of her favorite quotes is, *"Do the best you can until you know better. Then when you know better, do better."* Maya Angelou

Writing has become a passion for Dr. Poston. She finds it allows her to express thoughts that resonate with and encourage others. Writing is an excellent tool for self-healing and self-care. She was part of Volume 3, *The Wellness Universe Guide to Complete Self Care, 25 Tools to Achieve Anything: Using Imagination for Healing Body and Soul.*

There are many goddesses in Dr. Poston's life. Some have passed on, and some are living, but all continue to inspire her, like her mother Marcella, her daughter Amanda, daughter-in-law, Razan, and bonus daughter Elif, special goddesses in her life and the world. The Gritty Goddesses of the BBE book club, Diane, Elaine, Debbie, McCall, Dawn, and Barbara, inspire their friendship and love of books. There are many other gritty goddesses not mentioned here (you know who you are, Susan).

Dr. Poston would also like to acknowledge her mentors, goddesses Kathryn Macintyre, writer and spiritual guide, and Dr. Judy Schavrien, brilliant teacher and artist. She is grateful for the newest goddesses, Anna Pereira and Laura Di Franco, who have opened a world of opportunities through the Wellness Universe and Brave Healer Productions books, not just for Pamela but for countless others.

Dr. Poston can be found at https://www.thewellnessuniverse.com/pamelaposton/

# CHAPTER 15

# RECLAIM YOUR HEALTH

## HOW TO NEVER BE TIRED AGAIN

Lidia Kuleshnyk, B.Sc., M.E.S., Chronic Health Specialist

## MY STORY

### FROM NOTHINGNESS, ALL IS CREATED

I was born in 1965, a year of powerful change. I was born with chronic health conditions with a constitution that was supposed to seal my fate of dependency and decline and obedience to authority that would determine my quality and length of life. My story is the story of the collective, of the journey from an old paradigm of oppression and control into a new paradigm of freedom and responsibility. A paradigm that recognizes the one within the oneness, that I am neither separate nor distinct, yet ever unique and highly valued. My story is how I reclaimed my health. And in my quest to never be sick or tired again, I learned how to be secure and sovereign. I learned that from nothingness, all is created.

We are living in a time of unprecedented change. This period has been prophesized as a great awakening. At the core of this transformation is the strengthening of feminine power. This Goddess energy is already part of the yin-yang balance of life. It radiates from the trees and trembles in the land. It howls in the wind, shines in the sun, and glitters in the starry night sky. It is part of the spirals of life. This feminine power exists within every human being. The goddess energy is the force blossoming our evolution from Homo sapiens, an intellectually-based consciousness, to Homo spiritus, a spiritually-based consciousness. This feminine power is yearning to roar.

The patriarchal dominance of the past 2,000 years has had its chance to serve the planet. And since life is ever-changing, the opportunity now exists to evolve into a new paradigm. In this new paradigm of light, the sacred feminine is celebrated, in both men and women, through the honoring of life.

Right now, humanity has the greatest opportunity to return to its original role and responsibility—to be humane, conscious stewards of the planet.

Each human can become a conscious leader through embracing the divine feminine of goddess energy—a leader who has both immutable strength and limitless compassion through honoring of the self and others. This is the time for humanity to return to its true power of conscious leadership and create through unconditional love.

How do you love and honor life? How do you step into your goddess power, individually and collectively? You do this through healing, through your yearning to be free and whole. The goddess power is the feeling in your soul, the inner knowing that you are ready to release the old and create the new. The knowing that a new life awaits beyond the darkness, emptiness, and pain. A life that is your birthright. You can create a life of health, happiness, and peace. A life where healing is a lifestyle because you are evolving through a deep relationship with the self.

In my journey of healing, I found the deepest relationship with myself in the center of my being; in my womb of creation.

## THE WOMB OF CREATION

Women have the power to create life. The sacred space of the womb, the uterus, is the empty vessel, the nothingness from which all human life is created. At the point of conception, a powerful spiraling force activates life. This goddess power to create from nothingness permeates through a woman's whole being. A woman does not have to experience pregnancy and childbirth to connect with this power. Her power of creation already exists within her. I was born with a deformed uterus. Interestingly, my uterus was shaped like a heart, with a wall down the center. And like many women, it was tilted.

My uterus was a source of my greatest physical pain and rapid spiritual growth.

My teacher Michio Kushi always taught, "Everything that has a front has a back. The bigger the front, the bigger the back." The uterus is an organ and a muscle. The body's 12 major energy meridians run through the uterus. To say that the uterus, the womb of creation, is powerful is an understatement. In my 25 years in professional practice as a chronic health specialist and health and energy coach, the only time I advise clients not to remove an organ is when they are considering removing the uterus. Without the uterus, all the major organs and systems in the body become weakened, and a woman has to make extra effort to regenerate her energy. Without a uterus, it is easier to become tired, drained, and depleted.

In my late 20s, as I entered the classic "Saturn return" of my astrological chart, I found myself immersed in 18 months of deep healing. I call this the "cocoon of healing," wherein the stillness of rest, you allow every cell in your body to transform into a greater state of being. My body began to heal at a depth beyond my intentions and desires. I just wanted to heal my chronic digestive conditions so I could get back to work as an environmental policy analyst. I had no desire for spiritual awakening. And I certainly had no desire to reshape my uterus. But as I always say, "Energy never lies; you can't fool Mother Nature," and Mother Nature took over with such power that my entire being was renovated at the cellular level. Without notice, my uterus would rumble and explode in horrific pain; the volcano in the center of my being was erupting. My life force was returning. I felt wholly alive. I received spiritual messages to sit in a very hot bath to release the contractions and put hot salt packs on my belly. As I went through these birthing experiences, I realized I was healing my constitution. To heal one's constitution is an accomplishment only achievable by those who want to become so aligned and strong that they will never again suffer from chronic degeneration. Freedom was my goal. I decided I would never be weak or dependent again.

## UNIVERSAL ENERGY

At the age of 29, I was finally in charge of my health and my life. I experienced the tremendous energy that the human body can access when it comes into alignment. I began to understand the universal principle: Yin and Yang are greater than willpower. My willpower could not stop the earthquake of transformation in my womb. Nothing could stop the power of the universal energy flowing through my body. I began to more fully respect that I am a part of the infinite universe. I became humble and strong. I now honor my energy as a source of power and the foundation of my security. My power, my connection to source energy, is always present to support and help me. I honor life. Through my own healing, I have reclaimed my rightful role as a humane, conscious steward of life, as a conscious leader. I have learned how to live as a sovereign being and never be tired again.

# THE TOOL

The Capacity Principle of Conscious Leadership and Success: Know Your Limit, Live Within It

## RELATIONSHIP WITH SELF

My deep relationship with myself, and the fullness of universal energy, was made possible through diet and energy work. It was through macrobiotics and reiki that I was able to heal my chronic health conditions. And it is through my 25 years supporting clients with my Apona Healing Method of reiki, macrobiotics, and coaching that I created a simple, effective tool to help you reclaim your health, regain your energy and refine your power. This tool is my Capacity Principle of Conscious Leadership and Success: Know Your Limit, Live Within It.

For both myself and my clients, I discovered that the key to success in healing is not only to support cellular regeneration but also to develop a strong relationship with self. This is why I always remind clients *your chronic health condition is the gateway to your empowerment*. It is through your commitment to honoring the self that you are able to maintain your newfound state of health.

The Capacity Principle is based on Taoist principles of non-attachment that allow you to be in full presence, commitment, and engagement without absorbing external influences. You become the Buddha sitting in the middle of the burning inferno untouched by the events around you.

## FOUR DEMANDS ON YOUR CORE ENERGY

The Capacity Principle teaches you how to connect with yourself and recognize your energetic state of being so that you do not use more energy throughout the day than your present capacity. This is part of the art of living, knowing when to apply oneself and when to pull back, so that your core energy always remains strong enough to meet its major demands of 1) basic biological functioning, (2) mental-emotional requirements, (3) demands of external stressors and (4) providing substantial and powerful energy to heal a chronic health condition.

Through strengthening your core energy, you expand the energetic capacity of your cells, supporting healing and personal growth. By learning The Capacity Principle, burnout, exhaustion, depletion, and chronic fatigue are avoided, and you can continue to balance your life with enough energy and vitality to face any circumstance with inner ease.

## YOUR FLASHING RED LIGHT INDICATORS

We each have "red flags" "warning signs" telling us when we are living beyond our energetic capacity. The Capacity Principle teaches you to identify your unique indicators to determine if you should slow down or continue full speed ahead.

*Your flashing red light indicators* are like the red lights on the dashboard of your car saying, "Hey, something is wrong, pay attention and act now!" Your car's operating system informs you, before your car breaks down, to get help. When the red "engine" or "fuel" lights come on, do you ignore them and risk a breakdown or do you respect them, stop, and address the issue?

How do you find your secret keys, your *flashing red light indicators*, to manage your energy?

**First Step:** *Set aside 3-5 minutes.*

Turn off all phones and devices. Remove distractions. Sit comfortably in a quiet space.

Get a pen and paper.

**Second Step:** *Identify your "capacity expressions:" What Do I Say?*

Ask yourself, "What do I say when I'm not centered?" Remember a moment when you "had enough" of something. What are the first expressions you spontaneously said? These are your *capacity expressions*. If you can't think of any, ask friends and family if you often say the same expressions every time you are out of balance.

This indicator is evident in expressions such as: "This is just too much. I can't deal with this. This is crazy. I really need a major break, some time off. I'm out of here. I'm done. I can't believe this."

On a piece of paper, write down your *capacity expressions*. These are your *flashing red lights* that you have reached your limit.

**Third Step:** *Identify your "capacity responses:" What do I feel?*

Ask yourself, "What do I feel when I am not centered?" Remember a moment when you felt a sudden sensation, the first response to a stress or circumstance. Did you feel a certain physical ache, an emotion, or a mental response? These are your *capacity responses*.

You may feel a specific body ache, like a pain in your back or neck, upset stomach, tight chest or throat, burning or blurry eyes, or tightness in your jaw. You may feel a specific emotion, such as frustration, anger, irritation, apathy, despair, or feel numb, frozen. You may feel a specific mental response, such as poor concentration, lack of focus, or brain fog.

On a piece of paper, write down your *capacity responses*. These are your *flashing red lights* that you have reached your limit.

**Fourth Step:** *Identify Your Flashing Red Light Indicators: What Do I Do?*

Circle one or two of each of the *capacity expressions* and the *capacity responses* that feel most dominant.

Your *flashing red light indicators* are these *capacity expressions* and *capacity responses* telling you that you have reached your limit.

When you ask yourself the question, "What do I do to manage my stress and energy?" The answer is: use your flashing red light indicators as your first go-to tool to manage your response.

Your *flashing red lights* are your personal ninja tools that you can use immediately to create balance and conserve your energy.

As an example, when I say, "Not now" and feel "resentful," I have gone beyond my energetic capacity. These are my first *flashing red lights* telling me I am off-center. If left unchecked, I start to feel frustrated. If my resentment and frustration don't slow me down, then my second *flashing red light* is the feeling of tightness in my kidneys. When my kidneys are tight, I know my core energy is depleting. This is the final warning sign for me to slow down and regroup. If I continue to use my mental force to push myself beyond my capacity, I become very tired and drained.

When I live beyond my capacity, I lose my center, connection, and power. Life becomes a struggle. When I live within my capacity, I continue at full speed, with little time wasted.

Living beyond your energetic capacity is like driving a car with a flat tire all the time. At first, you can manage it, but eventually, it takes extra effort and energy to keep the car on the road. What happens if you continue to drive with the flat tire and ignore those red light indicators? Eventually, through your sheer determination to keep driving, your car breaks down or crashes. The result, you can lose everything, including your life.

The collapse or crash of your core energy is called illness, otherwise known as an acute or chronic health condition. What kind of life would you like? A life of extreme ups and downs, living with struggle, drama, and depletion? Or a life of balance, abundance, and confidence?

## NEVER BE TIRED AGAIN: WHAT DO I CREATE?

The Capacity Principle teaches you to *know your limit and live within it,* so you will never be tired again. It also allows you to expand your capacity, so you can be more, do more and live more.

To use The Capacity Principle to create the life you truly want, follow these four steps and create a greater connection to yourself:

1. *Reflections*

    Remember the four fundamental demands on your core energy.

    You demand a lot of your core energy. Respect it. Rejuvenate it. Regularly. Regenerating your core energy should be as fundamental as filling up the gas tank of your car. Take the time to do it.

2. *Habits*

   Get into the habit of asking yourself:

   i. What is my energy being used for throughout the day? Is this creating my highest quality life?

   ii. How are my thoughts, beliefs, actions, and choices affecting my quality and quantity of energy?

   iii. When do I feel depleted, and why? When do I feel energized, and why?

3. *Tools*

Identify and utilize your *Flashing Red Light Indicators* as your ninja tools to manage your energy. When your red lights flash, pause, assess, and take action to rebalance yourself immediately.

4. *Supports*

Develop an easy self-care kit to help you rebalance the moment you reach your capacity, before your energy becomes depleted, such as taking a deep breath, smiling with gratitude, going for a walk, repeating a mantra, or taking a nap. And if you need extra support, my Apona Healing Method of reiki, macrobiotics, and coaching will help you get back on track, fast, and regenerate your core energy.

The Capacity Principle shows us that life doesn't have to be a struggle. It's a reminder that you can manage your energy and your health simply and effectively. In doing so, you can live from a place of inner ease, confidence, and knowing that you can achieve success in any situation. The Capacity Principle empowers you to be a free, sovereign being, a conscious leader of our time, and a guide in The Paradigm of Light.

**Lidia Kuleshnyk**, B.Sc., M.E.S., is a Chronic Health Specialist who helps overworked, stressed-out, high achieving men and women resolve their chronic health conditions so they can achieve their health and wealth potential.

In private practice for 25 years as a Health and Energy Coach, Lidia utilizes her "Capacity Principle" of Conscious Leadership and Success to help activate the energetic potential of her clients so they can reclaim their health, regain their energy and refine their power.

Lidia supports clients with serious health conditions, including anxiety, arthritis, auto-immune conditions, cancer, concussions, brain injuries, COPD, heart and stroke conditions, and injuries. Lidia's Apona Healing Method provides a step-by-step process to guide clients through the process of healing, so they stay focused, on track, and centered, connected, and conscious - the 3 keys to unlocking the power to heal and achieve one's mission and potential.

What Lidia is most passionate about is empowering conscious leaders to feel secure and confident in their knowing so that they can turn any crisis or situation into success and activate human potential to turn lead into gold.

Through her own incredible journey, starting at the age of 10, Lidia healed her chronic health conditions and now loves sharing her experience, knowledge, and wisdom with others.

Lidia is the creator of The Apona Healing Method, the Chronic Health Breakthrough Program, and the Turn Stress Into Success: 3 Steps To Regain Your Energy and Reclaim Your Power program.

Lidia also shares her passion as a speaker, leader and an Award-Winning International Best-Selling Author, in her multi-author books "Navigating The Clickety-Clack: How to Live a Peace-Filled Life in A Seemingly Toxic World. Pt. 2" and "Evolving On Purpose: Mindful Ancestors Paving The Way For Future Generations."

To connect with Lidia and learn more about how Lidia's Apona Healing Method, Capacity Principle, Programs and Retreats can help you reclaim your health, regain your energy and refine your power, please visit https://www.thewellnessuniverse.com/world-changers/lidiakuleshnyk/

# CHAPTER 16

# BEYOND WORDS

## FEEL INSTANTLY EMPOWERED THROUGH SOUND

Rosemary Levesque, Licensed Spiritual Healer

*"Short, or long, or in-between, Tressy's hair makes her a queen . . .*
*A beauty queen with crowning glory, but listen girls, here's the rest of the story.*
*There's a beauty secret her hairdresser knows."*

I bet you can finish the jingle.

## MY STORY

The natural rhythm in the above jingle feels almost like a heartbeat. It resonates with human speech and emotions, the inner child, mystery, royalty, and even glory.

I can't say that having a Tressy doll when I was ten years old made *me* feel like a queen, but I never forgot the rhythmic words that sold me on wanting her. A special key inserted into her lower back released long tresses from inside her head that could be fashioned into a fancy hairdo or eased into luscious waves cascading over her shoulders. Since I also had long hair, I could relate. The jingle stuck.

My friends, more than myself, were into popular music and could sing along to any popular tune. Because I loved ballet and all forms of dance offered at the studio where I took lessons, I danced to Tchaikovsky, Bach, and other masters, fully embodying rhythm and tone. Though I struggled with form, I always felt the music flow through me, guiding my steps.

"Pretty hands," my ballet teacher reminded us. To this day, my hands express ballerina moves in yoga poses and exercises while my feet quietly glide across wooden studio floors. Muscle memory; that's the lasting power of embodied sound. Whether the sound that's embodied is empowering, graceful, and nurturing, or the opposite, your body, mind, and soul remember.

Sound is wordless, vibrating energy that creates and animates all matter. Sound resonates with and awakens the Divine in all forms. From Fibonacci spirals in sunflowers and snail shells to hexagonal patterns in snowflakes and quartz crystals, all patterns come from specific sound frequencies influencing physical form.

Though I was never trained as a musician, I deeply enjoyed choir, harmony, and the feeling of strength that came through my voice. My interest in using sound for healing began with listening to gongs, crystal and Tibetan bowls, and tuning forks. Unlike loud sounds coming through speakers at a concert, pure-tone frequencies in subtle volume feel powerfully cleansing, liberating, releasing, or spiritually enlightening and empowering, depending on the frequency of the sound and your own state of receptivity.

For many years I tolerated a small cyst under my right eye. When it appeared to increase in size, I began to employ natural healing methods from my toolkit, such as essential oils, clay, or abrasion. Nothing worked until I began giving myself sound facials. I used the vibrating stems of two weighted body tuners to gently massage my face, pausing on acupressure points, and made sure I applied the vibrating sound frequency directly to the cyst. Within days, the sebaceous cyst I endured for years was gone. In addition, my face looked more youthful with fewer wrinkles.

Sound provides more than physical healing. It works on emotional, mental, and spiritual levels as well. More importantly, from my point of view, Spirit communicates with me through the entrainment of sound from activated tuning forks in the etheric field of the body.

When I first began using tuning forks during healing sessions, the techniques came easily to me. Using energy tuning forks in solfeggio frequencies, I followed a training protocol to revitalize and balance energy centers (chakras). These tones are commonly called UT, RE, MI, FA, SOL, and LA. The protocol uses the concept of resonant and dissonant tones. A resonant tone means that when a solfeggio tone is used, the body vibrates in sync with that frequency to create balance and revitalization. A dissonant tone is created when two specific solfeggio tones are activated together. Dissonant tuning fork sounds find dissonant, or out-of-balance, vibrations in the body.

In either situation, resonance and dissonance each cause vibrations in the physical, emotional, and spiritual body. This is important to note. Think of it this way. You've likely heard of the opera singer who can hit the exact note which causes a glass to vibrate and shatter. The perfect pitch of her voice matches the frequency of the glass. They resonate and vibrate together.

In the case of using tuning fork sounds, aspects of the person vibrate in sync with tuning forks. Resonant sounds replenish healthy tissue and emotions, while dissonant sounds find and vibrate dissonant emotions, unhealthy tissues, and old wounds to ultimately release vibrations that don't support the soul. Both are fundamental to healing and empowerment.

My tuning forks can be held by the stem, upside-down, to act as pendulums. If you've worked with pendulums before, you know that there's a skill to having valid feedback from the divination process. In the sound healing technique, I use tuning forks as pendulums that move with the client's energy, first filling, then balancing each energy center before moving on to the next chakra. The movement is called entrainment.

Several important things happen during this process.

- The tuning forks pick up on the energy of the client and read their energy.
- The sound frequencies resonate with energy in the body to affect changes in physical, emotional, and spiritual healing.
- The sound coming from the tuning forks entrain with the body's energy to inform me of balance or imbalance, full and functioning or depleted, blocked, or non-functioning.

One client, in particular, stands out, expressing what I learned to be the magical power of Divine frequencies.

In this particular session, as my client lay face-down on my session table, the tuning fork behaved differently than expected as I held the tuning fork-as-pendulum over her heart. Rather than swinging in nice even circular movements indicating replenishment and balance, the tuning fork moved incessantly in clockwise, then counter-clockwise circles, as if digging deeply into her soul. She began to cry loud sobs as she felt the specific sound frequency move through her.

I felt more than intrigued by what I witnessed. The pure power of sound not only detected her deeply hidden heart pain but also persisted in its action until she completed her release. After her session, she commented, "The tuning forks directly affected a pain body in my heart chakra that I dreamt about last night. When all six (tuning forks) were used, I saw and felt the emotional joy and exultation of the rainbow. I felt white light and my energy expanding out to unity."

Sound vibrations can shake off low frequencies of poor self-esteem, guilt, anger, and pain. Use sound to heal unwanted calcifications, growths, wrinkles, injuries, and wounds. Shift your energy toward regeneration, healing, new tissue, and new awareness.

The opposite is also true. Dissonant frequencies, harsh words, memories of trauma, and injuries embed themselves into your body, especially the heart. Harsh words, judgmental tones, criticism, frustration, anger, hatred, and unworthiness reveal themselves as dis-ease (not at ease) with self and soul. The disconnection from Spirit happens when you embody these wordless frequencies that make you forget your innate power brought from soul to self. The Goddess within awaits your remembering.

## HEALING AND EMPOWERING THE HEART

When I taught biology years ago, we discussed the role of the heart as a pump in class. Its sole function was to pump blood throughout the body to pick up oxygen from the lungs and release carbon dioxide to the lungs for elimination. As the heart muscle pumps blood, it delivers nutrients and oxygen to all cells, carrying away waste to be filtered by other organs (kidneys, liver, etc.)

It's all very systematic, precise, and intellectual. I remember being fascinated as a child with the diagram of the heart in the encyclopedia, which showed (with transparencies) the outside of the heart and cross-sections of the chambers, arteries, and veins. The heart as a pump had me hooked on studying biology at an early age. My brain was fed with knowledge, while my heart was filled with passion for learning. Yet, in biology classes, we never discussed any intelligence associated with the heart. Even so, the heart has its own neural center with about 40,000 neurons.

The energy center of the heart, the heart chakra, is exactly in the center of all the major chakras. The heart generates an electromagnetic field greater than any other area in the body. It has an electromagnetic frequency 60 times stronger than that of the brain. As the centrally located chakra, it's a bridge between a person's mental and physical states, where thoughts are transformed and interpreted into feelings that manifest in physical form.

## THE BRAIN AT THE CONTROLS

As the brain develops with priorities for intellectual superiority, the brain *takes over*. It becomes a thinking machine. In biology class, the brain was depicted as the conductor controlling everything, every bodily function, including breathing while sleeping. As an important organ in the body, it's responsible for receiving information from the outside – from culture, religion, education, society, etc., to develop a belief system. Thoughts produce chemicals in the brain that, when you repeatedly think about an idea or belief, creates a groove in the brain – like a record groove, much like the one I created from Tressy's jingle.

The world is an unfriendly place for the brain. It protects you constantly, being aware, ready to fight and defend. For some people, the thinking machine is hard to turn off or bypass.

## THE HEART-BRAIN RELATIONSHIP

Empowerment to humans as Divine embodied beings comes from bypassing the brain's control and learning how to improve your intuition, feel more heart-centered, be guided by inspiration, and be empowered to live life fully. What is inspiration? According to the Merriam-Webster dictionary, inspiration is a divine influence or action on a person believed to qualify him or her to receive and communicate sacred revelation. It's also inhaling. Isn't it interesting that the breath of life is Divine embodiment?

In my training as a Certified Vibrational Sound Master Teacher, sound provides the means of communication from the Divine, inspiration, sacred revelation, and empowerment through sound in pure tone frequencies.

The brain is intellectual, whereas the heart is intelligence–which is driven by universal consciousness. Even though the heart is not limited by intellect, the brain often uses and exploits the heart. By the time you reach adolescence, the brain takes over, making the heart a slave. The brain perceives the world through ordinary senses and feeds the heart information. The brain says, "I want you to feel what I'm thinking." If the heart receives the message of fear from the brain, fear becomes an emotion that manifests in the body. Fear is a dissonant frequency.

Heart disease can be considered the manifestation of dissonant frequencies to the heart. Can heart disease be an overuse of the brain to the heart, in that the heart feels useless and unable to be what it was created to be? Does the heart commit cerebral coronary suicide? If so, does the brain become the executor of the heart?

## WHAT DID THE BRAIN MAKE THE HEART FORGET?

The heart is intelligent and, in fact, has its own source of intelligence through a connection to the Divine. Research shows that the heart's EMF (electromagnetic frequencies) are transmitted through touch and intention (physical and emotional stimuli).

You are much more powerful than you can imagine. You have a super connection to Source when you connect through the heart—bypassing the intellect of the thinking brain. Though the brain is useful in helping you to survive (fight or flight, ego, etc.), you surrender too much of your purpose in life to it (the brain). In re-establishing the heart as the center of spiritual intelligence, you can become inspired beyond your limiting beliefs. Sound helps you break through that barrier.

# THE TOOL

I m providing you with three powerful steps which work together for the feeling of instantaneous empowerment. The first is *breath*, the second is *sound*, and the third is *embodiment*.

1. Breath

    The Still Point – Breathing Through the Heart Exercise

    Practice breathing only six times per minute—a count of five seconds on an inhale, five seconds on an exhale. This heart-focused breathing activates the vagus nerve, which affects all organs in the body. Imagine that your breath is coming from and through your heart. (There's a reason why your lungs are included in the heart chakra and have such close proximity to the heart. It isn't only biological placement!)

    Try to pause at the end of an inhale before you exhale. This is the still point – the moment of freedom, no stress, no time or space; it's the moment of presence.

2. Sound – Affirmations, Voice, and Solfeggio Frequencies

    Affirmations – Aligning to the Divine

    Affirmations are positive statements that reflect what the *soul* wants. Your brain may want to override your thoughts with patterns and beliefs already engrained into deep neuro-pathways. As a result, when you write or say an affirmation, it may feel like a stretch, like you don't believe it.

    The beauty of working with affirmations is that they help retrain the brain to allow it to come into alignment with what the soul already knows to be true. It's important to verbalize your affirmations. Use your voice! Saying affirmations aloud, singing, shouting, and even moving to them helps you profoundly embody these new thoughts.

Use a representation of the chakra system to inspire you to write and verbalize similar affirmations for each chakra. For example, the root chakra represents the state of being. The affirmation offered is "I am." You might also say, "I feel safe," "I am protected," or simply "My home is my sanctuary." Be sure also to use powerful words in a positive tone. "I am safe" is completely different from "I'm not in danger."

If you start with the upper chakras, the affirmations you use will bring Divine wisdom into your crown. If you start with the root chakra, you create a solid foundation on which to build (or rebuild) your confidence and creativity. You choose.

## SOLFEGGIO FREQUENCIES – REPLENISHMENT AND BALANCE OF DIVINE ENERGIES

Solfeggio frequencies are based on sacred mathematics or sacred geometry. The numbers represent the vibration during a span of time (called hertz). The lower numbers are deeper tones, while the higher numbers sound higher-pitched tones. These solfeggio frequencies form the basis of Gregorian chants and new age music based on ancient wisdom.

Listening to these pure tone solfeggio frequencies helps to realign the physical body with Divine intention. Voicing these tones out loud works in tandem with the vibration of the tuning forks. Embody your inner Goddess with sound to manifest each intention associated with these frequencies.

UT – 396 Hz – Liberating Guilt and Fear

RE – 417 Hz – Undoing Situations and Facilitating Change

MI – 528 Hz – Transformation and Miracles (DNA Repair)

FA – 639 Hz – Connecting/Relationships

SOL – 741 Hz – Expression/Solutions

LA – 852 Hz – Awakening Intuition

3. Embodiment – the Integration of Breath and Sound

You breathe every moment. Sound surrounds and penetrates your day, mostly without your awareness or conscious involvement. However, you change your vibration when you choose *how* to breathe, *what* to say, and what sounds you *want to hear.* The magic comes with your intention to embody these frequencies so that you come more into alignment with your Inner Goddess, the highest version of yourself, your perfect soul blueprint.

Movement helps embed codes and memory into your cells. For example, tension at your shoulders, a wrinkled brow, and even forgetting to breathe (holding your breath) may be almost entirely subconscious. Yet, these subtle movements partner with emotions to become embodied as fear, anger, worry, and pain. To embody the Divine frequencies of sound and breath, specific affirmations help. The magic of sound with meditative movement crystalizes your efforts.

My favorite forms of movement involve dance, yoga, and Qi Gong. The important elements to include with these practices require you to let go of thought, become meditative, breathe and listen to your inner voice. External sounds you hear with your ears become insignificant when you tap into the feeling and rhythm of sound in your body—joy, peace, enrichment, balance, or relaxation. The opposite is also true. When you remember the feelings of peace and joy, your muscles relax into remembering that you are Divine. You are Goddess embodied. You remember your perfect blueprint, which is unspoken and *beyond words*.

Owner and founder of Second Nature Healing®, **Rosemary Levesque** brings to life ancient wisdom for the modern world. She is a Licensed Spiritual Healer trained in Vibrational and Spiritual Energy Healing designed to help you access your innate power to heal – physically, emotionally, and spiritually. Heal your soul and create a new, vibrant version of yourself.

Throughout the years of working with detoxification, energy, animal guides, nature, and healing, Rosemary incorporates Shamanic practices in her intuitive sound and Reiki classes, and healing sessions as well as her life's work to remind us how to BE in the world, to heal your spiritual ancestry in your sacred contracts, and access the power within All That Is.

Rosemary Levesque is a Licensed Spiritual Healer, Reiki Master Teacher, Certified Vibrational Sound Master Teacher, and Medicinal Aromatherapist. She was born in Hawaii and feels like she brought the energy of the islands into her work from the moment she was born. Trained as a Biology teacher, Rosemary taught in public and private schools around the world until she paused to raise her family in Portland, OR.

As a natural teacher, mentor, and psychic intuitive, Rosemary helps to awaken the healer within you to incorporate healing wisdom for stress release and personal growth into your life. Receive blessings and healing from your own inner wisdom through Rosemary Levesque's teaching, sessions, online courses, and coaching. She offers integrative natural healing alternatives for personal detoxification and optimal healing for animals and their humans. She helps to open the pathway for Spiritual Growth for Lightworkers and offers in-person and online courses for Lightworkers on their journey to the 5th Dimension.

To contact Rosemary, please reach out to her through this link: https://www.thewellnessuniverse.com/world-changers/rosemarylevesque/

# CHAPTER 17

# SHADOW SPOTTING

## A TOOL FOR SOUL ILLUMINATION AND LIBERATION

David D Mcleod, Dd, Ph.D., CMLC

## MY STORY

I stood with 25 other people around the outer edge of *The Carpet*. I was pumped with energy because I knew that today would be a very powerful and special day.

"This *Carpet* is sacred space." The facilitator stood in the center, turning slowly to address everyone. He spoke solemnly and reverently.

"Many have come before you," he continued. "They stepped into the center, declared what they were here to do, and then broke themselves open to reveal—and to *seize*—the gold and the beauty within. Today, if you choose, you will have an opportunity to do the same."

He paused to allow his words to take root in our hearts.

"This is serious work, my friends, perhaps the most important you will ever do. If you take this opportunity, you will come away transformed. Your life will change in ways you cannot even imagine right now. You all came here for a reason. Your minds might not know that reason, but your hearts have no doubt that you are here to reclaim something that you left behind long ago."

My body was ringing like a bell. I could feel energy swimming through me, and I just wanted to leap into the center of *The Carpet* and do my work. Tears began to flow out of me as the facilitator spoke. He wasn't done yet.

"People have cried their eyes out on this *carpet* to get what they came for."

"People have emptied their guts on this *carpet* to get what they came for."

"People have cracked their hearts wide open on this *carpet* to get what they came for."

"People have bled on this *carpet* to get what they came for."

He paused again for effect. Then, barely above a whisper, he said, "You can pass if you choose—and believe me, there is no shame in passing. I ask only that you let your heart make the choice, not your mind. For your heart knows the truth about who you really are and why you are here."

The more I listened to his words, the stronger I felt about stepping out. I couldn't wait any longer; I could barely contain myself.

"Who will be the first one on *The Carpet* today?" he asked. But suddenly, I felt completely frozen, as if cement encased my entire body. Everything seemed to slow down, and I watched helplessly as one of the other participants moved tentatively into the middle of the carpet.

As powerful deep work unfolded, I became mesmerized. I watched person after person take center stage, do some amazing healing work, and then, about 20 to 30 minutes later, march off the carpet like a completely changed being. Each participant seemed to transform from a weak and frail shell into an empowered and unstoppable force that now had a true purpose for being. It was magical. It was beyond amazing. It was transcendent.

After about ten people were complete, I began to feel my muscles loosening again, but my heart told me to wait a while longer. Apparently, my earlier impetuous desire to "get it over with" was completely counter-productive, and my heart had held me back from making a big mistake. By slowing down and witnessing other people going into their darkness and coming out the other side shining like blazing suns, I was able to connect to each person in the most spiritual sense of *oneness* I have ever experienced. As it turned out, this delay contributed to one of the most profound experiences of my life.

At last, my turn came.

I took my place in the center of the carpet. The ringing and buzzing in my body had long since vanished, and I was entirely present for the moment, with no expectation and no agenda.

The facilitator was masterful in his guidance, and I trusted him completely as I had never trusted anyone before. He asked questions to get some context of what was going on for me, but those questions didn't matter because they were just a vehicle to get me to begin feeling the emotions inside me that I had kept hidden away for so long. And then it happened.

A dormant volcano within me suddenly exploded, and hot blood-red rage just spewed out of me.

*Screaming.*

*Cursing.*

*Raving.*

I felt the handle of a tennis racket suddenly appear in my palm, and I immediately began pounding a pile of pillows in front of me. But I did not see pillows! I saw Mother, Father, bosses, associates, priests, leaders, and yes, even God, all of whom I had unconsciously held responsible for the current state of my life. I kept pounding and raging until I could barely move, my voice was a hoarse whisper, and my inner volcano had emptied itself.

I remember saying that I just wanted someone to love me for who I am. From out of nowhere, a person came to my side and assumed the role of my "ideal mother" and held me in the most loving way I could ever have imagined.

That's when the tears came.

My body shivered and shook with uncontrollable sobbing. My "ideal mom" repeated words like "I love you so much" and "You are my amazing and beautiful boy." So much stuff came out of my nose and eyes and mouth, I could not believe it.

After a while, the emotional energy subsided, and I was spent like a sponge squeezed completely dry. But there was an incredible peace within me, and when I stood up, a surge of power blossomed within me like a flame of gold and blue. I put my hands on my chest and smiled softly and effortlessly. I could not believe how amazing and alive I felt.

The facilitator stood in front of me with a huge grin and asked me a very simple question: "And what is true about you right now, David, in this moment?"

Despite my raspy throat, I summoned enough power to declare, "I am a divine being of boundless light and love, and I'm here to make the world a better place for everyone."

The people standing around the carpet erupted into cheering and applause, and I felt immense gratitude billowing in my heart. In the beginning, I had been worried that if I revealed my inner darkness, people would hate me and judge me and spurn me and that I'd be left alone to die in the wilderness. But the exact opposite happened! Instead of condemning me, here they were celebrating me and what I had done!

At that moment, everything shifted. I felt such love for everyone— including myself. I knew that I would never again hide my feelings or my truth. I knew that, no matter what happened in my life going forward, I would never again deny the truth of who I am to please anyone else. My life would never be the same.

---

As a result of this powerful experience, I have learned several things that have guided my life ever since:

1. I am not who I *think* I am. Rather, I am a boundless expression of the Divine engaged in a temporary journey in the physical world.

2. In my human journey, I experience both the physical and the spiritual at different times. When I occasionally forget about my spiritual nature, I slip into the unconsciousness of ego, which sees me as limited and weak. My ego-mind encourages me constantly to hide aspects of myself that it judges as defective, inappropriate, unacceptable, bad, or wrong. After all, if no one sees these parts of me, I can be welcomed into society.

3. Ego-mind experiences lead to the emergence of shadows in my psyche—that is, aspects of myself that I have disowned, hidden, or repressed because of my ego-mind's judgments about them. These shadows have a disempowering influence on my life, keeping me from expressing and experiencing all of who I am.

4. To transform my life and rise above my limiting beliefs, I must uncover, illuminate, heal and integrate these shadows. In other words, I must recover the parts of myself that I have hidden away and heal them so that I can transform their dysfunctional behaviors into energies that positively serve me in the future.

I was deeply inspired by my own visceral experience and by what I witnessed in the other participants. This led me to spend several years studying the darker side of the human condition. In the process, I learned powerful facilitation techniques to help people investigate this side of themselves to discover gifts and capabilities they didn't know (or forgot) they had.

I now understand that every human deals with *Psychic Shadow*, individual instances of which can be traced back to disempowering beliefs that arose out of psychological or spiritual wounding—most commonly in connection with unpleasant events during childhood.

But *Shadow* is not something to be feared and avoided, as I used to believe. On the contrary, intentional investigation of your *Shadow* can help you to reconnect to natural gifts that may have been hidden along with aspects or behaviors that childhood caregivers didn't like. Indeed, in my opinion, illuminating *Shadow* is one of the most powerful pathways back to your *Natural Divinity!*

# THE TOOL

This technique is a relatively gentle way to help you spot your shadow and then do some deep introspection to help you understand what it is trying to do for you.

## PART 1: SHADOW SPOTTING

Because shadow behaviors often happen unconsciously, positively identifying a shadow can be challenging. It's like trying to find a sub-atomic particle: you probably can't see it directly, but because it always leaves a trail, you always know where it's been!

After much study, I've identified six high-level classes of behavior that seem to identify a shadow.

1. **Acting Out.** This can show up in many ways, from active forms like temper tantrums or china-smashing rages to more passive forms like whining or sulking or slinking out of sight.

2. **Triggers and Emotional Charges.** If you experience that someone or something "pushes your buttons," you will probably have some internal emotional reaction. When such a trigger is fired, you may react physically, possibly to the point of moving into "acting out" behavior.

3. **Judgments and Projections.** Everyone has judgments virtually all the time. But when the judgments elevate to the point of evaluating someone else critically, negatively, or harshly, it may result from a triggering event and lead to a verbal assault or worse (a form of "acting out").

4. **Compensatory Behaviors.** These are behaviors we learn when we are young that help us to protect ourselves from emotional pain. For example, if you are constantly told, "You never get it right," then you may find yourself becoming a perfectionist. Or if you were raised in an environment where everyone talks over everyone else, you might come to believe that "Nobody ever hears me!" and so you compensate by becoming a shouter or a loud-mouth, just because you want to be heard.

5. **Ego-Defenses.** Whenever you are faced with stressful situations, your ego-mind looks for ways to keep you safe. This sometimes results in defensive strategies such as denial, dissociation, conversion, or minimization.

6. **Rigid Beliefs.** If you believe something strongly—regardless of whether it is true or false—your ego-mind will always find ways to make you right about that belief and make others wrong about their contrary position.

Take some time to review some of your recent behaviors. Do any of them fall into one of the categories mentioned here? If so, you have probably identified one of your shadows, and you can take some time to interview that part of yourself to find out what it's trying to accomplish in your life.

## PART 2: SHADOW INTERVIEWING

To do a successful interview, you will need a quiet space to set up two chairs facing each other about two feet apart. Designate one of the chairs the *Interviewer* chair and designate the other the *Shadow* chair. Make sure you have a journal and pen available and place them on the *Interviewer* chair.

Prepare your space by lighting some candles and, if you like, burning some incense. Set the room lighting low enough to feel comfortable but bright enough that you can still see what you are doing.

Stand in the center of the space between the two chairs with your hands on your heart. Close your eyes and take several deep, cleansing breaths. When you feel ready, say the following words (feel free to adjust to your sense of what needs to be said):

"I come here in vulnerability and openness to heal myself so that I can know the truth of who I am. I call upon God | Supreme Consciousness | Spirit | Krishna | (your choice) to join me in this space and provide guidance, love, protection, and wisdom as I connect with my shadow to create integration and healing. I am grateful to have you with me on this journey."

Feel free to repeat this prayer meditation as many times as you like. Take a few more deep breaths. Open your eyes and take your place in the *Interviewer* chair.

Recall the behavior that you noted from part one of this exercise. For the sake of this example, suppose you were having some intense negative judgments about your friend Bob. Then begin the interview by speaking into the empty room. It might go something like this:

"The other day, I found myself thinking some pretty awful things about Bob. He had made a sexist comment about my sister, and I was stunned. I think he thought it was a joke, but it really stung me, and I had a hard time stopping myself from slapping his face. I remember thinking that he was such a pig, and I just wanted to roast him on a spit."

Of course, the details of your initial "confession" will be different, but you get the idea. Continue with the following words:

"I invite that part of myself that had such a strong reaction to come forward and have a conversation with me. I just want to speak with you to understand more about what is going on."

You will feel a shift in your body when that part of yourself is ready to be present. Don't rush it; let it happen in its own time.

Even though you won't be able to "see" this part of yourself, recognize that it is still here, and invite it to sit in the *Shadow* chair. Use your imagination to visualize this part sitting across from you. There is a good chance you will recognize yourself as a small child, so be gentle and compassionate as you begin your interview.

"Thank you for joining me here today. I'm really glad you decided to come."

Imagine the responses from your *Shadow*, and take the time to write them down in your journal.

Here are some questions you can ask that your *Shadow* will most likely be delighted to answer for you.

"What was it exactly that got you so angry when Bob made that joke about my sister?"

"Did this remind you of something that happened to you when you were a child? If so, what was that?"

"What did you hope to accomplish with your reactive behavior?"

Somewhere along the way, you will very likely find that your *Shadow* will admit to trying to protect you from being hurt. When you get to this point, try to shift your questions to understand more about the intent behind the behavior. Specifically, try to determine what the *Shadow* wants for itself. For example, you might say

"I'm honored that you are trying to protect me. Thank you so much. But I'm curious, if you knew I was safe and protected, then what would you have for yourself that you really want?"

By expressing compassion and gratitude, you deepen your understanding of the *Shadow's* ultimate purpose in your life. If you continue with this line of questioning, eventually, you'll discover that your *Shadow* is trying to create one of the following for you:

*Being, Serenity, Oneness,* or *Love.*

All of these are just different expressions of the Divine, aren't they? And that is ultimately what your *Shadow* is trying to create for you: a deeper connection to your true *Divine Nature*. The only problem is that the *Shadow* may have an immature and possibly dysfunctional way of creating that. So to end the interview, you can say something like the following:

"Thank you so much for everything you do for me. I am so grateful to have you in my life, and I want to work with you going forward. I am an adult now, with adult powers and capabilities, so I know how to handle things these days. From now on, you tell me if I missed something, and I'll take it from there. And in return, I promise to love you and keep you safe. Deal?"

When you believe the interview is complete, close the session by inviting your *Shadow* to resume its rightful place in your heart. Then, stand up and give thanks to the spiritual entity you invited at the start, wrap yourself in a big loving hug, and revel in the knowledge that you truly are a Divine being—in every sense of the word!

Fighter pilot. Author. Software engineer. Mentor. Aerobics instructor. Poet. Janitor. Lifeguard. Musician. Radio host. Graphics designer. Father. Student. Teacher. Photographer. Ordained minister. Yogi.

These roles—and many others—add up to a *LOT* of life experience, which **David McLeod** brings to bear in his capacity as a transformational speaker, life-mastery coach, experiential facilitator, and writer/storyteller.

As a Certified Master Life Coach with a Ph.D. in Metaphysical Sciences and a DD in Holistic Personal Coaching, David creates and shares powerful *Life Mastery Tools* that enable adult men and women to transcend triggers, challenges, and obstacles so that they can express and experience the fullness of who they really are and thereby manifest truly magnificent and fulfilling lives.

Connect with David at:
https://www.thewellnessuniverse.com/world-changers/davidmcleod/

# CHAPTER 18

# BALANCE YOUR POWER

## A GODDESS' PHYSICAL, EMOTIONAL, AND SPIRITUAL STRENGTH

Birgit Lueders, MH CCII

## MY STORY

The Merriam-Webster Dictionary describes a goddess as *a woman whose great charm or beauty arouses adoration.*

Throughout the years, I've wondered what it would actually feel like to be a goddess. But I never thought I should arouse adoration to be called a goddess.

I grew up like every other little girl, dreaming of being as strong as Wonder Woman. Later I changed my ideal to becoming more like Mother Theresa, so I could show my true impact in this world by caring for others. Now half a century later, after many emotional ups, downs, triumphs, and tribulations, I'm wondering if I'm any closer to being a goddess.

I grew up in Austria in a little village outside of Vienna. I was the youngest of three daughters. Talk about female power in our household! Each one of us exhibited her goddess power in different ways.

Sonja is the eldest. She was quiet and always polite but insecure with her beauty. Karin is the middle child. She was mischievous, and everybody called her beautiful. I am the youngest and tried to be that boy my dad never had. I was the tomboy of the family. Adding my mom to our family's female dynamics, she was always concerned about her appearance. This certainly didn't make it any easier for me to find my female power.

I remember Sunday mornings as I watched my mother, hair still in rollers, put her makeup on. She carefully chose her dress to match our church outfits. I can still see her big smile after each compliment from friends about how beautiful we all looked. My dad was just as proud as my mom; he loved knowing he had such a beautiful family.

What did I learn from all this? That I did not want to be measured by my beauty. I played the role of tomboy quite well. Unfortunately, nature had a different plan, and when I turned sixteen, God changed things for me. I woke up one day and had a beautiful womanly body. I was suddenly tall, thin, and had a nice C cup.

You might think this story would have a happy ending, but it didn't. I was so upset about my female body. I wanted to be a warrior, not a woman whose great charm or beauty aroused adoration. This is where I started to exhibit female body dysmorphia. Any time I had the chance to hide my breasts behind sweaters, I did. My identity crisis only got worse, especially when my sister Karin made fun of my boobs.

Now 49 years old, I'm happy to announce that I left those years behind me and became a body-confident woman who traveled worldwide as a flight attendant. A flight attendant for Austrian Airlines with a sexy red skirt and high heels!

Only later in life did I discover the healing powers of plants and nutrition, which led me to become an herbalist, iridologist, and wellness coach. This blessing allowed me to empower and support other women in finding their Goddess power within their physical, emotional, and spiritual realms.

# THE TOOL

Dr. Pillai, a spiritual teacher, once said that the most powerful energy is the female energy. He said that power and energy are not masculine but feminine. He stated that the man always wants to prove himself to the woman because she embodies the power of love as well as destruction.

I couldn't agree more. After I became the mother of two girls, I truly experienced both powers within me. I was able to switch from loving and caring to warrior mode if I felt my girls were in danger.

During my quest to find my female power, I studied female spiritual deities. I especially loved the story of Lakshmi, one of the most popular goddesses in Hindu mythology. She is known as the goddess of wealth, beauty, luxury, happiness, and abundance. It's no surprise then that many Hindu men worship Lakshmi because of her many powers.

Within my religious upbringing as a Roman Catholic, not much was mentioned about the power of women besides the motherly love of Mother Mary and the mysterious relationship of Jesus and Maria Magdalena. The bible even downplayed Maria Magdalena's importance by claiming she was a prostitute, a ruined woman who needed saving from Jesus, but some early Christian texts showed her as Jesus's wife.

Even today, women still struggle by not understanding their true power, especially within relationships. Some women are too dominant, aggressive, and masculine, and some seem too empathic and intimidated, with no voice of their own. As a wellness coach, I have worked with many women over the last 15 years. My work with these women helped me realize that women need to find harmony within their physical body, emotional state, and spiritual being to feel like a Goddess.

## A GODDESS' PHYSICAL BALANCE

I have been a personal trainer and fitness instructor for over 20 years. I have seen many women in the fitness centers look stronger, lift heavier weights, and outdo their boyfriends and husbands with ease. This all sounds great until it becomes an obsession. Many women start working out because they feel ashamed of having too much body fat around their hips, butts, and thighs. They idealize Victoria's Secret models with their wings and million-dollar bras. And Wonder Woman, too, since she didn't show any cellulite on her butt and thighs during her stunts!

I'm reminded of a woman who came to the gym twice a day. She was chasing this perfect body, but she began to look more like a 12-year-old boy than a Goddess after a few years. It turns out a few years later, her husband left her for a woman who didn't worry all day about her weight and spent more time with him than in the gym.

Unfortunately, women are constantly bombarded by that "perfect" body image. But what is a perfect body image? One of the earliest models of perfect bodies was the Venus of Willendorf 25,000 BCE. If you don't know her, well, today she would be considered more on the heavy side, obese even. You can go through history and discover a constant switch between idealizing curvy, boyish, anorexic, or athletic female bodies.

During my teenage years, I idealized an athletic body shape. I remember watching the movie Striptease with Demi Moore and envying her body. No wonder I felt embarrassed about my curvy chest. It turns out Demi Moore recently opened up about her years of exercise and diet addiction. She said there were days she only ate one cup of oatmeal, drank only water, and exercised all day. There was even a time in her life after she gave birth to her daughter when she lost her body fat so quickly that she needed to stop breastfeeding because she ran out of breastmilk for her baby!

To find your goddess' physical balance, you have to tune out all the noise around you. You don't need a California nose, Brazilian full lips, or a butt like the Kardashians to feel better about yourself. Neither should you feel embarrassed about the wrinkles around your eyes or your too small, too big, or droopy breasts! And those little dimples on your hips and your stretch marks on your belly should not define your female power. Do you really think Lakshmi, the Hindu Goddess worried about her appearance?

You will always be that powerful Goddess, no matter what the scale says. The moment you feel broken, body shamed, old, or less than perfect, you give away your Goddess power. Don't chase an ideal weight, a wrinkle-free look, or that bleached fake smile; instead, support your physical body with self-love and self-care.

Many women end up in my office broken and defeated from years of dieting. Most of them end up body-shamed and insecure about their true beauty. They sometimes even lay on the operating table risking their life for surgically invasive procedures just to lose those few inches around their midsection in the hope they might fall in love with themselves again.

As a wellness coach, I help my clients find their inner and outer beauty. I start by educating them about food as medicine. If we choose the right food according to our specific needs, our bodies will feel healthy, nourished, and happy. Too many times, other holistic coaches put women through rigorous juice and water fasts to attain beauty, but I believe nourishing the body is always better than starving it.

## TIP #1:

Implementing little changes like having fruit for breakfast instead of black coffee can positively impact your health, mood, and beauty. How about a green juice made from fresh celery, cucumber, ginger, kale, and apple instead of a glass of wine in the evening? Eating high nutritional plant-based foods can invigorate a woman's beauty.

For thousands of years, women have been the main food supplier for the entire family through harvesting herbs, fruit, and vegetables. On many days men came home empty-handed from their hunts, but women always had a plant-based meal ready for them regardless of their hunting success. Stay true to your wise woman's knowledge and start eating more colorful food, the more colors you eat, the more vitamins and minerals your body will absorb. Remember, a Goddess is a warrior and empath, and because of that, she needs high vibrational and energetic earth-based food.

## A GODDESS' EMOTIONAL BALANCE

A woman's body is a fine-tuned emotional machine. Throughout the ages, people have associated the moon with female energy. Just think about it; a lunar cycle from one new moon to the next takes around 29 days. A menstrual cycle from one period to the next takes around 24 to 30 days. Even studies state more women have their period during the full moon than the new moon.

Now compare the roller coaster of emotions all humans, not only women, experience on a full moon. No wonder women seem quite emotional all the time. Science has discovered that a full moon can cause insomnia, anxiety, and even depression. My sister Sonja, a nurse, told me that hospitals have more staff on duty during a full moon. Evidently, people are doing crazy stuff during a full moon which doesn't always turn out well.

Is this all a coincidence? I don't know. But one thing is for sure; women have a complex energetic cycle just like the moon. Each month we go through emotional ups and downs. For example, during an estrogenic peek, aka ovulation, a Goddess feels ready to get pregnant. Imagine if that feeling would not come over her, mankind might simply die out. If there is no pregnancy, the cycle ends with the shedding of the uterine wall, resulting in a period and more energy release.

Thousands of years ago, women would meet in "menstrual huts" called Red Tents. It was a place for women to meet while on their periods, to share stories, rest, cry, and support each other, to gather emotional and physical strength for the next month's cycle.

Unfortunately, this kind of practice is long gone. Wouldn't it be great if today's women would meet once a month for a few days and share each other's deep-seated secrets without being jealous or competitive with each other?

## TIP #2:

A Goddess should never feel embarrassed about her emotional sensitivity. True strength only shows through vulnerability. But, of course, if you feel emotionally overwhelmed, you can always rely on herbal remedies.

The wisdom about herbal potions and tinctures has been passed on from female to female throughout the generations.

For example, evening primrose oil is an amazing oil for women. It nourishes the female reproductive system and helps ease or eliminate premenstrual symptoms like depression, bloating, irritability, and cramping.

Black cohosh should be your favorite pick as you get closer to menopause. It not only takes care of your hot flashes but also helps with fatigue, depression, and insomnia.

And my favorite herb for all Goddesses would be holy basil. A daily cup of holy basil can calm your mind and body through its ability to reduce your stress hormones.

## A GODDESS' SPIRITUAL BALANCE

History books describe women as highly intuitive. Many women have a "sixth sense," a feeling of concern that can't be overridden, especially about their children. I recently talked with a woman who told me that she woke up in the middle of the night with an anxious and worried feeling about her son. It turns out an hour later, her son called her and told her that he had had a car accident.

We have all heard stories like this numerous times, but somehow, we still don't trust our instinct or believe in ourselves. Like I said at the beginning of this chapter, a Goddess is the highest form of vibration and energy.

## TIP#3:

In case you feel less than perfect, try to surrender your mind to meditation. A quiet mind allows you to connect to your higher source, which is your higher knowing. Meditation creates a mind that is fully present in the here and now.

Feeling less scattered or less overwhelmed allows you to access your inner wisdom, guidance, and knowing.

I usually refer my clients to listen to theta brainwave music for ten to fifteen minutes daily. Theta brainwaves are usually present during our deep sleep cycle but listening to them as meditation can enhance creativity and intuition.

Keep your Goddess power balanced; stay in your presence through daily journaling, singing, laughing, crying, yodeling, and what else you might like to do. Once you feel centered, your feelings of unworthiness, anxiousness, and unhappiness will be a memory from your past.

There is the saying that behind every great man, there is a greater woman. During my flight attendant years, I had the pleasure to serve the former Russian President Mr. Gorbachev and his wife on one of my flights a long time ago. When I asked him what he would like to eat, drink, or read, he turned towards me and said I should ask his wife since she has always made better decisions than he ever could.

## TO ALL THE GODDESSES, YOU ARE PERFECT JUST THE WAY YOU ARE!

**Birgit Lueders** is the mother of two wonderful daughters Emma and Lisa, living in Philadelphia, PA. She is a certified Master Herbalist, Yoga Teacher, Iridology Instructor, and Wellness Coach.

Birgit first learned the values of an organic herbal lifestyle in her home country of Austria. Since 2009 she has operated BirgitCare -- a business focusing on health, wellness, and natural healing in Philadelphia, PA. Through BirgitCare, she offers personalized wellness coaching to support her clients' emotional, physical, and spiritual wellbeing by using modalities like Iridology, Herbalism, Nutrition, and Colorpuncture.

In 2012 Birgit founded the Center for Iridology, where she teaches Iridology Courses worldwide and annually in major cities in the USA. In 2020, during the pandemic, she adapted her Iridology Courses for online certifications and moved her wellness coaching program online.

Throughout the past ten years, Birgit has been a known speaker in her field at numerous national and international EXPO's, best-selling author on Amazon while being consistently featured on radio and TV. After being a Fellow, a Diplomat, and the Vice-President of the International Iridology Practitioner Association (IIPA), in 2020, Birgit became President of IIPA.

Birgit Lueders, MH, CCII, Diplomate of Iridology

Need WU Profile link

# CHAPTER 19

# HEALTHY VIBRANT GODDESS

## A S.A.C.R.E.D. DAILY SELF CARE GUIDE

Nancy Stevens, Lifestyle Specialist
and Co-founder of Uplift Clean Beauty

## MY STORY

I'm a self-care goddess with a specialty and personal brand focused on vibrant wellbeing. My brand sits solidly on the foundation of all things self-care! What centers and provides balance for me is found in the elements of my sacred daily practice. It's one I've carefully cultivated as I've journeyed through life. It's not complicated and fits this goddess on the go!

My goddess guide includes things that work with my needs and values. I've included my skincare routine, healthy eating, and exercise, along with compassionate personal affirmations and downtime. Each of these provides nourishment for my body-mind and spirit. To me, these are vital to having and enjoying a vibrant goddess life!

As integral as these elements are; during a very busy season, including our last son's graduation from high school, going on two out of state trips before our big summer trip, and hosting lots of company, my goddess place within the elements of my sacred guide was put to the test. I was left feeling as if I were chasing after my practice.

I didn't anticipate being disconnected from my daily practice because this is simply part of my day. I naively assumed being away from work and household obligations while traveling and visiting family would offer more time for deeper bliss and flow.

## THE BACKSTORY

Enter the energy of a thoughtfully planned long trip!

Beginning in January 2021, my husband Chris and I began discussing and planning the details of a long extended travel trip throughout the upcoming summer. *We've sure earned this special road trip. We'll have downtime and more time for me to spend with my parents and my husband's mom, and our siblings. This is exactly what we need as we move into the energy of being full-time, empty nesters.*

A one-week stay at our vacation home in Sedona, Arizona, was our touchdown launch point. I consider Sedona my Goddess home base, the ultimate energy renewal place! From here, we would travel by camper-van through national parks with stops along the way through Utah and Nevada before reaching our final destination, Oregon. This would be home away from home for the next eight weeks.

*I can't believe that we both have extended time off from our work. This past year has been full of ups and downs for me with starting a new business and handling some unexpected family issues. Time away will give me time to simply live in the moment without deadlines and any drama. We are going to focus on slowing down, enjoying, and taking our time.*

Prior to our Sedona launch, I was fully aware I had overextended myself in every aspect, from work to household to social. I reacted more negatively and responded less calmly to everyday life situations.

This was not typical at all for this high-energy, positive goddess.

## WEST COAST BLISS BEGINS.

The first leg of our trip began with a smooth flight to Phoenix and a leisurely drive to our place in Sedona. I'm ready for our trip to take place.

I instantly found release gathered in the scenic beauty of those magnificent, energizing red rocks. *Hello Sedona! It doesn't get any better than this. I feel I'm back in touch with myself.*

I took time to recharge with plenty of nourishing hikes in the Sedona energy vortices. I embraced my sacred daily routine with intentional compassionate downtime.

Part two of our journey began as we took off from Sedona in the camper van and headed towards Utah and through parts of Nevada while on the way to Oregon.

I paused elements of my practice given our travel agenda while maintaining my skincare routine and gentle yoga stretching—these were vital as we hiked in full sun and dry high heat.

We arrived with joy in beautiful Bend, Oregon, our first stop during our extended trip. I was ready to resume the fullness of my sacred daily routine placed on pause while on the road. In the beginning, I got out my yoga mat, did my workouts, made my healthy smoothies, gave myself quiet downtime with time for meditation and loving affirmations. I paid attention to getting good sleep and feeling rested. I am a high-energy goddess whose energy is replenished daily by the living soul food found in flow with my practice. I was renewed and ready!

## THINGS UNRAVEL!

Slowly and stealthily, due to things I wasn't prepared for, my trip steamrolled into eating off schedule and a daily mix of vacation foods coupled with giving generous amounts of my loving attention and energy to family without sharing downtime with myself. The high summer temps played a role as well, throwing off the quality of sleep, not to mention I was going to bed much later than normal.

I felt the sting of being out on the road front and center in my presence as our trip continued. "Chris, I don't know what's going on with me, but I feel off. I'm tired even though I'm not on the go. I feel like I'm expected to be on even though I have total permission to be myself. I'm enjoying myself, but I need more time to chill, so I can reset."

My sacred daily practice was at odds with the energy I chose to extend by sharing and doing life with everyone. Until I felt the impact of its departure, I was not fully aware just how much I need daily downtime in stillness to reset, renew and re-energize. *Today I'm going to find time to rest outdoors under Mom's beautiful willow tree and do nothing so I can recharge. Doing this is exactly what I've missed.*

I didn't realize the vital role my practice delivered to my energy/ wellbeing reserves until I felt the impact of being drained. Chris looked at me sideways when I half-jokingly at a low point asked, "Do you think I can get a ticket next week back to Nashville because I'm ready to go?"

## SACRED TURNING POINT

Of all the elements in my practice, my daily early morning walk takes front and center as a connecting piece within my day. While on our trip, I made time for my morning walk before the day began. This was non-negotiable.

I woke earlier than normal one morning and went for my walk, hoping to find some calm before the day took off.

I've always felt nurtured being in nature, and here in this moment, I connected to the golden light, soft warmth of the sun, and feeling nourished in the joyful sounds of birds singing. All of my hats worn on this trip (mom, daughter, sister, friend, aunt, cousin) slid off my head. I only had on my hat. Bubbling up from my soul was love. This early morning moment was a divine gift meant to get my attention. *I am and have all I need to feel balanced and whole in my practice.* Tears softly rolled down my cheeks. The tightness I'd felt in my throat released. Happy energy replaced my heavy energy. *Thank you, God, for this beautiful gift. I am grateful to be here with and in your energy today.*

We all want to feel cared for and whole. Instinctively I knew I was back home in the vibrancy of my sacred practice. I was gifted with a renewed perspective that I am my practice, whether or not each element unfolds entirely on any given day.

My practice is the fabric covering my being; it's my foundation!

I learned the art of pivoting and using self-compassion when unexpected energy moves in. Today my practice is stronger than ever with new learning that as a goddess, I'm okay and able to thrive even when all elements aren't gathered during a season of life.

What makes you and me a healthy, vibrant goddess? A sacred daily practice done in and with self-love and compassion. This is you, and this is me. Namaste!

I'm excited to share my healthy sacred goddess guide with you. It's simple, direct, and easy to follow. It's sacred. All you need to do is gather the word SACRED into your beautiful goddess self!

# THE TOOL

## THE S.A.C.R.E.D GUIDE

Each letter in this guide has a corresponding physical, emotional, interpersonal action. All are designed for ease of use while reminding you that you are as sacred as the elements found here meant to flourish your beautiful self!

Once you grow into this guide, you'll easily remember this by asking yourself, "Have I treated myself to sacred care today"? That's all there is to this guide!

Here are the powerfully simple elements found in my daily guide:

S Skincare Routine

A Affirmation

C Compassion

R Rest

E Exercise/Eating

D Daily downtime

### S—SKINCARE ROUTINE

How we treat our skin enhances and maintains healthy glowing skin.

Implementing an A.M and P.M skincare routine is the essence of goddess love shining through on your face. When you look good in your skin, your energy output increases because you feel good! The skin is your body's largest organ. When you take care of your skin, you keep your skin barrier healthy and enjoy a glowing complexion!

Follow these easy steps every day:

1. Cleanse in the morning and evening. Cleanse your skin upon waking to remove any sleep residue. Your evening time cleanse is an absolute must for removing any makeup, sunscreens, environmental pollutants, or buildup from your skin shedding.

2. Apply a spritz of toner. Using toner keeps your freshly cleansed skin moist and hydrated, so you're ready to apply the next product.

3. Apply serum/moisturizer. Use this product as directed to dampen skin, so the skin absorbs the ingredients. Serum goes on first, followed by morning or evening moisturizer.

4. Apply sunscreen (morning only)

## A—AFFIRMATION

If you want to bring change into your life, harness the sacred found in crafting and using personal affirmations. This is crucial to honoring the goddess inside! When using the power of personal affirmations, you create positive change, which helps you achieve your highest potential.

Think of personal affirmations as a loving, trusted friend who is always with you in all situations!

What is a positive affirmation? This is a powerful statement for something you want, which you then bring into your life and essence by lovingly stating this daily. As you get into the habit of making time for your daily affirmation, you'll begin to feel and notice a shift in your energy and how you show up. This expands outwardly and how you are treated takes on all new energy!

When should you use affirmations? I like to use mine at the start of the day as part of my morning routine. If I need a boost, I use these when needed. I also use my affirmations to counter triggers and reactions. The goal of affirmations is to keep your energy positive and open while training your mind to move from old habits attached to limiting beliefs, scarcity, or fear into positive possibilities.

What we believe and share, we live out and become!

Being the goddess, you require clean, clear, positive energy!

Affirmation support: Use the three P's formula: Use present tense, make these personal, and with positive energy.

Examples:

I am confident because I know who I am, and I live in my truth.

I am smart and resilient.

I have everything I need to accomplish my goals today.

## C—COMPASSION

In the absence of self-compassion, the sacred goes missing. Filling your cup with sincere self-love from a place of abundance is the foundation from which the sacred flourishes. Recognizing yourself as a sacred loving person is the essence of a goddess. This energy lays the foundation for practicing self-care. When we extend self-compassion, we come into our power, and from there, we tend to all others and life with the fullness found in compassion.

## R—REST

Getting enough rest is crucial to functioning with vibrant goddess energy. Rest is so vital to wellbeing that it causes physical and emotional issues in body-mind and spirit when depleted. We spend all of our time getting things done and little time focusing on sleep. Sleep replenishes energy so we can get it all done and feel great instead of depleted!

Goddess sleep tips:

- Keep your sleep space dark, quiet and cool for optimal rest.
- Turn off electronics. The light from iPhones, tablets, laptops or other electronics can wake up your brain, making it hard to fall asleep.
- Wind down. Your goddess body and mind need time to shift into sleep mode. Before bed, engage in calming activities such as listening to a meditation app or soothing music—mist your sheets and pillow with some lavender spray. Be thoughtfully intentional in releasing energy before you get into bed. Place your emphasis on sleeping so you'll shine like a goddess upon waking!

## E—EXERCISE AND EAT HEALTHFULLY

Find something that you enjoy physically and give yourself the gift of moving. Being sedentary is depleting not only physically but emotionally. Exercising awakens energy, while being inactive depletes energy.

Exercise Options:

Walking, hiking, yoga, swimming, tennis, dance, pilates, kickboxing, cycling.

Intentionally moving at least 15 minutes daily increases immunity, enhances creativity, brings on a good mood, and improves sleep.

Goddess Eating Tips:

"You are what you eat" is cliche and true. Eating processed foods with added fats, sugars and sodium is not a friend to goddesses. These deplete energy and potentially increase health issues like obesity, high blood sugar, high cholesterol, and high blood pressure.

Stock your kitchen with fresh fruits and veggies to eat on the go and enjoy in salads, side dishes, or as an entree. Include healthy nuts, seeds, beans, whole grains, gluten-free options, and eat clean unprocessed proteins. If you eat out frequently, look for healthier alternatives. Eat your favorite comfort foods and enjoy eating out while keeping your eye on including whole and plant-based foods in your day today!

## D—DOWNTIME

We need this element more than ever, in my opinion, to counter being busier than ever and dealing with so much in our lives.

Downtime is the space of reduced doing and inactivity, allowing body and mind space to unwind. Being still and silent reduces stress and renews energy while restoring balance.

This often-overlooked element is key to wellbeing in all aspects of life. Downtime is my go-to goddess element.

In the short space of being still and silent, our overactive thoughts are placed on pause. This pause resets our emotional center allowing for increased productivity and creativity.

Simple steps:

1. Find a time during the day where you can be still without distractions.
2. Choose the amount of time available to you. For some, this is less than ten minutes. For others its's greater than thirty minutes or more!
3. Immerse yourself completely at the moment, giving as much attention to this space as you would your work or family obligations.
4. When your downtime is over, notice how you feel and lovingly move back into your day.

I hope you'll use this guide to shine your goddess light brighter within as you go through your day-to-day life!

*"A self-care specialist"* best describes **Nancy Stevens**' life's work. Her specialties and interests with self-care cover multiple areas. She is passionate about supporting women in finding and extending loving, authentic care to themselves as a way to thrive in all areas of their life.

Nancy is a certified health and wellness coach providing her clients with support and tools, so they find inner balance in today's busy world.

Nancy's accomplishments as a self-care specialist include:

-Two #1 best-selling Amazon books: *The Beauty of Authenticity* and *The Wellness Universe Guide to Complete Self-Care 25 Tools For Stress Relief.*

-Leading over 1500 hours of yoga classes to all age levels and abilities as a certified yoga instructor, including The Wellness Universe event SoulTreat.

- Several speaking presentations, both online and in-person events.

-Co-Hosting *Soul Empowerment* on The Wellness Universe Learn It Live platform.

- Hosting *Authentic Self-Care with Nancy* on News For The Soul Radio. com

-Founding *UpliftCleanBeauty.com*, a skincare company focused on sustainable, clean, vegan facial products.

Nancy lives in Nashville, Tennessee, with her husband, Chris. They enjoy family time with their four adult sons and daughter-in-law along with their fur baby Doug, the dog! Together Nancy and Chris have enjoyed traveling overseas and look forward to traveling in their camper van, taking in the scenic wonders found in the national parks! A hiking and nature enthusiast, Nancy enjoys walking and hiking as much as she can, including re-energizing and relaxing at their vacation home nestled in the red rocks in Sedona, Arizona.

To learn more and connect with Nancy visit
https://www.thewellnessuniverse.com/world-changers/nancystevens/

# CHAPTER 20

# OWN YOUR BATTLE GODDESS OF COMPASSION

## USING VOICE DIALOGUE TO TAP INTO YOUR DIVINE FEMININE POWER

Carolyn McGee, Sacred Haven Living Guide,
Intuition Coach & Teacher

## MY STORY

*What did I mess up this time?* was the pervasive thought that ran through my mind when something didn't go right in business or life. It flowed so quickly in and out of my consciousness that I wasn't aware of it half the time. Even after I did a lot of self-development work, it still lurked in the background.

I grew up ultra-responsible and often took on obligations that weren't mine under the guise of being helpful, which did bring me joy. Unfortunately, there were emotional attachments to giving and receiving for my family and me. Nothing was ever free. I felt this underlying string of expectations when I received anything. I eventually realized I also had an expectation when giving; perhaps it was that the person would love me or accept me if I did something for them. I got my validation and love externally by doing for others.

Part of my external validation was not following my passion for helping others by going into healing or social work. I'm blessed to have a highly logical and analytical brain, and I followed the family's encouragement to go to engineering school. I excelled and worked for 25 years-plus in high-tech manufacturing. I was very successful but never fulfilled.

I overdeveloped the masculine, producing energy. The women I worked with were competitive instead of collaborative, and it was every person for themselves. Living and working in this energy reinforced that it's not safe to receive. There was always a condition to receiving any support. It was also not safe to be seen as feminine. Being nurturing, feminine, or cooperative brought unwanted attention and sexual harassment.

There was an accounting error in one company, and my job level and pay rate were increased by mistake. A male coworker found out about it, and he started spreading the rumor that the only reason I could've been promoted was by sleeping with the boss. When I brought this to Human Resources, he was told it was an error but not to apologize or tell people he made a mistake. I got to keep the level and pay increase, but the cost of receiving them was my reputation.

At another privately held company, the owner gave promotions for sex. He was not happy that I did not conform. When I was pregnant with my daughter, he came up behind me at the copy machine and trapped me by putting his hands on my very pregnant belly. He whispered, "This could've been our child." It was during a recession, and I had been unemployed for nine months when I started working there. I felt trapped in many ways. It was not safe to be feminine, a creator, or not give in to masculine demands.

This cycle of toxic masculinity and fear of my femininity continued for years. Along the way, I released myself from an unhealthy marriage and started working on myself.

A piece of my journey was remembering how to communicate with animals and angels. As I allowed in the unconditional love of the animal kingdom and the divine world, I felt unrestricted love and acceptance for the first time. This allowed me to expand into unconditionally loving myself. I found myself drawn to the powerful goddess energies but was fearful of their strength and presence.

I wasn't present enough in my energy and body to accept the support of the strong independent goddess energy.

Meeting Alan Davidson, the creator of *Evolutionary Mystic Meditation*, opened a new way of understanding my mind and body. For the first time, I could feel my energy aligned in my body. I felt magnetic and open to possibilities. Life seemed much richer, more fun, and easy.

Opportunities flowed as I embraced being safe in my physical body and refined my intuition and connection to the divine. However, I still had that voice of ultra-responsibility and *what did I do wrong?* running in the background.

Using Voice Dialogue along with the Emotional Freedom Technique (EFT)—or "tapping"—provided an opportunity to make friends with those unevolved voices running the show in the background of my life for years and decades.

Voice Dialogue is the recognition that we are made up of many different thought patterns. Originally developed by Hal and Sidra Stone, this technique involves someone moving across the room into a different chair to acknowledge their voices. Some examples are the voice of resistance, the voice of the inner critic, the voice of procrastination. These are all aspects of ourselves that we often look at as the shadow aspect. We don't give credit to how powerful these pieces of ourselves are and the value they bring to our personality and spirit. Only by understanding these aspects of our humanness and the "shadow" self of those unevolved voices can we learn to love those aspects of ourselves and give them the opportunity to mature.

Shifting into each voice and tapping with the energy of the voice allowed it to be heard and release the unhealthy hold it had on me. I learned to honor and accept my inner critic, judge, saboteur, and not-good-enough. Making friends with fear so she is seen and honored rather than stamped down had the counterintuitive effect of making me feel safer and allowing me to feel more energy in my body.

The voice of *what did I mess up this time?* no longer ran nonstop in the back of my mind.

Working through all these aspects of myself, I became more intuitive, more connected, and more powerful. That overdeveloped sense of responsibility became balanced with boundaries to filter through what's mine and what isn't.

Once these aspects of our self are recognized, nurtured, and loved, we can step into the divine aspects of our self. These divine parts are powerful to expand our awareness of the multitude of energies available to support us. We all can connect to the healer in Christ Consciousness. We have the nurturing heart of the Divine Mother. We can connect to Stillness, which is an aspect of the divine masculine. Once we understand this, we can expand our connection, healing, and energy.

Learning to love all pieces of myself gave me the courage to open to what Alan called the Battle Goddess of Compassion. She is the piece of us who is might for right. She is the part who advocates for those less fortunate. She is the aspect of us who volunteers time. She is the wise model and leader. She is the one who interjects and does not allow others to be put down. This fierce energy is unconditionally loving yet accepts no bullshit.

As I tapped with and embodied this voice, I stood more firmly in that which I believe. Allowing anyone to cross a boundary of what I felt was good for me was out of the question. Tapping into this aspect of myself expanded my mind, intuitive connection, and energetic boundaries into a new dimension.

I deeply understood that the word "no" is a complete sentence, and it felt natural to set a boundary because it's the right thing to do for me and those I love. It gives them the opportunity to step up and take responsibility for their actions.

Owning the Battle Goddess of Compassion—mama bear energy—by not allowing anyone to hurt my children or hurt those I love empowered me. My love is truly boundless, so I love everyone and stand for everyone. How can I stand by when those who I love are being hurt because they don't know how to receive, or they don't know how to say no?

This energy of the Battle Goddess of Compassion is being you! It's understanding the energy of Wonder Woman, of Athena, Kuan Yin, Isis: these strong energies who've nurtured, loved, encouraged, and cared for those they love. When someone attacks them or tries to take away the divinity of their existence, this energy will not stand for that.

The first defense is deflection, pushing back those words, actions, and energies of "not good enough," "didn't try hard enough," "don't have what it takes." Those are all lies.

The second defense is standing ground by making a clear boundary: this is my belief, and you are accepted in your belief but do not try to force your beliefs or your way upon me.

The third defense is that I will repel you from my energy, space, and people I love. You are not allowed to attack me or my loved ones with your unconsciousness.

As you connect with and own your Battle Goddess of Compassion, you step into your divine feminine power. You become a powerful, charismatic, and caring advocate for love and connection.

# THE TOOL

Voice Dialogue was developed as a method for working with sub-personalities in the early 1970s by Hal and Sidra Stone. This methodology invited you to imagine a part of yourself as separate from yourself. The self would stay in a chair, and the part or voice would physically move into another chair somewhere in the room. The facilitator would then speak to the part to understand the driving motivation behind the voice. Their insight gained by allowing this aspect of the self to have an independent voice was profound in its healing aspects.

My mentor Alan Davidson created a methodology of shifting in your chair to move from one aspect of the self to another and added the Emotional Freedom Technique (EFT) or tapping to anchor in the energy of the voice. He invoked the energy of the Controller, who is the conductor of all our voices, by getting permission from the Controller, whose main job is to keep the self safe and be the gatekeeper of which voices get to be heard.

With this approach, the facilitator can communicate easily and clearly to understand the motivation and how young or old the energy is that has created that voice. These voices are often termed the "voices in the basement." They are the immature aspects of our personality that unconsciously force us to make certain decisions. Learning to honor the energy that created these voices and keeps them strong is deeply healing.

If you are not familiar with tapping, you can get information on my profile.

https://www.thewellnessuniverse.com/world-changers/carolynmcgee/

## STEP 1 – CONNECT WITH THE CONTROLLER

Shift in your chair by rotating your hips and body in a circular motion in the direction that feels correct to you and ask to speak to the Controller.

Use the following tapping script to become the voice of the Controller.

- I am the Controller
- I am the voice that keeps the self safe.
- I control everything I can.
- I control the voices and what the self does.
- I have been with the self for as long as I can remember.
- I am on guard for the self 24/7.
- I never get a break.
- I love the self.
- I am the Controller

Acknowledge that the Controller is on guard 24/7, never has a vacation, never gets a break. As the Controller, you love the self so much that you are willing to do anything to keep the self safe.

Then ask your Controller these questions.

a.  Do you give permission to speak to some of the other voices?

b.  Will you provide a crystal clear channel to the other voices?

c.  Will you let me know if they don't feel safe?

## STEP 2 – BE THE VOICE OF STILLNESS.

Stillness is beyond the beyond and infinite. It is that aspect of all-knowingness without needing to do. It is a divine masculine presence.

Shift in your chair by rotating your hips and body in a circular motion in the direction that feels correct to you and ask to speak to Stillness.

Use the following tapping script to become the voice of Stillness.

- I am Stillness.
- I am beyond the body.
- I am beyond the heart.
- I am beyond the mind.
- I am beyond the will.
- I am beyond the self.
- I am beyond heaven.
- I am beyond time.
- I am the sound of silence.
- I am Stillness.

Feel as your awareness extends beyond your body and connects into infinite space and stillness. This is the stillness at the center of all being.

## STEP 3 – BE THE VOICE OF THE DIVINE MOTHER.

This feminine aspect balances stillness with unconditional love for all. She is nurturing unconditional love.

Shift in your chair by rotating your hips and body in a circular motion in the direction that feels correct to you and ask to speak to the Divine Mother.

Use the following tapping script to become the voice of the Divine Mother.

- I am the Divine Mother.
- I am the heartbeat of the earth.
- I am the creator of all life.
- I am the mother to all sentient beings.
- I love all my children unconditionally.
- I am infinite love.
- I am nurturing.

- I am healing.
- I am divine healing.
- I am the Divine Mother.

Allow this nurturing, unconditional love to fill your heart, bringing healing and serenity into your entire being.

## STEP 4 – OWN THE VOICE OF THE BATTLE GODDESS OF COMPASSION.

The Battle Goddess of Compassion is the wonder woman who lives in all of us. This might for right energy unconditionally loves all sentient beings. She is kind and collaborative and recognizes the divinity in us all. When someone or something threatens one of her children, she takes out her sword of righteousness and goes to battle to protect. There is no offense yet a fierce defense.

Shift in your chair by rotating your hips and body in a circular motion in the direction that feels correct to you and ask to speak to the Battle Goddess of Compassion.

Use the following tapping script to become the voice of the Battle Goddess of Compassion.

- I am the Battle Goddess of Compassion.
- I am the Divine Mother and Stillness.
- I am the Divine Feminine arising as the warrior priestess.
- I am might for right.
- I am fierce in my loving.
- I seek out ignorance and offer connection.
- I transform cruelty and suffering into healing.
- I am love in action.
- I am in service to all.
- I am self-compassion.
- I am strength and stamina.
- I am light and wisdom.
- I am the Battle Goddess of Compassion.

Invite this fierce and unconditionally loving energy to help you heal any voices that are holding you back. Ask for balance with the divine feminine and divine masculine energy. Notice how you are enlightened, fully embodied, caring, and aware. There is no need to act, yet you respond or defend as needed.

## STEP 5 – BE YOUR CENTERED SELF

The Centered Self integrates all the voices with ease and grace. You can access Stillness, the Divine Mother, and the Battle Goddess of Compassion as the Centered Self. You live authentically, connecting to all.

Shift in your chair by rotating your hips and body in a circular motion in the direction that feels correct to you and ask to speak to the Centered Self.

I invite you to journal your new understanding and feelings. I would love to hear what awareness opened for you. I have a recording on my website of the tapping to help you connect easier and deeper to the different voices. There is also a journal prompt PDF. You can download it and other gifts at https://www.thewellnessuniverse.com/world-changers/carolynmcgee/

You may also message me from my profile with any questions, comments, or observations.

**Carolyn McGee** is the creator of the Sacred Haven for Empowered & Intuitive Living Community which includes North Carolina retreats, virtual gatherings, powerful workshops, private coaching, and soul-nurturing VIP weekends. She serves women ready to connect with their inner wisdom, trust it to make empowered decisions, then take inspired action and discover the power of nature's cycles to create a life that lights them up.

Carolyn specializes in Amplifying YOUR Intuitive Superpower to listen to, trust, and follow your soul's path to living the most joyful, healthy, connected, abundant, and purposeful life. She has taught thousands of women to trust themselves and their intuition so they can show up in their full power in business and life.

By showing you the way back to your intuition, she helps you enhance your ability to receive messages and understand your guidance 24/7. This empowers you to take inspired action so that you release second-guessing for good, and you feel 100% confident in making crystal clear decisions.

Carolyn is one of five Advanced *Evolutionary Mystic Meditation* Facilitators.

With a background of 20-plus years in high tech, Carolyn knows firsthand the importance of living from a blend of her masculine and feminine energies. Carolyn has co-authored 10-plus bestselling books, is a popular radio and TV host, sought-after speaker, and blogger. To learn more about Carolyn, or to contact her, visit

https://www.thewellnessuniverse.com/world-changers/carolynmcgee/

# CHAPTER 21

# FREEDOM FROM ABUSE

## A PATH TO CREATING A NEW LIFE

Victoria Soto, JD

## MY STORY

I am Victoria Soto, spiritual leader, teacher, protector, bestselling author, and lover of life. I currently reside with my family in the United States of America. We live in one of the prettiest towns in the state of Texas. I, like countless many, am also a survivor of many forms of abuse, from emotional, physical, professional, sexist, labeling, and short-changing, etc. Name it, I know of it, or it could have happened to me. It's not something I've sought. This is a cup I pray passes me. Unfortunately, human beings are abused in many ways, and it's my mission to help them by writing about the tools that helped me break through the abuse and find and create a new and glorious life.

First, I feel compelled to say something about the relevant universal abusive stressor happening today. This type of abuse falls under the realm of emotional abuse. The unbelievable and inconceivable stress of the unknown and known comes to and at us through negative information we receive each day. Our minds are sponges for negative streaming abuses from what we lovingly refer to as our "media devices" for one. It can also come at us from every direction, face-to-face, in any given moment, in our homes, crosswalks, or workplaces. This emotional abuse is what I call *the noise!* This noise can be a painful and brutal attack on our senses. I call it the ultimate enemy. You may know it as fear. In my opinion, fear is the most loathsome and dangerous reaction because it brings debilitating stress. In this form of abuse, stress can kill, steal and destroy, wreaking havoc on our minds and bodies and steal our hopes for a future. It breaks down our physical immune defenses, and that can be deadly. This kind of abuse can be considered a greater threat than an invisible killer that is airborne because it comes through our thoughts. Whoever you are, you must find a way, tool, and/or weapon to defeat this.

One particular and very vivid past abuse I experienced gave me the foundation of the tool that helps me today. This abuse situation was what I like to call my "snapping out of it" moment. This abuse was so brutal it had me forgetting my value. It made me lose my focus and path to God (my center). Unfortunately, I found myself in a state of survive or die for so long I forgot who I was to God and who He was to me. I had lost my way. From one day to the next, I wondered if this would be my last day on earth. Finally, my chance came. I finally snapped after hearing my abuser, who was sitting across from me, tell me how much joy it brought him to beat me into a pulp. Hearing someone casually say to you that beating you was the best feeling of euphoria for them really brought it home for me. I realized the abuse would never end. I knew I would die at the hands of my abuser. This realization broke me in the best way possible. There was only one choice to make; I had to stop it right then. I knew then that I would never be touched in violence again!

I can speak of this abuse now without feeling any sense of hurt or sadness because I was absolutely freed of it. This absolution and clarity of heart and mind worked for me in that moment. In that moment, I snapped and came back to my center. You could say that "I came back to my senses." I was so young and would never have dreamed in a million years that this would've been my lot in life. Now, 25 years later, I'm a woman of strength and courage. I wear my power like a crown with pride. I hold my head high and am filled with humility and grace given to me daily by my center of love, my Lord God. As a professional, I'm fortunate to protect and help others find their rescue out of situations. But first, I had to understand what it felt like to be rescued before I could do the rescuing. My life is fulfilled and joyful. I am poised to receive both the good and the bad. I am armed with love and tools in my chest that I carry every day. I have been living this new life of balance. You can too!

# THE TOOL

## FINDING YOUR CENTER AND ALLOWING IT TO WORK FOR YOU

We're living in unprecedented times where we see death, destruction, and division all around us. How does one escape an impossible onslaught of emotional abuse like what we see every day? My tool for you is first to be very still and find your center. Your center, your true core of self, is what balances you. It's what brings you back to the place where you're meant to be. Your center is the space where you're safe and unwavering. It has always been part of you. Once you tap into that center, it's the start of taking back control and escaping your abuse, whatever that might be. We all need to remember or recall our center amid this noise to find our peace and escape the abuse to survive what is now and what lies ahead.

I created a list for myself that allows me to find my center and start breaking through abuse. How can you find yours?

Ask yourself the following questions:

1. What is the one thing I'm absolutely sure of that brings me a sense of peace?
2. What is the one thing that allows me to feel more accepted and loved no matter what my mess of the moment might be?
3. What is the one certain fact I believe is my all-time rescue, no matter the difficulty or impossibility of any given situation?
4. Who or what is my strength when I'm weak and can no longer go on?
5. Can I count on this thing, person or fact always?
6. What always allows me to know that it's not too late to live my best life when the entire world seems to be falling apart?

7. What is the one thing I know when nothing else makes sense, and there is no longer any rhyme or reason left?

8. What or who can I rely on to pull me out of my impossible place so I can be there for others to pull them out of theirs?

9. When I'm pulled down into deep murkiness, who or what is my life preserver?

10. When I'm trying to hold my peace face with today's division and catastrophic hate and am listening to the ranting of complete insanity, where do I find peace and quiet?

However you answer the ten questions listed above, the most prevalent answer is where you'll find your center today. These answers will change, of course, as you grow, but their effect will always give you the power you need to begin your escape from an abusive or stressful situation. There may be more than one answer for you or one solid answer that truly fits each question. I find that when I see my answers spring into moments of enlightenment and realization, I know it's at the core for me. This happens when answers come to you in fractures of brilliant light and love that you see within yourself and in the people most important to you. It's different for everyone, given your circumstances. My solid answer to every one of those questions is God! I examined this today and found it was the joy and love on people's faces in general as they interacted. I found it in the love I received from my son and the smile on his face. I search for my center in any given moment when I feel the abuse sinking in and trying to take hold. Asking myself even a couple of these questions brings me back to my center, back to "me." It's the love of my God! This love is magnified in the memory of the sound of the great, booming voice of my father, the giggles and voices of my two beautiful sisters, the loving smile and bear hugs from my brother, and the memory of the touch and loving voice of my mother. It manifests in many ways all around me if I reach for it. This tool has helped me to do it every time. Find your center and name it, claim it, and let it rescue you from an impossible and unthinkable stressful existence.

## REMEMBERING TO COUNT YOUR BLESSINGS. THIS ALLOWS YOUR CENTER TO WORK FOR YOU

The second gem from my tool chest is to count your blessings. I've found that counting my blessings is a great tool to stave off the abusive horrors of today. It has helped me escape my past, present, and future abusive behaviors, whether it came from a swift punch in the face that broke my jaw or from the noise of social media.

It can also come from negative thoughts. I have been through so much heartache and pain that there are too many to recount (for one chapter). I know I'm in good company along those lines. Show me a sad person who has been in a bad place, and there is always someone who has been in a worse predicament. The feeling of isolation is another trick the enemy loves to play on us when we're caught in the grip of abuse. Therefore, don't believe the lie that you're alone. We're never alone in our abuse, stressors, and misery. We should also remember that the sun can and does come up every day. We will experience indescribable moments of joy and elation that will overcome these bad moments. It's the stuff that makes life worth living. Holding on to the certainty that there are many more blessings to come, even amid nightmares, is another step toward freedom from abuse.

How do we hold onto our blessings? By counting them, one by one. We bring in perspective instead of focusing on what was taken away from us when we do this. It brings your focus and vision to you and who you truly are. I hope you realize that you're magnificent! Know that you can and will overcome monstrous odds in the face of unimaginable abuse. Count your blessings and remember!

## TAKE OWNERSHIP OF YOUR EXPERIENCE AND USE IT FOR GOOD:

When I snapped out of my predicament, I realized and understood, on every level, that I was not a rag doll to be torn apart by allowing my shoulder to be pulled out of its socket. I was not a football to be kicked in the stomach until my ribs fractured. I remember hearing the phrase "drop kick" for the first time. It was not a memory from watching a sporting event. It was my abuser referring to me as the ball and how awesome it was to throw me on the floor and kick me repeatedly. I was living in my own Hell on Earth. Still, I remember feeling something holding me to my chair as I sat across from him. I stilled myself to continue to listen. He continued going down his memory lane of his abuse, and finally, the words came out. He said, "Beating you is the best high of my life." I started seeing my life slowly flash before my eyes in stages of reflection. In these flashes of my life, I remembered my loving family. I remembered my strong and amazing mother, a woman who lived almost her entire life in pain. She broke her hip as a child. As a result of a poor decision, she endured countless surgeries and lived away from her family for months while doctors (in an attempt to have her legs be even again) broke her bones over and over. I cannot imagine the pain this caused her, and yet, she smiled and gave others joy her entire life. This is the stuff of which I was made! My father was a brave, strong, and wonderful giant of a man who never let another human being make him feel small. His integrity is still, today, not to be matched in my eyes. This is the stuff I am made of! I came back into the knowledge that I was worthy of better. My God created me for better! Better love, better peace, and a better existence. One of freedom and joy! I wanted to live in a healthy body and mind and not in a cage.

## WHO AM I? THE ANSWER TO THIS QUESTION FREES YOU AND GIVES YOU GREAT POWER.

When I snapped, I began to pray. Through my prayers, I began to remember who I was. The night the physical abuse came to an end was when I found myself and my truth again. I found "me." I could tap into this superpower of praying, remembering, and counting my blessings. Prayer is now one of my favorite superpowers. My praying was tantamount to my escape.

We should all ask, "Who am I?" This is not only a question but a tool to add to discovering your truth and freedom from the abusive stressors of today. We should continuously ask this of ourselves as we change and evolve each day. We are a product of what we experience, including, but especially not limited to, our spiritual relationship. We would not exist without that. For me, that is God! That, my friend and reader, is golden. That is where you will find your ultimate truth and freedom to be happy and at peace in a world seemingly going haywire more and more each day. Embracing who we are and the common truths about ourselves and respecting others is essential to our growth as a world. It's part of our growing up and evolving into the great beings we were created to be.

## THE BEAUTY IN FORGIVENESS

One of the best ways to use the knowledge of who you are is to accept all that you are. Knowing who we are and accepting that we are ever-changing and fallible is a healthy place to start—coming back to the person we were meant to be before the abuse brings us rejuvenated peace and strength. We find ourselves free of the chains that kept our joy buried. We were muted in our independent thoughts and decisions. We were reduced to a fraction of who we were. Now, free, we can be all that were called to be. We can think for ourselves again. We can also decide to forgive our perpetrators or not. I recommend forgiving them. Even though it's difficult, I know it's the fastest way to heal. Also, if they're still on the prowl and come to understand that we've forgiven them and living our glorious, purposeful life, it drives them crazy (if that makes you happy).

More importantly, when we use the power of forgiveness and understand who we are as fallible creatures, we're apt to know the value of forgiving ourselves. Once you've honed this tool of forgiveness, it'll serve you well throughout your entire life. There is great power in knowing who you are, imperfections and all. It's humbling, but in humility, we find strength. Those of us who know this truth are at peace and can count ourselves blessed. We should all want to breathe life into others and into the world around us. However, we're human and apt to have our good moments and not-so-good moments. Due to a misstep of our own doing, we could cause others pain, and when this happens, we should apologize and ask for forgiveness. We must use the tool of forgiveness to forgive ourselves and to move on, whether the people we hurt forgive us or not.

## BREAKING THE CYCLE OF ABUSE WITH LOVE AND EDUCATION

Our society and world have a long-storied history of putting people in checkboxes to make someone else feel better about themselves. "I may be this, but I would rather belong to this box than be associated with the other one." This is just one example of a habit of people assigning levels of intellect and class structure based on another's desire to dominate. This has been a stain on humanity and a shameful reality for far too long. I believe that the only way to stop this is through love and education. We should love one another. This is not a novel idea! In my belief, I'm commanded to love my fellow human being. It's a good and beautiful way to exist. Love is the great equalizer. Love and education are, in my opinion, a great tool to break at least this one nasty cycle of abuse in the world.

We must delve into the possibilities that what we were taught may not be correct. If what you have been taught puts any person above or beneath another, then you've been taught wrong. Therefore, moving forward, we must learn that we are all the same being. We are physically joined together on this planet for a purpose. Spiritually and lovingly, we can choose to think differently and re-educate one another so that we may live harmoniously in peace and not in abuse.

My idea may be a utopian one, but I believe that since we've all been abused in some shape or form in our lives, we are all on equal footing. We can choose to end the cycle of abuse on a universal scale. Let's do it!

**Victoria Soto**, JD, is the president and CEO of the Law Office of Victoria Soto, with offices in Austin and Round Rock, Texas. She concentrates her practice on defending healthcare providers before their licensing agencies. In this field of practice, Victoria seeks to protect her client's ability to continue to do what God created them to do, which is to heal the sick and suffering and to prevent illness throughout the world. For this opportunity, she is thankful and counts herself honored. Victoria is also honored to be an Attorney-Affiliate and Of Counsel to the Lucas/Compton Firm in Washington, DC. Victoria's Healthcare administration law practice also serves as a consultant for the healthcare institutions. The Victoria Soto Company for Success approach also offers consulting services in strategic and dynamic public relations regarding debate/election. and candidate preparation. Victoria is also a published author of the World's Best Doctors, released in 2016. This publication was written as a tool for doctors and healthcare providers to improve their way of practice in aspects of the human element for better outcomes. Victoria is also a contributing author to self-care and faith-centered books and is honored to be a part of the Wellness Universe.

# CHAPTER 22

# YOUR ANGEL TEAM

## CLEARING THE BAGGAGE AND BLOCKS WITH DIVINE ASSISTANCE

Ingrid Auer, Spiritual Teacher

## MY STORY

I still remember him very well. His name was Walter. He was a small, unimpressive man and had taken up residence in my kinesiology practice as an astrologer. I was naturally curious to learn from him what I had planned for my earth life as a soul. "Ingrid, you will be working with a lot of women; I can see that in your birth chart." "Me, with women? After all, I'm not a gynecologist, a midwife, a women's coach!" But Walter was right. In the course of my kinesiological work over two decades, 95% of my clients were women.

At the same time, angels entered my life. At first, I perceived their presence skeptically and cautiously, but they have become the center of my life over the years. In 1998 I received an order from the spiritual world to bring spiritual tools "from heaven to earth." On the one hand, to open people's hearts and, on the other hand, to provide them with spiritual tools for healing their souls. Help for self-help, so to speak.

When my work with angels became more and more known and spread over Europe to the USA, Central and South America, Japan, and Australia,

I gave up my kinesiological work. I was busy starting a small company and bringing my spiritual tools to the world in the form of highly energized symbols and essences. It's not surprising that all my employees are women; my father and my husband are the only male supporters in my company.

Also, as a lecturer, seminar leader, or coach, I was to work almost exclusively with women, although I had no influence over that. It just happened that way. I think of the wonderful and profound women's seminars or women's rituals I've held for various countries with great joy. So, what Walter predicted for me many years before came true.

Even when I walk through rooms where my spiritual tools stand in rows on shelves waiting for their journey into the big wide world, the topic of femininity and womanhood runs like a thread through all the different products.

The majority of my angel essences, oils, and aura essences focus on female issues, such as hormonal problems, pregnancy, childbirth, menstruation, female sexuality, or menopause. But there are also some which rebalance the various emotional injuries in a woman's life on the spiritual level. It doesn't matter if these are female emotional problems being dealt with as a toddler, schoolchild, teenager, young adult, wife, mother, girlfriend, lover, or grieving widow.

What particularly fascinates me is the relationship between the subtle energy centers in the female body and spirituality. If they are blocked, our entire life is blocked. Therefore, this is my call to you:

*Isn't it time to free your female chakras from the old ballast of your clan, your childhood, and your present life?*

*What would it be like to once and for all discard old beliefs and patterns that no longer belong to you?*

*How would it be to start clearing out and throwing off ballast before your energy system collapses?*

*What would it be like to discover a new, free, loving, and joyful approach to your own female body?*

# THE TOOL

## WOMEN! LET'S HEAL YOUR FEMALE CHAKRAS!

*Living a healthy life in a woman's body
can be downright fun - even ecstatic!
And that's good news for everyone!*

– Christiane Northrup M.D.

*Female chakras, are there such things at all?* That was my first thought when I read about them in Dr. Northrup's book *Women's Bodies, Women's Wisdom.* This remarkable American gynecologist has observed for decades that there are energy centers in the female body that are closely related to the imprints and experiences of our lives as women.

But: how can we rebalance our female chakras?

As with all the other chakras, there are different ways to strengthen and balance our chakras, such as:

- On the **energetic** level, through physical exercises or yoga
- With the help of body-energy-work
- With the help of meditation
- On the **emotional** level through talking therapy, family settings, kinesiology, astrological sessions, etc.
- On the **mental** level through positive thinking, mental training, etc.
- On the **spiritual** level through transformation with the help of the archangels.

They are not "tools" in the conventional sense, but their energies are available to us as spiritual aids. This may be unfamiliar and new to you, but it's worth trying and experiencing. Whether you've worked with angels before or not, know about angels, or are an angel novice, just try it! Invite them into your life and ask them to help you. I've also given practical tips on interacting with angels in The Wellness Universe Guide to Complete Self-Care books one through three.

## WHAT CLAN COMPULSION HAS TO DO WITH THE FIRST FEMALE CHAKRA

As soon as a small crab is kept in a bucket with other crabs and tries to climb out and escape, the other crabs keep pulling it back.

But what has this got to do with us women, particularly with our first chakra, the energy center at the bottom of our spine, from where we absorb earth energies? Well, the first (female) chakra is closely connected to our clan awareness. The focus is not on love, friendliness, or tenderness, but loyalty. The clan does not concentrate on individual needs but the preservation and survival of the collective and the family. Even when the clan talks about love and solidarity, it means compulsory clan formation that has nothing to do with affection or love.

Let's go back to the crabs. If one of them wants to leave the bucket, the others react the same way as when a woman wants to free herself from tight family patterns. There it's normal for family members also to try and sabotage—at least in the beginning—her efforts.

Our first chakra is influenced by education during the early years. Most families do not intend to hurt their members deliberately. They only pass on their 'knowledge' which they consider as the sole truth. Even if it's about painful and restrictive structures, they're usually not ready to rethink them or let them go. "We have always done it like this." Which woman does not know this sentence?

*Connect with Archangel Uriel and feel his presence. He embodies power and strength and gives you the energy to release old blockages related to your family of origin, clan, or ancestral lineage. Ask Archangel Uriel to send his transformative energy into your 1st feminine chakra with the help of his red healing ray. Ask him to dissolve all blockages and help you to be well-grounded and rooted.*

## WHAT BONDAGE HAS TO DO WITH THE SECOND FEMALE CHAKRA

Many women are still expected to concentrate on satisfying the needs of immediate and extended families. Without consciously being aware of it, they're directed by emotions, rooted in their clans, and connected with their first, and particularly their second, female chakra.

This energy center is situated in the area of the uterus. Therefore, we must not be surprised that many women suffer from health problems connected with their reproductive organs.

The second chakra has to do with relationships. First of all, the relationship with ourselves, and secondly, the relationship with others. At the same time, this chakra is an energy center that reacts to the quality of relationships and everything emotionally closely connected to us. Therefore, it not only reacts to burdens within our family and our circle of friends, but also to our financial situation and lack of financial security.

We women are often educated so that we assimilate the problems of our family members (second chakra), or we care for sick and old members of the family tirelessly. We often take on others' big burdens and make them our own. As a result of our education, we refuse to see that this often happens against our will. However, our body and soul often react.

*Focus your thoughts on Archangel Chamuel, even if you have never heard his name before. He is the angel of love and self-love and holds you tight. Chamuel's magenta healing ray transforms your emotional injuries, especially those related to your second female chakra.*

## WHAT SELF-EMPOWERMENT HAS TO DO WITH THE THIRD FEMALE CHAKRA

Some women literally feel powerless. It's because they have never learned to stand up for their own needs. Therefore, they are incapable of granting themselves permission for their actions and decisions.

Whereas the first female chakra has to do with grounding and balancing, but also with imprints from the clan, the second female chakra with emotional securities, creativity, and children, the third female chakra is about personal power and self-authorization. The energy center is above the navel and is also called the solar plexus. When we are nervous or scared, we feel an unpleasant tension in the stomach area around the navel chakra (which it is also called).

For centuries a woman's personality was entirely judged on whether and how they were beneficial to others and how they could find their place within the family unit. Therefore, many women were only judged on their domestic duties and motherly qualities, and as a result, treated accordingly. They were normally not allowed to live their individual personality. And if they did, only hidden from public view. I do not think I need to comment on the effect this had, and still has, on the collective female self-worth

The strength and weakness of the third female chakra are connected with performance, competence, inferiority, and immaturity. And, of course, with our rights. This means that we women (as well as men) must have the power to make decisions regarding ourselves and our lives. On the other hand, we must not give voluntary or involuntary permission to others to make decisions for us and our lives.

*Call Archangel Jophiel to your side and ask him to restore your lost joy of life or serenity. Send his yellow-orange healing ray into your third female chakra and feel your solar plexus relax. Your body straightens up, and you know that no one except yourself can give you permission to live happily and self-determined.*

## WHAT LOVE AT EYE LEVEL HAS TO DO WITH THE FOURTH FEMALE CHAKRA

Many women lose themselves in a partnership and would give anything to be accepted and treated equally in return. They keep waiting for years for equal love in their partnership! Love on equal terms. However, as reports about sexual and sexist assaults show, gender equality has still not reached everybody.

The fourth energy center in a woman's body lies in the area of her heart and her breasts and is called the heart chakra. Energetically it is closely connected with the second chakra, the sexual chakra. Whereas the uterus is sometimes called the 'lower heart,' the physical heart in the chest is called the 'upper heart.' If one of the chakras is hurt, it has a negative effect on the other.

If a woman experiences abuse, incest, or rape, she usually closes her heart and her heart chakra. Due to disturbed sexual morals, which are still widespread in our society, and are passed on from one generation of women to the next, many women close their second chakra and therefore cut themselves off from their sexuality or their erotic needs.

Female disorders in the heart chakra area can often arise when a woman does not exactly know how to combine her love energy (energy of the fourth chakra) and her creativity, or the wish to express herself and be completely herself (energy of the second chakra). There might be an additional inner conflict caused by a belief that she is only worthy of love when needed and can give what others need. This applies both for the care level (job, household, cooking, etc.) and the sexual one.

*Archangel Raphael does not only stand for healing but also for inner freedom. Therefore, ask him to your side and send his green healing ray into your fourth female chakra. Feel how his loving energy begins to heal old emotional wounds in your heart and feel the relief within you.*

## WHAT BOTTLING THINGS UP HAS TO DO WITH THE FIFTH FEMALE CHAKRA

It's sometimes claimed (usually by men!) that women have a more pronounced need to talk than men do. However, I know men who talk at least as much as women do, if not more! But it's not necessarily the length of a conversation but the content that counts. Even if we women like to chat about handbags, shoes, or mascara, we also have just as many conversations about personal feelings and experiences.

However, many women amongst us have never learned to talk about their feelings or needs. Since their childhood, they have carried on their family's way of thinking without questioning it.

The fifth chakra is located in the area of the larynx, or the thyroid gland, which causes problems for a lot of women. Symbolically and energetically, this chakra stands for the natural need to express oneself and say what is important.

The throat chakra also stands for the inner life plan which we have brought into this life. If we deviate too much from it by not expressing and living our true feelings, talents, wishes, or desires, we can feel the effects in our fifth chakra. Therefore, excessive will, stubbornness, or fixations, can cause thyroid problems.

*Ask Archangel Michael to come to you and feel his calming presence at your side. His healing ray is blue and can release your blockage in the throat chakra. Ask Michael to send his healing energy into your fifth female chakra and dissolve anything burdening so you can feel free to express your feelings without reservation.*

## WHAT THE "SIXTH SENSE" HAS TO DO WITH THE SIXTH FEMALE CHAKRA

You've either got it, or you haven't, people say. I am talking about the 'sixth sense,' this extraordinary ability which enables us to perceive far more than our five sensory organs allow. Everybody has got a sixth sense, but usually women are more likely to use it than men. Women listen to its signals and messages when we have to make decisions, or we sense something that is in the air but not (yet) visible.

Have you ever thought the so-called sixth sense might have something to do with the sixth energy center? The sixth chakra is situated between the eyebrows and is also called the 'third eye.' Why? Because we can 'see' and perceive more with it than with our physical visual organ, the eyes.

But why do we women still question our sensitive perception? Do we refuse to accept abilities that connect us with other levels and other worlds? Because they are not scientifically proven? Because we are not taken seriously? Because we are laughed at?

Many of our female ancestors had a strongly developed sixth chakra. However, they closed it, as they feared ending up as witches at the stake, for their abilities. Even today, many women close their third eye. Their special abilities, such as clairvoyance and being a medium, are still questioned, not appreciated, and degraded by most people.

Although most women would say their intuition is placed in their heart because they follow their feelings or stomachs because they trust in their gut feeling, it's actually situated in the sixth energy center. The third eye works like a receiver transmitter, absorbing all the vibrations and unspoken messages around us.

*Archangel Zadkiel is unknown to many people. His ray is violet, and he helps you to integrate your innate spirituality into your everyday life and to develop your medial skills. Ask him to direct his energy into your sixth female chakra and activate it so you can bring heaven to earth.*

## WHAT THE DIVINE IN EVERY WOMAN HAS TO DO WITH THE SEVENTH FEMALE CHAKRA

In mythology, the spiritual woman has always been called the great wise one, primeval woman, the knowing, or the great goddess. Old tradition portrays her as the life-giving creator and nourishing mother. At the same time, she is a healer and destroyer in one. But what has this got to do with the seventh female chakra?

It's located in the middle of the head and is open toward the top. Through this chakra, women and men are connected with the mystical, the universal, the Divine, or whatever you want to call it. Hence, a higher level of awareness or creation.

In the relationship with the Divine, women have always played a dominant role, even in the patriarchal religions. However, this has often been written out of history, and up to now, this important role of women is often kept secret.

Particularly now, in these scientifically orientated times, many women neglect their female spirituality. But, at the same time, an increasing number of women are looking for themselves. They have got stuck in a dead-end road or have other problems. In the course of the search, they discover their natural and intuitive access to spirituality. Some even open up for the spiritual world, contacting their higher self or other spiritual beings for the first time in their lives.

*Are you ready to connect with Archangel Metatron, the King of the Archangels? Ask him to your side and feel his fatherly, loving energy. His golden angel ray activates your seventh female chakra and connects you with the wisdom of the universe, the cosmos, the great Goddess. Recognize the Divine feminine in you and consciously integrate it into your life as a woman!*

**Ingrid Auer** is one of Europe's leading mediums, channeling messages and energized symbols and essences from the angels, Ascended Masters, Mary Magdalene, the Patron saints, and the Lemurian Goddesses. Since 1998 she has been writing spiritual books, which she has received as a medium.

At the center of her work, she manufactures high vibrating, energized symbols and essences, which are not only used by private individuals but also doctors, midwives, healing practitioners, energy practitioners, therapists, and teachers, with great success.

The energized symbols and essences have also proved to work well in the areas of pregnancy, childbirth, and childcare. Additionally, they are effective during care for the terminally ill and those who are grieving.

For many years, Ingrid Auer has been in close contact with the Ascended Master, Mary Magdalene. She publishes Mary Magdalene's messages, which she receives medially, and was offering spiritual journeys to Southern France, the center of the worship of Mary Magdalene in Europe.

Ingrid founded and manages her companies "Lichtpunkt & Ekonja" (Austria, publishing and worldwide distribution) and "Ingrid Auer LLC" (California, distribution in the US). She lives in Vienna, Austria, and Mallorca, Spain, and is a regular visitor to the US. Ingrid is also a Leadership Council Member of The Wellness Universe:

https://www.thewellnessuniverse.com/world-changers/ingridauer

# CHAPTER 23

# CALMING THE INNER MENTAL STORM

## HOW TO BECOME YOUR BEST FRIEND

Nicole Batiste, Intuitive & Attuned Inner Life Coach

*"The greatest gift you have to give is that of your own transformation"*

– Lao Tzu

## MY STORY

My relationship with myself started off rocky at a very young age. Trust, safety, and my voice were taken when I was just four years old. I hadn't developed a sense of who I was, but I certainly developed a sense of who I needed to be to survive. I learned early on that I needed to be compliant, agreeable, and quiet.

It was a typical elementary school day. You could hear the voices of children as they moved about the hall heading to their next class. As I started to head out of my classroom to join the bustling hallway, I heard Ms. Collins call out, "Nicole. I have something I want you to do." *What did I do wrong?* I tried to recall how the class went. *Did I say something wrong? What could she be calling me for?* I turned around and started walking towards her, avoiding eye contact. I wasn't afraid of her; Ms. Collins was one of my favorite teachers. I always called her a teenager because I loved seeing how it lit up her eyes and smile. However, the constant fear of doing something wrong had taken hold. I stood there waiting for her to correct me about something.

Ms. Collins: "Nicole, I want you to write down something nice about yourself every day."

Me: "For what? None of it would be true anyway."

If she said anything else after that, I don't remember it. That was my first exposure to the power of our words and the importance of our relationship with ourselves. Unfortunately, I wasn't in a place mentally or emotionally to recognize that loving gesture. I was in elementary school and already hated myself. Her kind words rolled right off me, and I continued on the abusive road from which she tried to pull me. There were two roads for me: one I lived on, the hidden road, and one I existed on, the compliance road.

Keep quiet, yep, that's the hidden road. My eyes are open, yet I'm in complete darkness. I hear conversations, or are those my thoughts? *You're stupid. You look like a boy. No one notices you. You're worthless. Don't try too hard. You don't want to fail again. What makes you think you could?* Oh, those are my thoughts. I drifted back to the hidden road again. I kept this road a secret because I was afraid that telling someone would result in my feelings being downplayed as always. After all, I was always "so sensitive." I was determined not to ever feel those feelings again, at least not in public. Embarrassment, shame, isolation, and loneliness were common for me, even among family, but I did everything to hide that. *You're so needy. You don't think. You're so emotional. Cry baby.* I drifted here at all hours of the day and night. My sadness and disdain for myself were normal to me, though. *Hmmm, I wonder what that feels like?*; I saw happy people and was both jealous and curious.

"You're such a sweety deety," my grandma used to say. Behind the smile, *you wouldn't say that if you knew me.* In public, I traversed the compliance road. It's the one where quiet, well-mannered, soft-spoken, and obedient Nicole showed up. No opinions; go with the flow. Having a different idea or thought may get me yelled at (which translates to disapproval, unlovable, having done something wrong). I was too fragile for that. I couldn't risk having to cry or seem upset. I had to make sure I controlled my environment so I ensured to keep the unlovable hidden. The smile did the trick. There was always a smile or at least no signs of distress. If there were, people ignored them. *I wish I were never born. I bet I was adopted; there's no way I'm a part of this family. They wouldn't even notice or care if I was gone.*

I carried my first attacker's burden for more than twenty years, which created a magnet for more like him to show up throughout my life. That burden caused a perpetual abusive relationship with myself. The words of disapproval didn't flow as much as I got older. I didn't have to say them anymore since I successfully drilled them into my head so early in life; now, I just embodied them. My external language, even when trying to be positive, all had a negative self-hatred undertone.

My life started to turn around after reading my first personal development book in my twenties. I had a new outlook; I had hope. What I didn't have, and kept me on life's treadmill, was a solid relationship with myself. The funny thing is—if "funny" is the right word—I hadn't realized my sense of self hadn't improved. I felt better about the direction of my life, but the quiet moments revealed otherwise, and I often retreated onto the hidden road. "It seems like you can never be happy," my mom said that to me one day. "I am happy," I replied with a half-hearted smile. I wasn't happy; I was deeply depressed. The abuse was deep in my bones. The sadness, depression, and pessimism flowed through my veins and were a part of every fiber of my being. I had no idea how to rid myself of those toxins. Yet if you asked anyone what they thought of me, I was a sweet young lady. You never know what is going on inside someone's mind.

*What's wrong with me? Why can't I be happy?* I continued to read one personal development book after another, searching for ways to "fix" me. I bought course after course that touted some sort of betterment. My debt started to grow due to that addiction. I loved learning but was I learning or hiding? The debt kept me stuck; the courses were incomplete, the books, while read, were not put into action. It was as if I was at a pep rally, getting hyped and motivated, with a short-lived feeling of accomplishment at the end. The accomplishment was that I finished the book, and that's where it ended. But I didn't see that. And a few short hours after reading a great book, the nothingness and stagnation returned. And the craving for those feelings came back. I bought another book, registered for another course.

*What am I doing? There has to be more to life than this. I'm tired of being here, tired of being sad for no reason, tired of being depressed. How is it that people are happy and I'm not? Outside looking in, I should be happy. I have a steady job, a roof over my head, food to eat.* There was so much guilt.

I got married when I was 23 years old. He was a friend and a nice guy. I married him because people said he was a good guy and I should marry him. He is a good guy, and we are still friends but no longer married. The recurring theme in my life is happiness creeps in, and I find a way to push it out.

My friendship with myself didn't start to flourish until I met a co-worker who pointed my words out to me. I hadn't realized that despite trying to improve myself, my words kept throwing me back down. My mindset and perspective were constantly in the mode of lack, victimhood, self-dislike, and any other word you can think of that makes growing and flourishing nearly impossible. He woke me up. The darkness started fading away, and I formed an ear for all that I read in those books. If I had met him years earlier, though, I wouldn't have heard his words. Funny how life has a way of making things happen.

As the sun started to shine brighter on my life, I realized that the most important relationship you can have is the one with your mind. What you feed it, what you say, what you think truly matters. The more I became aware of and changed my thoughts and words, the more the hidden road turned to dust and blew away. Don't get me wrong; it still appears from time to time. It is faint, I recognize it right away, and instead of fear, frustration, and hate, I embrace the awareness because I know what to do to work through it.

I wanted to find a way to teach people how to hear themselves to become their own best friends. Today, I validate myself. I can genuinely celebrate others' success and lift others when they fall. I am enough, and so are you. You just have to see it for yourself. Are you ready to see the amazing person someone else already sees and has been trying to tell you is there? If so, let me introduce you to the N.I.K.K.I. Method of befriending the beautiful soul within.

# THE TOOL

*"Nature does not hurry, yet everything is accomplished."*

–Lao Tzu

It is so empowering to truly see and hear yourself with love, compassion, and grace! If you're reading this right now, that may sound like a fairytale in a far-off land. Let me assure you; you can make it happen. And while the N.I.K.K.I. Method is not something that will happen overnight, if you're intentional, it will happen. Warning, it usually sneaks up on you.

Huh? Sneak up? Yep. When you were younger, do you recall a relative or friend of the family commenting on how much you've grown since they last saw you? Did you feel like you grew? Nope, you were just doing what you do, and it happened.

That's how this will work, with one exception. This time, you're going to be intentional with your thoughts and actions because you will set the intention of becoming your best friend.

Before we dive in, I want to offer a companion journal and workbook that you can download and print on my W.U. profile (link in my bio at the end of the chapter). Go ahead and grab it to work through it as you read the rest of the chapter.

Let's get to it, shall we?

The steps in the N.I.K.K.I. Method are what I use to ensure I continue to cultivate a healthy relationship with myself. It stands for **N**otice, **I**ntrospection, **K**nowledge, **K**indness, **I**mprovement. This method is quite adaptable to many areas, but I'll focus on the internal relationship for now.

**Step 1:** Set your intention for the type of relationship you want to create with yourself. Remember how I used to read books and never did anything with the knowledge shared? I don't want you to make the same mistake; change happens when you put in the work, and to maximize, you have to know what you want as a result. As an example, my first intention was to have more self-confidence. (I had not yet realized that confidence came from knowing and believing in yourself.)

To help get your brain moving, here are some journal prompts to consider. Make sure you don't overthink your answer, go with what first comes to mind, and see where it leads. You can always work through these again.

1. What do you feel is most hindering to your quality of life at this moment?

2. If you could change one thing about your relationship with yourself overnight, what would it be?

3. What quality do you like about yourself that you'd like to further enhance or cultivate?

4. What part of you do you secretly like that you've been hiding from yourself?

After you've answered those questions or questions you came up with yourself, go ahead and move to step 2, breaking down N.I.K.K.I.

**Step 2: Employ the N.I.K.K.I. Method of compassionate transformation. Become your best friend.**

**Notice. Become aware of your thoughts**; the words you use to describe yourself in your head and out loud to someone else are what create your reality. How do you talk about yourself? As I shared above, I called myself stupid all the time in my mind. I called myself slow and ugly. And because I continued to feed that to my subconscious mind, I consistently perpetuated scenarios to prove myself (my words/thoughts) right. As you start to become aware of your thoughts and words, use these journal prompts to increase the awareness:

1. Do the thoughts carry me towards or away from the intention I set for myself?

2. How do I feel in my body when I say/think certain things about myself? (notice any tension in the chest, jaw, shoulders, etc.)

Bonus points when you reframe what you said or catch a run-away thought before you complete it.

**The key:** Become keenly aware of thoughts and words that drain and deplete your energy, then counter them with kindness and without judgment.

**Introspection. Examining your own mental and emotional process,** you'll notice you've already started doing this when you responded to the journal prompts under **Notice**. To go deeper, examine times when you get angry with yourself or start a downward emotional spiral. Instead of judging those feelings, understand them. Allow them.

Journal prompts:

1. Will it be helpful for me to dig further into how I'm feeling right now? (This question is to help discern when it's best to explore and when it's best to accept and move forward). If yes, then the second question is a good place to start.

2. What am I feeling right now? (there's a feelings wheel in the complementary journal).

**The key:** Gather **knowledge** about your emotional state without judgment. And do not allow yourself to stay down too long. You have more control than you think. You are stronger than you allow yourself to give you credit for. Not after this, though!

**Knowledge. Gather knowledge from introspective work as well as other sources.** The knowledge about the way you respond to situations is giving you an invaluable skill of self-awareness. That skill empowers you to be in control rather than allowing your mind to control you. You will also use other sources to gather knowledge. For instance, as simple as this sounds, I stopped calling myself stupid when I looked up the actual definition of intelligence. As you explore, you'll likely use other sources to help get a better understanding of things.

Journal Prompts:

1. I notice I get sad when (someone else seems genuinely happy, someone else seems to be doing well, someone else appears to have it all together, or I realize I should feel fine). Change the word sad to any emotion you need at the time of your knowledge gathering.

2. When I feel myself slipping into depleting emotions, I will _____ to bring myself back up. Or I will allow [emotion] to process through me with loving kindness and self-acceptance.

**The key:** Don't judge what you've learned. Be kind and give yourself lots of grace. You didn't know then what you know now. Every day you're choosing to be your best self. Celebrate that.

**Kindness:** How you treat yourself during the process matters; you're teaching your mind and brain how you want to be treated and how you want to feel. If you treated your friends the way you treat yourself in your mind, how long do you think you will have them as friends? It's no different, except you're not able to escape yourself. That's just rude (kidding, not kidding).

Journal prompts:

1. Am I treating myself as I would a very dear friend?
2. How can I be kind to myself today?

**The key: Notice** how you're speaking to and about yourself. Become aware of how you speak about your possessions and life in general. It's a form of personal judgment (see how sneaky being mean can be!)

**Improvement:** You've put in so much work. One thing I know is you can't unlearn what you learn. Doing so is a choice.

Journal prompt (do this one daily and celebrate as many improvements as you can recall). One improvement I love to point out to people is simply becoming aware of their behavior change or having stopped a thought that wasn't going to be very kind.

1. I am celebrating the fact that I've improved in _____.

**The key:** You are worth this work. You have a gift that needs to shine. You are a light in this world. You'll dim it no longer.

*"Mastering others is strength. Mastering yourself is true power."*

–Lao Tzu.

Embrace the tears that will stream once you finally hear and see yourself the way others see you. You'll feel the shift; you'll realize how powerful you truly are. You'll want to be your friend. When you sit in that place, that's when you shine.

Dear Goddess, the world needs your shine. Let it be!

**Nicole Batiste** is an Intuitive & Attuned Inner Life Coach and Speaker. She has a passion and a gift for helping women see how amazing they are, allowing them to step into their powerful selves.

She founded Be Well with N.I.K.K.I. to support those who know what it means to feel like they live two lives that are not in alignment. One inside their mind and one that everyone else sees. She helps her clients bridge the gap between where they are and where they want to be using her created method. Realizing the foundation of "stuckness" in the "real" world is the "stuckness" we hold onto in our mind— most of the time without knowing it— Nicole created the N.I.K.K.I. Method to help clients push past those holds, and teaches clients how to support themselves. Self-acceptance, self-compassion, self-trust, and self-care are common results. To learn more, visit:

https://www.thewellnessuniverse.com/world-changers/nicole-batiste/

# CHAPTER 24

# SUGAR FREEDOM

## EFT/TAPPING FOR FOOD CRAVINGS

Rev. Jennifer Elizabeth Moore, Accredited EFT Master Trainer

## MY STORY

Sunday 7:00 PM: *You are a Goddess*, I affirm.

I stand before the mirror in my uncomfortably tight vintage dress. I want to feel sovereign in my body. I want to feel luscious and sexy.

*You are a Goddess!*

Regardless of how many times I repeat this audacious claim, I don't buy it. Instead, I crave M&Ms and despair over the inconvenient truth that I outgrew half my wardrobe.

*Goddess? More like Miss Piggy. You shouldn't have eaten that entire quart of Rocky Road.*

The magical feminist replies: *Screw patriarchal standards, you're perfect.*

Feeling divine is but wishful thinking. Sugar's got me by the throat. I vow to myself this will be the last binge.

Monday 4:30 PM: *I'll just have a little piece. That should be okay.*

I break off a portion of the massive chocolate bar I'd bought 20 minutes earlier from the bodega. Ahhh, here it is—that sweet surge, the molten bliss. All is well in my world.

4:33 PM: I grab a roll of aluminum foil, hoping it will thwart my desire. Three layers of foil wrap around the remaining four fifths of my temptation.

*I'll savor this over the rest of the week.*

I pry bags of broccoli and nearly empty quarts of ice cream out of frost. I toss my chocolate behind the ice trays. I stack frozen dinners on top.

*That should do it. Out of sight, out of mind—done!*

4:38 PM: *Just a little more. That should be okay.*

*No. Willpower! Girl, get a grip.*

*Oh, F-it.*

I grab my paring knife, slice the bar into four equal sections. I break one into squares. I put them in my bowl from high school pottery class.

*OMG yum!*

*You fat cow. You spoiled brat! You have no control. Put the rest back. Eating half is better than eating all of it.*

4:43 PM: *You might as well eat it all. You know you're going to, why wait!?*

*No.*

*Come on!*

*No!*

*You know you want to.*

*No.*

*But it's so delicious.*

*Okay fine. But this will be the last time. I'll start dieting tomorrow.*

Except we all know what happens.

Tuesday 4:00 PM: I exit the trolley two stops from home.

*Just a little something sweet. That's all I need. Halloween candy is two for one! Well, I can't pass this up.*

I hand the cashier my last five bucks, and she hands me three pounds of fun-sized treats.

5:00 PM: I sit in my cornflower blue corduroy chair. The cat bats crumpled balls of wrappers across the carpet. I shove the two remaining pounds into my underwear drawer.

*I'm never doing this again!*

If you've ever been in the clutches of sugar addiction, you know what I'm talking about; countless hours lost in the struggle between discipline and defeat. It hurts walking up and down the stairs. You're puffy and bloated. Mental tapes of self-loathing run on repeat.

From the ages of 13 to 40, I fought sugar addiction. It was a constant battle between my inner good girl and ravenous appetite, and I felt anxious, moody, and hopeless. I was caught between adoration and aversion with my beloved nemesis, sugar. The first time I stopped, I was 23. I hit rock bottom after I quit smoking and gained 40 pounds in three months. I abstained from sugar for eight years. It wasn't easy. Eventually, self-will vanquished self-control.

As someone committed to women's empowerment and busting cultural ideals of beauty, I'd abandoned diets years earlier. Ironically, this made my relationship with food more challenging. I wanted my rally cry to be, "Eat the damn cupcake!" I wanted to believe abstaining from sweets and other starchy foods was an unnecessary deprivation. I wanted the truth to be that I could enjoy any treat I wanted in moderation if I got my emotional house in order. I hoped if I repeated enough acceptance and forgiveness affirmations, my body would magically find its perfect weight.

Unfortunately, this was not the case for me. Instead, I discovered that sugar impacted everything. I'd hoped to merely reduce my consumption, but after a tiny exposure, I'd slip into a vicious cycle of craving and avoiding. Reducing processed sugar was a recipe for failure. Instead of getting to the other side of withdrawal and being done with it, I'd let a starving tiger out of a cage and find myself in a perpetual state of white-knuckling. Anytime I ate candy, cakes, cookies, or even high carbohydrate savory foods, I faced a cascade of cravings and mental and emotional instability. I had to be honest with myself and admit that one was too many and a thousand never enough when it came to sweets. I had to accept that I'd love myself more by embracing my limitations than ignoring them.

However, self-imposed discipline can only last so long. If our only choice is enduring deprivation or scarfing down a pound of chocolate, eventually, the candy wins. I spent over two decades struggling with abstinence. I exerted crazy amounts of energy to keep cravings at bay. Every temptation required doubling down on my emergency brakes.

In comparison, the last decade has been effortless because I discovered EFT to address and soothe my cravings. Over time, the relentless hunger that defined the first half of my life vaporized. I went from deliberate avoidance of forbidden foods to indifference.

As I write, I realize there's a partially eaten six-month-old chocolate bar in my desk. If someone told me at 23 that I'd stop eating M&Ms by the pound because I wouldn't even want them, I'd say they were lying. Amazingly, I can now consume organic artisanal chocolate in moderation. Yet, I no longer want to! Aside from the physiological benefits of a whole food diet and healing my gut, EFT/tapping is the thing that completely transformed my relationship with my body and food. This is why I want to share this tool with you.

## EFT FOR CRAVINGS

EFT stands for Emotional Freedom Techniques. It employs tapping or light pressure on endpoints of acupuncture meridians while concentrating on an issue or challenge. It balances our body's energy system and reboots fight or flight reactivity in a fairly short time. Tapping calms our thoughts and feelings. It enhances relaxation. We can use it to dismantle entanglements with foods and other substances we use to self-soothe.

EFT looked pretty strange the first time I learned about it. I'd think, *how will tapping on my face keep me from eating a box of truffles?* However, I'd tried everything else, so I was willing to give it a go. I did not tap on sugar or chocolate at first. I actually started by tapping for sensitivities when my body would react to ingredients in processed food. I started to sneeze less. My brain fog decreased. Over time, my resistance to dietary restrictions subsided.

The first time I used EFT on cravings was for cheese. Instead of trying to avoid or deny my cravings, I leaned into them. I put a gluten-free pizza in the oven. I prepared a cheese plate for testing. The first taste of sharp cheddar lit up in my mouth. *How could I not want this savory flavor?* Yet after a single round of tapping, the same cheese that had set my taste buds ablaze five minutes earlier was sort of meh.

Not gonna lie: I ate the pizza and even had an extra slice. Initially, the shift was a lack of anguish over eating cheese. Eventually, I noticed bricks of unopened cheese remained in my refrigerator for months. I might eat a single portion and forget about it. It used to take massive effort to resist consuming an eight-ounce slab of cheese in one sitting; now, I easily ignore it. If I eat more than one serving of cheese on rare occasions, I'm blessedly spared my negative self-talk and relentless guilt. By tapping on cravings, the pleasure centers of my brain no longer hijack my self-care.

# THE TOOL

Now I'm going to teach you how to tap on a food craving so you can disengage from the addictive aspect to find ease and freedom instead. Before I explain this process in detail, I'll address some people's concerns about tapping for cravings. "If I tune into my desire, won't I lose control?" Fortunately, you'll probably be pleasantly surprised how quickly your hunger abates. However, for anyone with a substance abuse problem or allergies, it's better to tap without engaging directly with the substance.

EFT has three repeating parts called the Basic Recipe:

1. Identify and Rate
2. Acknowledge and Accept
3. Tap and Notice

This formula works whether you're addressing cravings, physical pain, stressful memories, negative self-talk, or any other kind of distress. EFT is surprisingly versatile while simultaneously incredibly simple. The key to success lies in tuning in precisely to the issue you're tapping on and being as specific as possible. While there are times when working with a skilled, accredited EFT practitioner will better serve you, tapping for food cravings is something you can do for yourself. I'm going to use chocolate as an example, but you can substitute any food you crave.

## TUNE IN

Generally, EFT starts by noticing thoughts, feelings, and sensations to identify what you need to tap on. With food cravings, we begin by engaging with our desire. Though it isn't necessary, it helps to have a sample on hand. This way, you can gauge shifts as they happen.

Let's imagine you've decided to address a lifelong passion for Kit Kat bars. Unless you already have one stashed away, plan ahead and grab one the next time you're shopping.

Before you even tap, pick up the wrapped candy. Hold it in your hand. Notice what it feels like to anticipate eating it. Think about how much you want it. Let yourself go there. Feel it. Then unwrap the chocolate and notice how you react to its smell and texture. Break off a piece and taste it. Take a moment to lean into the pleasure. Pay attention to your sense of taste and how it feels in your mouth. Then consider how you'd rate the level of intensity, desire, and excitement on a scale of 0 to 10. 0 has no energy whatsoever; 10 is so extreme you can't imagine anything higher.

## IDENTIFY AND RATE

You can use the following questions for further clarification:

- How much do I want this?
- How does this feel in my mouth?
- What sensations have I noticed?
- What makes this so appealing?
- How am I reacting or responding to it?

These answers provide a word or phrase for you to tap on. This will be the Reminder that you'll repeat with each point to help you focus. For example:

*OMG Yum! I love the sweet, velvety sensation of chocolate melting in my mouth. The contrast between the gooey caramel and the crisp layer of cookie makes this my favorite. I can't imagine not wanting this.*

Feeling caught between guilt and desire, I close my eyes and imagine how strong the pull is to eat another piece. It's heightened. I use these details to create a simplified set of Reminder words: "gooey, crisp, sweet, velvety chocolate."

Because shifts can occur so swiftly and effectively, ironically, we'll forget where we started. That's one of the reasons we use what's called a SUDS: Subjective Units of Distress Scale. This is to determine your intensity on a scale of 0 to 10. Ask yourself, "If 0 was no intensity at all, and 10 was the most extreme possible, how would I rate it?" Tuning in to the "gooey, crisp, sweet, velvety chocolate," it gets a rating of 8.5. With SUDS established, we move to the next step.

## ACKNOWLEDGE AND ACCEPT

The Set-Up Statement acknowledges our issue while also inviting new possibilities. The Set-Up has two parts. Part one states what is: "Even though I'm really craving this gooey, crisp, sweet, velvety chocolate..." Part two offers the counterbalance: "I love and accept myself anyway."

The Set-Up has three purposes:

1. To allow you to access your issue and express your reality.

2. To neutralize resistance by providing space for negative and positive feelings.

3. To define and express how you'd like to feel instead.

The traditional balance statement is: "I deeply and completely love and accept myself." If these words don't resonate for you or provoke dissonance, choose a statement that works for you. Take a moment to consider what feels best. It's important to use words you agree with.

Here are some examples:

- I'm willing to love myself as I am today.
- I'm open to the possibility I can change.
- I'm doing my best, and that's good enough.
- It's safe for me to release this.

- I welcome surprisingly easy, unexpected shifts.

## TAP AND NOTICE

The previous steps help you to tune in and define your issue. Now we tap. Using the tips of your three middle fingers, tap gently on the outer edge of the opposite hand just below the pinkie. As you tap, repeat your Set-Up Statement three times.

"Even Though... (state problem), I... (use any positive or neutral statement you prefer)."

Example: *Even though I'm really craving this gooey, crisp, sweet, velvety chocolate, I love and accept myself anyway.*

After you tap while repeating the Set-Up three times, you'll say the Reminder words aloud as you tap through all the points. The point list is in the next section.

Tune into your thoughts and feelings as you tap. Make note if any associations about the food come up or you recall any specific memories. When you finish your first round, take a deep breath. Notice how you feel. Break off another piece of chocolate and engage with it. Notice how the smell affects you. Notice how strong your craving is. Taste it and notice if there's any difference in the flavor, texture, and sensation. Reevaluate your SUDS and write your new number down. As you tap, perhaps you'll notice your craving details shift. The chocolate smell gets overshadowed by a scent of praline. What started as a gooey to crunchy ratio is now the salty-sweet combination. Adjust your words to reflect your new perspective.

Evaluate your new SUDS. Adjust your Set-Up and Reminder to reflect the differences. Tap again.

Set-Up: *Even though I'm still craving this salty, sweet candy bar, I love and accept myself anyway (repeat three times).*

Reminder: *This salty, sweet candy*

Even if a number of new thoughts or underlying issues arise for you, it's more effective to stick with the craving. You might tap on the chocolate craving and recall a memory about Halloween candy or even a fight with your mom over baking cocoa. Even if something new bubbles up, stay with the craving through the entire round of points. This allows you to track changes and systematically address them, one piece at a time. Don't get sucked into a narrative and go down emotional rabbit holes. Stories and brainstorms overcomplicate the process. Keep it simple. Attempting to address multiple aspects distorts the process. You may feel tempted to go off on a tangent, but I encourage you to follow the protocol I've shared. The purpose of this approach is to defuse the intensity of your craving. It is not to pull every skeleton out of your closet or dive into the drama. One of the things I love the most about EFT is how it addresses issues gently from a safe distance. While it may seem counterintuitive, less is more. Your precision will be rewarded.

At the end of each round, return to the top of your head and take a deep breath. Scan for shifts. Re-rate your intensity 0 to 10. If your rating is a three or higher, repeat the tapping sequence until it's as low as it will go. Repeat your exact phrase as you tap through all the points again.

## TAPPING POINTS

1. Side of Hand (the outside edge of your hand, below your pinkie)

2. Top of Head (the crown of your head)

3. Inner Eyebrow (just above the bridge of your nose at the edge of your eye socket)

4. Outer Eye (on your temple, just past the corner of your eye)

5. Under Eye (directly under your pupil on the ridge of your eye socket)

6. Under Nose (the philtrum, aka the groove between your nose and lip)

7. Under Lip (the space between your lower lip and chin)

8. Collarbones (the often tender spot just beneath your clavicle and above your nipples)

9. Under Arm (on the side of your upper ribs past your breast, just below your armpit)

10. Top of Head Again. Take a deep breath. Rate your intensity.

## PERSISTENCE

Tapping for cravings is both simple and effective. It often takes only a couple of rounds to dissipate a craving's urgency. As I mentioned about tapping for cheese, my initial results were fairly subtle. However, over the last decade, I've tracked significant differences. Tapping for new cravings and reactions to food sensitivities has had a cumulative effect. Today I marvel: not only am I free from desires for unhealthy treats, but also my appetite is significantly decreased. I feel miraculously full with portions that would have left me starving two decades ago. My willingness to use EFT persistently has truly changed my life. I invite you to make tapping your go-to tool. Take your time. Get familiar with the points. Practice leaning into your cravings, rate your SUDS, and tap them down. Most importantly, keep it simple and keep tapping.

Author of *Empathic Mastery*, Wellness Universe Expert, Energy Healer, and Master Trainer for EFT International, **Jennifer Moore** supports empathic, creative women. Born from a long line of world-class awfulizers, Jen spent her first thirty years struggling to control fear and overwhelm. This left her anxious, exhausted, over-medicated, and bingeing on sugar

After hitting bottom, Jen sought help. With recovery, life improved. This inspired her to pursue professional skills, including a Master's degree in Psychology & Religion, Emotion Code Certification, and additional healing modalities. Jen brings depth and compassion to her work through a combination of finely tuned intuition, the pragmatism of a Capricorn, and a wealth of knowledge gained from more than three decades of professional experience.

Jennifer lives in coastal Maine, surrounded by flowers, bees, and elderberries. She shares this paradise with her husband David, their tuxedo cats Neo & Livi, a herd of deer, a lone fox, and a couple of groundhogs. When she isn't writing, teaching, or working with clients, Jen loves to concoct healthy, sugar-free treats, play with crystals, and make flower essences.

To learn more and grab your copy of Jen's Illustrated EFT Guide and favorite sugar-free recipes, visit:

https://www.thewellnessuniverse.com/world-changers/jennifermoore/

# CHAPTER 25

# BEING UNSTOPPABLE

## HOW TO USE DIVINE DESIGN TO UPLEVEL EVERYTHING

Rochel Marie Lawson, RN, AHP, CMS

## MY STORY

As far back as I can remember, I always imagined what living my dream life would be like. I imagined graduating from college, having a successful business, and making seven figures. I envisioned driving my dream luxury car, a Mercedes Benz 450 or a big BMW 750 LI, living in a large white house with a pine green front door by a lake in a beautiful neighborhood filled with lots of big maple and pine trees. I imagined so many wonderful aspects of my life that I began to believe I could have everything I ever wanted.

When we set out to travel down our path to bliss, which starts the moment we're born, the journey is filled with all kinds of experiences and adventures. Some of them are perceived as good, and some are perceived as negative; however, all of the incidences we go through on our journey don't happen by chance and are not accidents.

The amazing thing is we can have more control of how our life ebbs and flows. Instead of living a life by chance, trial and error, or with disregard, you can live a life that leads to being unstoppable. Living life by Divine Design will up-level everything you experience on your path to bliss.

Everyone has the opportunity to release the energy of living a haphazard life and refuel it with the energy of Divine Design. When you understand this concept and step into utilizing the tools of Divine Design, everything in your life amplifies and changes for the better. You gain more control of your life by allowing the perfect plan for you to manifest without struggle, difficulty, stress, anxiety, or worry.

Let me explain.

I have always been a type-A person, a perfectionist, and to an extent, a bit of a control freak. I wanted to control the outcome of all I was involved in, to the point of absolute ridiculousness. It seemed like the more I attempted to control things, the more I struggled and experienced difficulties and the more powerless I felt. It became a vicious cycle.

I entered my tenth year running a successful business in Silicon Valley. My business received its first award as being named one of the Top 50-Women-Owned Businesses in Silicon Valley. On top of that, my company was in the running for a multi-million dollar contract that would take the business to a whole new level or, rather, up-level everything in the business I worked so hard to achieve. The truth was that I had not done anything. I actually hampered and slowed down the business's success because I believed I had to control everything.

And this was horrible. It made me sick to my stomach. Each time I thought about how I hampered the business's abilities because of my controlling, type-A behavior, I got a headache and felt a pit in my stomach. I didn't know what to do or how to change what I had let get out of control, which was myself!

When I began to look at all aspects of my life, I saw mirror images of that "darn" controlling behavior that killed my joy, disturbed my peace, and left me feeling out of control. My mindset lacked clarity; negative thoughts began to infiltrate my brain, sucking the positive thoughts from the forefront of my mind. This left me feeling drained and stressed, with a sense of uneasiness in my body and mind. I was moody, short-tempered, and downright icky to be around. My energy was heavy, stagnant, thick, and stuck.

I was so deep in the muck of it all that I felt stuck and stoppable for the first time in my life. I longed for the beautiful, loving, peaceful, joyful aspects of my life back. I longed for that enthusiasm I had when I first embarked on starting my business. I desired to have that carefree, imaginative, creative mindset that restored my spirit with peace and freedom.

And then something very profound happened.

All the work that my team and I had put in to obtain that multi-million dollar contract award was about to be for nothing.

The company awarding the project decided that my company was too small because I had my hands in everything. Although they felt my company could "most likely" complete the work successfully, they worried I would hamper the project's ability to be completed on time due to my involvement in too many aspects of the project and my micromanagement of the team.

This made them very uncomfortable because their thought was if something happened to me, my team of employees would not be able to fulfill the obligation of the contract for the project.

As I faced the fact that because of all my "control," I was about to face defeat, I stepped into a place of fear. I stepped into a place of lack. I stepped into a place of failure. I stepped into a place of loss. I stepped into a place of criticism. I stepped into a place of being stoppable for the first time in my life. And it felt awful.

Fear robs you of all power because when you step into a place of fear, you lose contact with the Divine powerhouse. Fear puts you in a place of being stoppable instead of being unstoppable. When you're fearful, you magnetize more of what you are afraid of. You become hypnotized by the racing, fearful thoughts.

This became a pivotal point in my life. The realization that I needed to make a rapid change and release control came to me in a most divine, unconventional way.

One day, I was taking my son to basketball practice and my daughter to dance practice. As I drove them to their desired destinations, they heard me talking on the phone to the project manager of that big project.

When I hung up the phone, my daughter asked me why I was so upset. Then my son said, "Mom, you just need to chill out. You can't control everything. You just need to relax and let all come to you by Divine Design."

My daughter then chimed in, "Yeah, Mom, you always tell Khrystopher to relax and let the game come to him, and that is what you need to do: relax and release and let the game come to you." Then they both said by Divine Design.

When we arrived at my son's basketball practice, he got out of the car and said, "See ya later, Mom," with a divine look in his eyes and a divine smile on his face.

As we continued to the dance studio, my daughter said, "Mommy, you always say we are most powerful when we learn to release and keep our poise. This allows us to be strong, confident, and faithful." I looked at her and said, "Lauryn, I don't remember telling you that," and she said, "It's not important that you don't remember; what's important is that I do remember." We arrived at the dance studio, and she hopped out of the car and ran into her dance class.

Those words from my children on that day changed my life. I knew I'd received a message from the Divine. I began to embrace the fact that I created the current situation with my business and life. I was not unstoppable because I was coming from a place of fear. I was not living life by Divine Design; I was living my life by default.

I would not let go of control and release my desires and request to the Divine. I was blocking my blessing. I was acting from fear instead of faith. I was not exhibiting the poise and power that was within me. I was curtaining and stopping the blessings meant for me to experience on my path to bliss.

Every woman has within herself a nugget of gold; it's her consciousness of a divine mind, which restores and brings peace into her life. That's what I tapped into to change my life.

Divine Design is the perfect plan that includes health, wealth, love, fearlessness, and unstoppability. It's the plan that brings perfect happiness into one's life. It's the plan that restored happiness, peace, and freedom in my business and my life. Through that conversation with my children, my mind was able to see that I needed to release the control to restore my unstoppability.

The discovery of living a life by Divine Design allowed me to regain my poise, which allowed me to regain my power which amplified the energy of unstoppability within me.

With Divine Design, there is only completion under grace with perfect ideas in a perfect way. No more running a business or living life in a haphazard fashion. When you choose to live a life by Divine Design, life's perfect ebb and flow becomes smoother and easier, and your dreams become a reality.

# THE TOOL

Over the years, many of my clients have asked me to share with them my method of using Divine Design to develop that feeling and energy of being unstoppable and up-leveling everything that they do.

I believe that this information was bestowed upon me from the Divine because I sought to understand how to be better and not live a life by default but a life of intention with integrity and freedom.

It gives me immense joy and pleasure to share with you what was bestowed upon me all those years ago.

When you begin using Divine Design, you become unstoppable, and your entire life will be up-leveled.

Here's my warning, though: I want you to be fully prepared for a life of bliss, as miracle after miracle begins to occur in your life.

Are you ready? Here it is.

1. **Ask For Guidance**

    There is truth in the phrase "ask, and you shall receive." Make it known to the Divine what it is that you seek assistance with. The instant you ask, the Divine knows the way of fulfillment and will deliver the Divine Design to you. Use active faith in the asking to impress your subconscious mind with the belief that you are ready to receive your plan of Divine Design.

2. **Tap Into Your Intuition**

    Intuition is a spiritual faculty above the intellect and does not explain but simply points the way. It's the "still small voice" commonly called a hunch. It is Divine guidance. It's the eye that watches over all that you do. To work with your intuition, you must give it the right of way and still the reasoning mind. This is where you will receive the information on creating that energy of Divine Design that leads to unstoppability.

3. **Do The Next Indicated Thing**

After checking in and receiving guidance from your intuition, do not hesitate to do exactly what it's telling you to do. If you are guided to relax, wait, and not take any action, then relax, wait and take no action. If you are being guided to move forward in grace and take action, then do that. Have faith and know that you are divinely guided.

4. **Keep a Journal**

One of the most direct means for connecting with the Divine Infinite Intelligence is with pen and paper. Writing helps you see through the confusion and clear out mental blocks and emotional cobwebs that can keep you stuck in a negative energetic cycle. It's a profound and wonderful way to document your Divine Design steps and journey as you transform and up-level your life.

5. **Become Unhurried**

This is the most crucial and difficult step with using Divine Design due to the busyness of life. Learn to value serenity over stimulation. It's okay to be busy but don't allow yourself to become driven. When you refuse to become driven, you can hold your priorities sacrosanct. You will no longer waste time figuring out where to invest your energies because you will know what takes precedence and make the bold choices you need to make with faith and grace.

6. **Watch Your Words**

The words we speak are creative as well as communicative. In the creative capacity of words, they form a bridge between mind and matter and play a vital role in shaping our reality. We give ourselves persuasive suggestions with our own words. Avoid speaking untruths, exaggerations, self-put-downs, diminishment, and aimless criticism. This creates a "fog" around your ability to tap into your intuition and may block the flow of important guidance that you need to receive.

7. **Practice Nonresistance**

Nonresistance leads to transmutation. You cannot lose blessings that belong to you. Trying to control every situation creates resistance because control is based on fear and constriction and not openness and freedom. As long as you act with resistance towards a situation, that situation will continue to appear in your life. It may appear in a slightly different manner or aspect of your life, but it will keep appearing until you act with nonresistance towards it. This leads to being unstoppable.

All perceived blocks or challenges on your path become looked upon as blessings and lessons to assist you with being unstoppably successful. When you practice nonresistance, you release the thoughts of the outcome and know and believe that the best outcome possible will occur.

To become nonresistance, all you have to do is release the day's outcome to the Divine as part of your Divine Design. Make an affirmation upon waking, such as "Thy will be done today. Today is a day of a perfect beginning and perfect completion. I am open to receive the miracles of life that are being bestowed upon me now."

The last thing that I want to add is one of the most important aspects of using Divine Design to create unstoppability and up-level your life:

8. **Trust Your Instincts.**

You know more than you think you do. Sometimes the only difference between being unstoppable and living a Divine Design life is being brave enough to trust your instincts. Your instincts are connected to your gut, your solar plexus chakra. Those instincts will never lead you astray. There's nothing weird about tapping into your intuitive capacity and allowing the sensations you feel within your body to guide you.

Pay attention to the quiet hints that come from within you. Don't dismiss them, ignore them, or cast them aside. They are real bits of information divinely designed to lead you on your path to bliss.

Once you start using Divine Design in your life, you will begin getting in the habit of noticing the beautiful synchronicities that appear in your life. A whole new world opens up for you where the realm of miracles and wonders becomes possibilities, and quick and seemingly impossible changes take place for your good.

As for the ending to the story I shared after that day with my children, I realized that I was the problem in my life. I had been blocking my blessing and was living by default, trying to control everything instead of living in poise, power, and unstoppability.

I opened up the portal of my inner being and allowed the wisdom of Divine Design to be bestowed upon me. I embraced the wisdom, used it in all aspects of my life, and my entire life up-leveled.

I watched miracle after miracle occur in my life. My health improved, my mind relaxed, my energy became more vibrant and positive, and my skin glowed with radiance.

My relationship with myself improved, and my relationship with others became solid and radiated with love.

My business grew tremendously, and yes, my company was awarded that multi-million dollar contract.

Namaste,

Rochel Marie Lawson

The Queen of Feeling Fabulous

Known as the Queen of Feeling Fabulous, **Rochel Marie Lawson** is a successful business owner, Registered Nurse, Ayurvedic Health Practitioner, Dream Lifestyle Transformation Facilitator, two-time #1 Bestselling Author on Amazon, two-time International Bestselling Author, and author of four other best selling books including "Intro To Holistic Health Ayurveda Style." She is a speaker and radio show hostess. She is the founder and president of Blissful Living 4 U, which was founded to bring wellness, wisdom, and wealth into the lives of individuals seeking a holistic path to living the life of their dreams.

Rochel Marie's energy, guidance, and enthusiasm have helped thousands of people improve their wellness, wisdom (aka mindset), and wealth by utilizing ancient, holistic principles that unlock the access for transformation to occur. She has been named one of the Top 50 Women-Owned Businesses in Silicon Valley and created The Unstoppable Women's Summit.

She has a weekly podcast, The Blissful Living Show, hosted on her own podcast network. She has been a guest writer for several blog publications as well as a featured core blogger for The Wellness Universe. She has been quoted in the Huffington Post and featured on Fox, CBS, NBC, and several other large media publication outlets.

Rochel Marie has spent over 25 years assisting people to achieve, elevate and sustain wellness and wealth through wisdom, to enhance the power of their minds, and to transform their lives so that they can live the life of their dreams with more abundance, clarity, energy, happiness, joy, peace, vitality, creativity, wisdom, prosperity, success and wealth.

https://www.thewellnessuniverse.com/world-changers/rochelmarielawson

# ABOUT THE AUTHOR

**Anna Pereira** is the Founder of The Wellness Universe and CEO of Soul Ventures, a woman-owned business, where her mission is to make the world a better place. She's an inspirational leader, mentor, and connector for business owners who are changing the world. As an author and creator of wellness events, projects, and programs, Anna is an expert at showcasing, promoting, and supporting the world's most talented wellness professionals.

Anna lives between Europe and her birthplace, New Jersey, USA, with her husband, sports expert, and investor, Hugo Varela. The couple has adopted pets (one dog and two cats) and cares for two strays. Big Red, their African Gray, loves to speak English and Portuguese and is the ruler of the house. Anna enjoys turning on the creative flow when time allows by painting, writing, and creating custom T-shirts and jewelry. Finding balance in nature or at the beach with friends is her joy. She's dedicated to serving her calling and leaving her legacy as a 'conduit for change' by bringing more health, happiness, and well-being to the world with a collaborative spirit and intentional action. Learn more about Anna and The Wellness Universe at TheWellnessUniverse.com

https://www.thewellnessuniverse.com/world-changers/annapereira/

# YOU MATTER GODDESS

## THANK YOU FOR INVITING US ALONG ON YOUR GODDESS JOURNEY

How can you use these tools to create your optimal life? Once you rest this book down, commit to yourself to try at least one of the tools and see where it takes you. Although inspiring, ultimately, it's up to you to take steps to experience your personal achievement and fully embrace your Goddess energy and expression of it. I shared with you in my introduction how essential the work you do on yourself is to open doors, build your resilience, and create the most optimal version of yourself. When you're living in your Goddess energy, your joy will follow, and you will inspire others too.

How about those stories?! I hope you enjoyed the personal stories from our expert wellness professionals, coaches, and guides. We have received wonderful feedback from volume 1, 25 Tools for Stress Relief, volume 2, 25 Tools for Happiness, and volume 3, 25 Tools to Achieve Anything, with specific expressions of gratitude from our readers about our expert's stories. We, too, find the personal stories to be incredibly valuable!

Sharing gives us strength, courage, and confidence. Our Wellness Universe experts have shared with us their vulnerabilities, celebrations, and insights to connect and express through your unique Goddess energy. After which, the tool each one shares—which has worked to transform their life—instills in us the confidence that it may change our life too. That right there, my Divine Goddess, is the key to motivating you. We gain faith and trust in the tool when we know it has worked for someone else, especially a wellness professional.

You matter. You are worthy of all the success in your hopes, dreams, and goals the Universe is waiting to gift to you for the Goddess you are!

## YOU ARE NEVER ALONE

Self-care is essential to our mental and emotional well-being and whole health. Our hope was to help you discover a new or better way to your best self and connect back to your inner Goddess to help you live your happiest, healthiest life.

All the experts here agree that empowering you by giving you tools to treat yourself at home is one of the keys to transformation and healing. When you take responsibility for self-awareness, self-care, self-healing, and self-development, you are much more apt to feel good and stay feeling that way. We've experienced those who take self-treatment to heart getting better faster, staying healthier in the long run and really enjoying their lives to the fullest.

The road to living in your unique Goddess energy does not have to be a solitary journey.

We also know many people need skilled assistance and guidance to support them to their greatest version of themselves. The clients we come across are in all stages of physical, mental, and emotional dis-ease or dysfunction that gets in the way of achieving their desired outcomes in life. Some need a quick tool and home program, while others require intensive or prolonged care. We all agree that having a transformational guide on the journey is paramount to peak performance, whatever stage you're in.

When you have a wellness professional, guide, coach, or healer in your corner, you'll reach your goals faster, but more importantly, you'll have someone invested in your progress and transformation, and you won't be doing it alone. Remember, that practitioner has been where you are and has healed the layers you're going through. They can hold a healing space for you and offer their best support to do that same work. Holding a healing space for you means they've practiced a conscious presence, an ability to ground and center themselves, and an ability to energetically enhance your healing and self-growth process. They have learned and practice modalities that work. That conscious presence is not something you find in all people. It's a practice that our wellness professionals, healers, coaches, and skilled therapists have worked for years to master. They've adopted a lifestyle that includes these skills and tools, so they can help others. They are special, amazing people.

This final note is to encourage you to seek out a wellness guide if you feel like you're stuck, not making progress, feeling more hopeless than hopeful, or just can't consistently get your mindset to stay positive, open, or clear. We encourage you to explore different modalities and different wellness guides, coaches, and practitioners. Find someone you vibe with and hire them to help you get to where you want to go.

Try asking: What else is possible for my transformation today? Just asking yourself that question should help you feel hopeful. Sit with that question without straining to hear an answer. Allow yourself to meditate on the possibility.

Another great question to sit with or journal about: What if there's something you haven't learned yet that could change everything?

We sit around and think we've read it all, done it all, and learned it all, and we stay resigned to our current mediocre physical, mental, emotional status because we think there are no alternatives or options left. I've been exploring self-care and the vast array of transformational modalities for an entire lifetime, and I'm here to tell you I won't have time to get to all the possibilities.

Life is constantly changing and creates new circumstances and challenges. When we recognize and have an awareness around self-care, we can better and more quickly serve ourselves.

The point here is there are people out there who will help you heal. There's a professional out there waiting to teach you something you didn't even know existed and expose you to another level of hope and transformation you didn't realize you could feel. This book outlines dozens of those approaches. Some traditional. Some alternative. Some you may have never heard of. Some you may have heard of but never tried. It's time to explore!

It's our job as authentic healers, practitioners, and guides to facilitate a process of healing and transformation in you, connect you with your inner healer and power, and super-boost that power inside you. And we're good at it. Try us!

Please go back to the chapters that drew you in, piqued your interest, or had you feeling a little excited. Look up the amazing author there and read a little bit more about them on www.TheWellnessUniverse.com. You might even contact them to say thank you for their words or set up a call with them to discuss what you learned. The authors I asked to be a part of this are extraordinary humans; they want you to feel better, be your best, and they are open-hearted, skilled, and very aware and experienced wellness professionals. They thrive when you thrive. It's part of their mission, like it is mine, to help make the world a better place.

I hope you enjoyed this book. Even more than that, I hope you're getting into action with it, trying the exercises and tools, and getting some results! I'd love to hear how you're doing. Please share your story with me via www.TheWellnessUniverse.com

Lastly, I have a personal favor to ask. If you enjoyed this book and have a couple of minutes to leave a review on Amazon, all of us in the guide would greatly appreciate it. Your review helps others see our book, and it spreads the good vibes. Thank you!

Signing off now with a final wish for your best health: May you find what you need to thrive, mind, body, and soul, and inspire others to be brave enough to give themselves the same.


To Your Most Amazing Life Goddess,

Anna

# RAMPAGE OF GRATITUDE

It is with deep appreciation and heart-felt gratitude to have such amazing, talented, beautiful people surrounding me and this book.

My thanks go to God, my higher power, and everyone looking out over me from above. My mom included. Thank you. I know I am a big assignment, and without you watching from above, I could not do what I do.

Hugo Varela, my husband, my rock, my inspiration, my teacher, my love, my Prince. The most amazing human being I have ever met. Thank you for always believing in me and all your blessed support and love. I love you forever.

I am truly blessed by my angels! My Godparents. My Best Friend Jeanne. My sister Irene. My in-laws Manuela and Antonio.

Heartfelt gratitude to all my friends, family and mentors who have supported and encouraged me throughout my life. Every ounce of support I received from you personally allows me to create more success professionally and aids me to keep to my mission and serve those making the world a better place and creates the space for well-being. Your love, compassion, and support are my foundation and springboard. At times you have seen something in me I did not see for myself. Without your love, support, and belief in me, I would not be where I am today. I am blessed and grateful.

My backbone and team at The Wellness Universe. Without you, we would not be The Wellness Universe. Thank you, Jenny, Vanessa, LE, and Julie.

Our Authors. Each of you have amazing gifts and share the mission to leave the world a better place. You touch countless lives with all you do as a resource for transformation, healing, and well-being. That takes a brave person. Thank you for being brave. Thank you for being a WU World-Changer.

Thank you to every member of The Wellness Universe community. You are what the world needs, now more than ever. Thank you for being a channel, guide, teacher, healer, coach, therapist, agent of change, way-shower, and support to all seeking to live their best life.

Thank you to everyone who helped this book come into existence: Laura Di Franco and her team at Brave Healer Productions. Our designer, Dino Marino. Lynda Goldman, whose original painting graces the cover.

Thank you to those who have reviewed and endorsed the book, those who have supported our launch, and those who keep sharing our books. Your support helps spread the word and helps us get more books to worthy causes and into the hands of people who need this information most.

And YOU. Our reader. You have taken a bold step and responsibility to help yourself. I applaud you for not only seeking your best life but taking the essential inspired action to create it. You have not only given yourself a gift, you have given a gift to all you love, and who love you. By creating a wonderful world for yourself, you create a wonderful world for those around you. My sincerest thanks.

# HOW THE WELLNESS UNIVERSE
## SERVES THE WORLD
## & HOW YOU CAN JOIN

A call to those seeking real-life experiences that ignite your soul, transform you to your greatest self, connect you to life-long friends, and support your total well-being, you are invited to SoulTreat!

Join us for our SoulTreat Retreat. Information on our retreats can be found at www.WUSoulTreat.com

## FRIENDS BETTER YOUR LIFE:

Find the people, conversations, and content that create more happiness, balance, ease, and well-being by visiting www.TheWellnessUniverse.com Whether you come to amplify more of the good stuff in your life, or you are seeking a solution to a physical, emotional, mental, or spiritual challenge, you will be welcomed here. Connect to a WU World-Changer via our directory of thousands of members.

## WELLNESS PROFESSIONALS:

If you are a coach, therapist, healer, teacher, guide, practitioner, or representative of anything wellness (services or products), and seek to stand shoulder to shoulder while being amplified for your contribution to the world, join us:
https://www.thewellnessuniverse.com/become-wu-world-changer/

A sample of what The Wellness Universe has in store for you:

- Book collaborations like this one
- Teaching your online course
- Hosting workshops or participating in SoulTreat Retreat
- Be included in a community of World-Changers
- Get published online
- Wellness business support
- Online profile in one of the top wellness directories
- Collaborations, special projects, social media exposure, interviews, and so much more

## ORGANIZATIONS:

Inquire about our corporate and group wellbeing programs:

If you have a group or organization and seek support for your members, reach out to us. We would be honored to serve you with our wellbeing programs that support organizations from the top down.

Email us at: ContactWU@TheWellnessUniverse.com

*"I have long held the desire to work within a collaborative environment - Anna Pereira embodies the essence of collaboration. Her natural leadership style garners support, attracting hearts and minds who share a mission aligned with her vision. Supportive, tirelessly giving, purpose-driven, and admired, Anna is someone who will champion you, uplift you, and celebrate you. The best decision I ever made in becoming a member of the Wellness Universe."*

**– Kathy Jerin**
HeartMath Trainer, Meditation Teacher


*"Anna Pereira is a shining example of what leadership should look like from someone with titles like Founder and CEO. She's a hard worker, she's driven, she delivers results; and, she does it all with caring, kindness, and a desire to see others succeed. Anna leads by being in service to all of us at the Wellness Universe (WU) so that we may be in service to our clients in each of our respective fields. What I most appreciate about her is what she doesn't do. She doesn't approach her position from the tired, worn-out, power-over leadership paradigm, and that, in and of itself, makes her a beacon in her industry. Anna truly cares and shows compassion for all of us at WU. Anna is the reason I stay with the Wellness Universe, and the example set by Anna is also why I have said no to joining other sites that are similar in their services. There is no personal touch with the copycat sites, and the human connection that Anna fosters within her community makes all the difference. If you want to work with someone who knows how to Be The Change, I recommend Anna."*

**– Jennifer Whitacre Gardner**
Strategist, Teacher, Visionary, Speaker, Author, Facilitator,
and Compassionate Space Holder

*"It's been my habit to pick very carefully when I align myself with an organization of any type. I want a group I choose to be supportive, with mature and responsible members and whose dedication to service is paramount. The person who founded such an organization is the setter of the culture. Such a person is Anna Pereira, founder of The Wellness Universe (WU). WU is a group in support of the success of people who seek to bring wellness to others. WU not only serves the wellness needs of people worldwide but also cares for the wellness providers. To be successful, it takes a leader's vision and tireless effort. Anna Pereira is such a leader. She is mature, incredibly responsible, serially creative, positive in outlook, allows herself to be personally vulnerable, inspiring, and carefully relates to each member of WU as if he or she were the only member! The team she has assembled to support the many intricacies of WU, which has several thousand members, is stellar. And with her vision and hard work, Anna also brings a sense of fun and joy. Anna Pereira is a remarkable leader and has created a remarkable organization--without peer"*

**– Ilene Dillon, M.S.W.,**
International Speaker and Best-Selling Author Emotional Mastery Expert

# GODDESS TREASURE BOX

**Includes:**

1 Signed Book – Hand signed by Anna Pereira

1 Matching Journal – Exclusive Author's Gift, not for sale anywhere

**Ritual Kit:**

Beeswax 'I Am a Goddess' Candle

Paolo Santo

A Rose Quartz Heart

A Crystal Gemstone Pendulum

Extra surprise gifts and bonuses from our authors!

## ORDER TODAY

https://www.thewellnessuniverse.com/home/goddess-treasure-box/

Are you highly sensitive?
Is your heart open to the angelic world?
Do you have a spiritual network?
Do you run your own American webstore?
Would you like to bring my spiritual tools to
the USA?

Get in touch with me!
Love,
*Ingrid Auer*

Special thanks to the support from our sponsor, Ingrid Auer

https://www.ingridauer.us/

info@ingridauer.com

## OTHER BEST-SELLING BOOKS
## BY ANNA PEREIRA
## & THE WELLNESS UNIVERSE

*The Wellness Universe Guide to Complete Self-Care, 25 Tools for Stress Relief*

*The Wellness Universe Guide to Complete Self-Care, 25 Tools for Happiness*

*The Wellness Universe Guide to Complete Self-Care, 25 Tools to Achieve Anything*

Made in the USA
Columbia, SC
06 December 2021